The Volleyball Coaching Bible

Don Shondell

Cecile Reynaud

Editors

Human Kinetics

Library of Congress Cataloging-in-Publication Data

The volleyball coaching bible / Don Shondell, Cecile Reynaud, editors.
   p. cm.
  ISBN 0-7360-3967-8 (pbk.)
  1. Volleyball—Coaching. I. Shondell, Donald S., 1929- II. Reynaud,
Cecile, 1953-
  GV1015.5.C63 V65 2002
  796.325—dc21

                     2002007964

ISBN-10: 0-7360-3967-8
ISBN-13: 978-0-7360-3967-3

Acquisitions Editor: Todd Jensen; **Production Editor:** Melinda Graham; **Assistant Editors:** Scott Hawkins, John Wentworth; **Copyeditor:** Bob Replinger; **Proofreader:** Anne Meyer Byler; **Permission Manager:** Toni Harte; **Graphic Designer:** Robert Reuther; **Photo Manager:** Les Woodrum; **Cover Designer:** Jack W. Davis; **Photographer (cover):** David Sanders; **Art Manager:** Carl Johnson; **Illustrators:** Tom Roberts, Brian McElwain; **Printer:** United Graphics

Human Kinetics books are available at special discounts for bulk purchase. Special editions or book excerpts can also be created to specification. For details, contact the Special Sales Manager at Human Kinetics.

Printed in the United States of America   10   9   8   7   6

Human Kinetics
Web site: www.HumanKinetics.com

United States: Human Kinetics
P.O. Box 5076
Champaign, IL 61825-5076
800-747-4457
e-mail: humank@hkusa.com

Canada: Human Kinetics
475 Devonshire Road Unit 100
Windsor, ON N8Y 2L5
800-465-7301 (in Canada only)
e-mail: orders@hkcanada.com

Europe: Human Kinetics
107 Bradford Road
Stanningley
Leeds LS28 6AT
United Kingdom
+44 (0) 113 255 5665
e-mail: hk@hkeurope.com

Australia: Human Kinetics
57A Price Avenue
Lower Mitcham, South Australia 5062
08 8277 1555
e-mail: liaw@hkaustralia.com

New Zealand: Human Kinetics
Division of Sports Distributors NZ Ltd.
P.O. Box 300 226 Albany
North Shore City, Auckland
0064 9 448 1207
e-mail: info@humankinetics.co.nz

A Tribute to Jim Coleman

Jim Coleman was a world leader in scouting opponents and evaluating team performance in volleyball. His chapter in this book was one of Jim's last opportunities to share his thoughts on charting and recording data. He passed away on August 3, 2001, the result of acute pancreatitis. One of the true pioneers of the sport of volleyball, Jim was remembered by USA men's gold medal coach Doug Beal as follows: "I seriously doubt that we will ever see anyone again who will combine Jim's technical knowledge, his inquisitiveness, his personality, and his enthusiastic energy."

Jim Coleman will always be remembered as a volleyball legend and will be sadly missed by the worldwide volleyball community.

CONTENTS

PHOTO CREDITS

INTRODUCTION

Opportunities and Challenges in Volleyball Coaching

Don Shondell

Volleyball is relatively new as a competitive sport. The intent of its inventor, William Morgan, was to create a mild, noncontact, recreational activity that middle-aged businessmen could play safely at the YMCA during their noon-hour break away from their workplace. The year was 1895, just four years after James A. Naismith created basketball for college-aged men at Springfield College. Basketball was devised as a rigorous game that could be played indoors on winter evenings, and it caught on immediately in high schools and colleges across the nation as both a recreational and competitive sport. In the year that Morgan invented volleyball, colleges and high schools in Massachusetts and adjacent states were already playing basketball competitively.

Volleyball's growth as a recreational YMCA noon-time activity was restricted by the small numbers of YMCAs located in the larger cities of nearby states. Over the years, the rules remained similar to those of the original game. If you examine the original rules for a moment, you will understand why the game was slow to spread. For example, any number of players were allowed to play on each side of the net, rotation of positions did not occur, one player could air dribble the ball as many times as desired, and there was no limit on the number of times that players could pass the ball back and forth to one another before finally returning the ball across the net.

Major changes did not occur until 1912. Those revisions established the number of players on a side at six and required a team to rotate before serving.

Four years later, because of the increased interest in the game, the American Sports Publishing Company decided it was financially feasible to publish a separate book for the emerging sport of volleyball. The timing was perfect, because the new book included four major rules revisions that were destined to be critical to the continued growth of the sport. These changes drastically altered the way the game could be played. The critical and much needed changes were as follows: (1) the ball could not come to rest in the hands, (2) a player could not touch the ball a second time unless another player had touched it, (3) the game would be played to 15 points, and (4) the net was raised to eight feet. The rules made no mention of a lower net height for women because they were not involved in YMCA recreational programs, the groups that at the time provided the leadership in the development of this relatively new sport. It wasn't until 1920 that the rule restricting contacts on a side to three was implemented.

The first confirmation that volleyball had become a competitive sport took place in 1922, when the YMCA sponsored its first YMCA national championship at the Central YMCA of Brooklyn, New York. The first champion was the Pittsburgh, Pennsylvania, Downtown YMCA.

In 1949, 27 years after the first national tournament, women finally had their first opportunity to compete in a national championship. The first women's volleyball championship was conducted under the leadership of the United States Volleyball Association, later renamed USA Volleyball, in Los Angeles, California. The champions were the Houston, Texas, Eagles. Also conducted for the first time in 1949 was the United States Volleyball Association men's national collegiate championship, won by the University of Southern California.

A major breakthrough for volleyball occurred in 1964, when it became an official sport in the 1964 Olympic Games. It was one of three trial sports selected by the host team, and the excitement of the sport gained it a permanent position in future Olympic Games.

The initial NAIA collegiate championships for men occurred in 1969. The host school was George Williams College in Downers Grove, Illinois. Earlham College of Richmond, Indiana, won the tournament. In second place was Indiana Technical College in Fort Wayne, Indiana.

The first women's collegiate national championship was conducted in 1970 by the Division of Girl's and Women's Sports of the American Association of Health, Physical Education, and Recreation. Long Beach State College hosted the competition. The champion was Sul Ross State University of Texas. UCLA finished second. The NCAA now sponsors this event.

The inaugural NCAA national championship for men was hosted by UCLA in 1970. UCLA won the tournament, and Long Beach State College finished second.

High school volleyball evolved at a similar rate, with competition for girls attracting more participants than competition for boys. As early as 1971, 14 states conducted high school championships for girls and 6 for boys. The first state tournament for boys was held in Pennsylvania in 1938.

Initially, volleyball for males at the high school and college level attracted little interest because the sport was stereotyped as a nonathletic activity played almost exclusively by old men at YMCAs. In addition, because its noncontact nature appealed to females, volleyball trailed far behind basketball as the indoor sport of choice in the United States for athletic young men.

When I attempted to initiate the men's volleyball program at Ball State, I felt that I had to overcome several myths. I was able to accomplish that by persuading outstanding athletes to come out for the volleyball team. I was confident that if I could get good athletes involved in the program, we could become more successful, develop enthusiasm for the program, and eventually win acceptance of the sport.

As a result, even when financial difficulty required Ball State to drop six sports, volleyball survived, and it continues to be one of the more popular sports for both men and women at Ball State.

Books and videos on volleyball didn't appear until the late 1960s. Only then could beginning coaches and teachers find information that would be helpful in attempting to initiate a volleyball program.

This lack of reference material was a major obstacle when I began my coaching career in fall 1959. Only two resources were available—a book written in 1942 by Bob Laveaga and a film produced in 1946. Many changes had occurred in the game during the intervening years. I knew I would have difficulty finding answers to my questions about the differences between the recreational game and the highly competitive game.

I found that YMCA players in the area were my best source of information about the competitive game. Some had played in the national championships and had observed the latest techniques and tactics.

I sent letters to schools in the four states adjacent to Indiana to find out if there were volleyball clubs that might be interested in organizing a league or association. I received a response from Jim Coleman, a volleyball coach at Wittenberg College in Springfield, Ohio. He not only had a volleyball club but also was a volleyball clinician and was planning to conduct a clinic in the Columbus, Ohio, YMCA in the near future. He invited me to attend. I learned more from Jim Coleman at his clinic than I did playing four years of club volleyball at Ball State as an undergraduate.

In the next several years, I attended the USVBA national tournaments and had the opportunity to take notes and film the top teams in the country playing volleyball at a very high level.

Another major breakthrough in my volleyball education occurred when Coleman received a State Department grant to travel to Poland and study volleyball in that country. His leave would also involve attendance at the world championships. Jim agreed to take five reels of 16-millimeter film of the top teams in match play for use by the coaches of the Midwest Intercollegiate Volleyball Association (MIVA). As league president, I had the responsibility of storing and mailing the films to the seven league members, who could then study them for two weeks. When the films were not on loan, I would have hours to study and analyze what the finest teams in the world were doing in terms of skill execution and team tactics. Largely because of what I picked up from these tapes, Ball State dominated the MIVA in the 1960s and the early 1970s.

When I look at the videotapes and coaching books now on the market, I realize how fortunate beginning coaches are to have so many excellent resources available to provide answers to their coaching problems.

When I received the freshly typed chapters that were to make up *The Volleyball Coaching Bible,* I couldn't wait to sit down and ponder everything these extremely qualified coaches had to say about their topics.

Cecile Reynaud, my coeditor, and I had spent hours discussing the qualifications of the nation's most successful coaches and identifying the chapter in the book we felt each would be best qualified to write. After completing our list, we divided our contacting responsibilities and outlined the junior tournaments and conventions that were forthcoming. Most of the top coaches attend those tournaments for recruiting purposes, so we felt that we would have the chance to sit down individually with each of the potential writers and discuss the opportunity we were presenting to them—to share their knowledge with fellow coaches. This process worked out perfectly. In almost every case, the coaches were eager and excited to be part of this extraordinary book.

We are extremely pleased with the first part of the book, "Coaching Principles and Priorities." Topics in this section are difficult to write about because they involve soul searching based on years of coaching experience. And experience is what we looked for in the writers of this section—Mark Pavlik of Penn State, Mike Hebert of Minnesota, and Jona Braden of Kentucky. I am confident that you will find this section inspiring as you plan for next season.

The second part, titled "Program Building and Management," provides a road map to success. As you read the five chapters on program building, you will notice similarities in the challenges faced by the five writers, although each is working with a different segment of the volleyball community. Olympic gold medal coach Doug Beal offers what he feels are the critical steps to building a competitive, successful team. His chapter, "Seeking Excellence in a Program—Going for the Gold," is worth the price of this book. Couple this with sage words of advice from Terry Pettit, the man who put Nebraska volleyball on the map, and you will have completed your quest for solutions to your marketing and program-building problems.

John Dunning, coach at Stanford, discusses the keys to developing a successful college program. Dave Shondell, one of the nation's outstanding high school coaches, outlines the factors that have brought him success. Tom Pingel, the current director of high performance national programs for USA Volleyball, was a key player in the success of the Munciana and Circle City junior volleyball programs. He is highly qualified to outline the keys to organizing and managing a junior program. After reading these chapters, I know you will have gained significant knowledge about program building and management.

The third part of this book, "Innovative and Effective Practice Sessions," is exciting reading for the inquiring coach, especially because the authorities presenting it have proven their expertise in the areas they have written about.

No one does practice planning better than Penn State's Russ Rose, coach of the 1999 NCAA women's Division I championship team. Mary Jo Peppler, outstanding clinician and member of the Volleyball Hall of Fame, divulges what she has found to be the keys to successful teaching. She has a new twist on some ideas about teaching that she is excited about sharing with readers.

Bill Neville, Olympic gold medal coach, is one of the best when it comes to drill construction, and he is eager to share what he has found to be successful in his years of coaching.

John Cook, fresh off winning a national championship at Nebraska in 2000, outlines some of the conditioning secrets that has brought him success throughout his coaching experience at Wisconsin, Nebraska, and in the USA national program.

Part four opens with Florida's Mary Wise covering serving instruction and training. Her teams are always in contention for the national championship, and serving has always been one of her team's strongest weapons.

Who is more qualified to discuss serve reception than Steve Shondell, who has won more matches and state championships than any other coach of girl's volleyball in the state of Indiana? We all know how much a team's success depends on its ability to pass the serve. This is a critical chapter for any coach.

The most successful NCAA Division III coach before her recent retirement was Teri Clemens of Washington University of St. Louis. Her team's setters were always successful because of their consistency and intelligence; she shares those secrets with you in her chapter on setting.

Former USA women's team player and currently on the coaching staff at the University of Southern California, Paula Weishoff is our choice to discuss the ins and outs of attacking, and she does an outstanding job.

The Buckeyes of Ohio State have a reputation based on their tenacious backcourt defense, and here to present his secrets to success is Jim Stone.

When it comes to blocking, we turn to former USA men's coach Rudy Suwara. Rudy has also been successful at the college level, coaching men at UC Santa Barbara and women at San Diego State.

Offense is complicated, and offensive systems are based on team personnel. For that reason we have two chapters on this topic. Fred Sturm, former USA men's national team coach, currently coaches women at Boise State University. He discusses offense from his position as a women's coach, yet he offers many tactical suggestions applicable to men's programs. Peter Hanson's Ohio State men's team is known for a quick, complicated offense best suited for the quicker and more powerful men's teams. The reader will enjoy and learn from both chapters.

The final chapter in this section is written by former USA women's coach Taras Liskevych, who has also had coaching experience with women at Pacific and with men at Ohio State. The principles of defense described in his chapter are applicable to both men's and women's teams.

The last part we call "Game-Winning and Tournament-Winning Strategies." The coaching abilities of the contributors to this section have proven time and again that they are in control when the game is on the line.

Successful coach of the Wisconsin Badgers, Pete Waite shares his thoughts on the importance of the mental aspect of coaching in giving players and teams the competitive edge.

Once the world's leading authority on scouting and recording data on volleyball performance was the late Jim Coleman. A former coach of the USA men's national team, Wittenberg University, and George Williams College, Coleman was the one initially responsible for the current system used in this country for recording proficiency in executing volleyball skills in game situations.

The book closes with a message from the most successful coach in college volleyball, Al Scates. Opponents of UCLA men's team have been the victims of Al's ability to prepare his team for major competitions and to make critical adjustments, offensively and defensively, during the match if the opponent employs tactics not anticipated in the original game plan.

Coach Scates, in illustrating the importance of scouting and practice preparation, discusses how the ups and downs of the 2000 season were beneficial in building his team's determination to win UCLA'S 18th NCAA championship. This total far exceeds the number of NCAA championships won by any other NCAA coach in any sport.

It is a great privilege for Coach Reynaud and me to be coeditors of what we feel is one of the finest sources of coaching information for volleyball. We are indebted to the outstanding coaches who have so unselfishly contributed their knowledge to this book.

PART I

Coaching Priorities and Principles

CHAPTER ONE

Living Up to the Responsibilities of a Model Coach

Mark Pavlik

Merriam-Webster's Collegiate Dictionary offers these definitions:

model: an example for imitation or emulation.

coach: one who instructs or trains a performer or a team of performers.

Does the model coach exist? Thousands of coaches in the world of sport work intensely at their craft, but are any of them a model coach? By precise definition of the term, a *model* is an example only. The imitator determines the worthiness of the model he or she chooses to imitate.

Coaching encompasses many facets, and the model coach (if one truly exists) has the facets in perfect symmetry. Viewed individually, we see each facet in a relative light. For instance, we might say, "He can really teach skills, but his administrative skills are poor," or, "She can really recruit, but she can't get along with her peers." So the model coach may be similar to the model diamond: each has perfect facets in a relationship that sustains the whole gem and warrants the label of being the very best. And everyone wants to copy the very best.

So it is with living up to responsibilities of being a model coach. All coaches have strengths and weaknesses—perfect and imperfect facets—of their coaching personae. Generally, we look to those who have achieved success at certain levels as our models. To correct deficiencies, a coach of a 12-and-under team may look to the 18-and-under coach. The high school coach may look to the collegiate coach, who may emulate the international coach, and so on. All coaches will be or have been models to others during their careers. What facets should we view in others and address for our particular situation? Although we may look at individual aspects, we should understand that the symmetry and structure of the diamond and the relationship of its facets form the strength and beauty of the diamond, allowing it to withstand just about any stress introduced to it. Pertaining to coaching, isn't that what is needed? Coaches must strive to be impervious to stress. They should have the ability to protect and insulate the team, to provide the team with a structure so strong technically, tactically, and socially that it will perform well under any stress. How does a coach approach this responsibility? I wish I knew! This approach seems to be a lot more about relationships than about Xs and Os, doesn't it? So let's examine the relationships that exist in coaching.

Coach-Self Relationship

The most important relationship, even above the player-coach relationship, is the coach-self relationship. Let's face it—most coaches will not become wealthy as a result of coaching. Knowing that coaching is calling may be the first twinge of the coach-self relationship. Questions will come to mind. Answers may not come easily, and those that do may not be comfortable.

The coach must analyze the coach-self relationship: Am I good at this? Can I make a difference? Is this something I am happy with? Don't I know anything else? Can I make it work as a career? Do I know what I am doing? Will I get better? Will I be good? And, quite possibly, at some point in a coach's career comes the real question: What am I doing? (This usually surfaces as I watch my team demonstrate a level of volleyball that borders on awful!)

So this facet of coaching, understanding the relationship with self, may be the keystone of the coach's structure. This facet will be the one that enables the coach to survive the stress induced by career and outside agencies. To many of us, model coaches seem to show a dogged determination to succeed with their teams—not necessarily in the win-loss criteria but in helping their teams achieve excellence. For example, these coaches appear confident in their ability to accept and even direct consequences in a manner beneficial to their efforts.

These coaches seem well balanced, emotionally healthy, and hard workers. Our models carry an air of confidence and leadership. "Let's get it done, and I will show you how!" seems to radiate from them without their saying a word. Our models have a terrific coach-self relationship. They are the real things: bright diamonds in a sea of cubic zirconium.

Coach–Player Relationship

The next facet is the coach-player relationship, the consequences of which leave grown (and reasonably rational) men and women shaking their heads. For most coaches, the rewards of their career or avocation are based on young people. The results which a coach gets can be downright emotionally draining at times.

The players are youths playing a game. Coaches want them to improve, but players want to play the game better. Of the millions of players we collectively coach, few reach the pinnacle of the sport. Many, however, continue to participate well past their association with their coaches. They simply love the game.

At some level, the love of the game may be the cornerstone of the coach-player relationship. Our model coach radiates a love of the game. Winning or losing, in or out of season, at the gym or at home, our model coach talks about, dissects, and most importantly, thinks deeply about the simple parts of the game. The players understand this much better than we may imagine. If our love of the game is sincere, then the coach-player relationship is on solid ground.

Our model coach shows a decided respect to and for the players. The coach is encouraging yet demanding, patient yet pushing, calming yet motivating. He or she manages to be equitable to the team but not necessarily fair to the individual. Nevertheless, team morale is high, and achieving excellence is the focus of the team.

Many coaches deal with student-athletes. Whether the level is elementary, junior or senior high school, or college, the model coach emphasizes the importance of successful academics. In the coach-player relationship, our model coach encourages players to be successful in other parts of their lives. He or she is always interested in the academic progress of the student-athletes and finds appropriate situations to review this aspect of their lives with them. The model coach is an adult concerned about the total development of the player.

Model coaches provide expert instruction. They are knowledgeable, experienced, and inventive. They teach. They convey. They care. They think and find a way to share that with their teams. No matter the personality of a team, our model coach enables it to achieve excellence. In viewing a training session of the model coach, we find that the players play hard. This manner of playing may be the greatest show of respect from the team to the coach. To go hard in a training session is all that players can control. In doing so they acknowledge that the structure of the session will ultimately improve team and individual performance. They are telling the coach, "We will follow you."

Coaches do it in different ways. Their approaches are as dissimilar as night and day. Some use a reserved approach, some use humor, some sarcasm and cynicism, but all have established a coach-player relationship that works. How do they establish a relationship? Another of the strengths of our model coach is listening—not only to what the players say but also to what they don't say. Soliciting input from players and considering the information they give helps the model coach establish the coach-player relationship.

Model coaches may obtain a measurement of this facet by the number of former players who have moved into the coaching ranks. Their love of the game was fostered, not inhibited. Model coaches are keepers of the game, passing along the love of the game to their players.

Coach-Administrator Relationship

Another facet of the model coach is his or her relationship to the administrators of the program. Whether it is a high school athletic director, the club board of directors, the collegiate athletic director, or the owner, the model coach maintains a professional and cooperative relationship with this person or persons. Our model coach is not a yes man or yes woman but one who has a stake in the success of the program. In cooperating with administration the model coach always finds ways to overcome whatever limitations are part of the job. If budget restrictions preclude the purchase of coaching aids, the coach finds a way to produce them. If other teams use the same gym, the coach works out a satisfactory schedule. Cooperation is also a facet of the model coach. The characteristics noted earlier regarding the coach-player relationship come into play in the coach-administrator relationship.

The model coach is a "player" within the administrative team and exhibits the traits of the players on his or her team. For example, when disagreements occur the model coach doesn't just complain—he or she is prepared with a solution. Our model coach also has a sense of timing in presenting arguments. Just as the coach asks players to present their concerns in an appropriate manner and time, the model coach does the same for the administrative team with one-on-one meetings and other suitable opportunities, foregoing the water-cooler ventings or antagonistic bitching-and-moaning sessions.

The model coach pays attention to the day-to-day office minutiae that is part of the administrative element of coaching. Adhering to timetables and deadlines helps the model coach maintain an effective coach-administrator relationship.

It seems to the outside world that the model coach has a harmonious relationship with his or her administrator. Harmony exists only when two or more parties work with complementary efforts. The model coach provides timely suggestions, accurate forecasts, and insightful rationale to provide the administration with a realistic view of the volleyball program. This activity is necessary because a coach cannot afford to think like an administrator, and an administrator cannot afford to think like a coach. The administrator is charged with the future direction of the club or program. The coach understands the importance of providing the information that will well serve the future decision-making process of the administrator. The two-way communication and understanding will help the program achieve the excellence toward which both parties are working.

The coach-administrator relationship can provide a larger sail to move the program even faster toward the desired shore of excellence. The model coach cares for this relationship as much as he or she does for any other.

Coach–Coach Relationship

Model coaches are always in a learning mode—always questioning, dissecting, and analyzing the game. They think best when discussions center on the game. Model coaches become animated and display their love of the game as they explore the topic. The best discussions usually occur coach to coach. Some of the best "clinics" happen during an informal setting. Coaches can convey and glean more information and experience in these settings than they can in any 30- or 40-minute lecture. The coach-coach relationship can pay great individual dividends.

The coach-coach relationship is a facet that all coaches find necessary. One of the main benefits of this relationship is that it enables coaches to take the game and themselves seriously. If we don't take the game seriously, why should we expect others to consider it important? Professionalism goes a long way.

The model coach realizes that professional growth originates from the respect one holds for the efforts of one's peers. If this were not the case, coaches would not try to improve as other coaches raise the bar. The model coach knows there is always a better way, a different perspective, or simply additional relevant information that can aid his or her efforts. The model coach knows that peers provide these.

How does one maximize this relationship? One obvious way is to network, to talk with as many coaches as possible. The many professional organizations for all types of coaches can serve this purpose well. Volleyball is blessed with some outstanding state and national organizations. The model coach becomes involved, attends clinics as a presenter, and listens to what other coaches have to say. The model coach started with a level of involvement that was comfortable and allowed for future growth. The coach has been able to build on previously gained knowledge and understand the new perspectives and thoughts presented.

Through maximizing the coach-coach relationship the model coach creates yet another mechanism to improve the game and those associated with it. Sharing ideas and experiences will always force reflection on one's own beliefs. Being forced to support a position when challenged usually leads to understanding the strengths and, more important, the weaknesses of that position. By beginning to challenge internally his or her personal belief, the coach gains a clearer understanding of the concept and develops more ideas about applying it or discarding it. Model coaches use the coach-coach relationship to improve their personal tenets of the game.

Those fortunate enough to be part of an athletic department that includes experienced and successful coaches of other sports can benefit from coach-coach relationships that cross the lines into those other sports. Many discussions center on the art and science of coaching and can provide insightful perspectives that the coach can apply to volleyball. For example, how a softball coach structures a warm-up, how a fencing coach prepares for a major competition, or how a football coach teaches footwork may supply the volleyball coach with new ideas. The more the model coach interacts with coaches of other sports, the better the coach will understand that coaching is a world unto itself and that ideas can come from anyone anywhere.

The coach-coach relationship provides an outlet for and with peers through which the model coach can review, recite, and reinvent ideas if necessary. The relationship ties all coaches together, gives greater meaning to what a coach experiences, and provides a support group within the coaching community.

Peers call on the model coach for support, thoughts, and, at times, constructive criticism. The model coach reaches this level in his or her career because of the willingness to be available and open with others.

This idea also extends to those within the athletic department. A genuine interest in the teams of other coaches and their efforts and successes fosters the coach-coach relationship. The volleyball coach goes to a field-hockey game, makes it to a baseball game, catches a wrestling match. The model coach supports colleagues and encourages them as they continue to strive for their own excellence.

Our model coach finds the coach-coach relationship necessary and fulfilling in a professional sense. It provides benefits both personally and to the team. The model coach knows that this relationship is important to the growth of the game, and he or she always strives to be part of that growth.

Coach–Official Relationship

How does our model coach handle the referees, especially when the duo is doing a great imitation of Stevie Wonder and Ray Charles, minus the music (unless whistles count)? No doubt our model coach feels frustration and may even be seen venting some of it, but even through this venting the model coach maintains a professional air, a dignity above reproach, while finding a suitable approach to questioning the referee's perspective of the situation.

The model coach realizes that the outcome of the match rarely rests on the efforts of the referee. They are human, and they will miss calls. We have all had calls go for us and against us. The model coach develops rapport with the officiating community, not necessarily to gain an advantage in dealing with them but to understand their approach to certain situations.

The officiating community, as a whole, seems to be open to discussion of interpretations and review of game situations. They seem to want the players to decide the outcome of a match.

As in the coaching profession, experience is the best teacher, and first-time officials have much to learn. The model coach improves the learning experience by providing accurate, constructive feedback. Being honest and specific works for the model coach and the referee in this situation.

The model coach knows the rules of the game for the level within which the game is being played and maintains knowledge of rules changes and updates. To achieve this, the coach must generally have discussions with the officiating community. As mentioned before, these conversations are beneficial to the game.

When a situation arises in a match, our model coach understands that the team will notice how he or she reacts to it. Our model coach rarely explodes from the bench and charges toward the second referee to question a call. The model coach perceives a controversial call as something out of his or her control. The coach understands that until he or she can learn all the facts from the officials, it does no good to introduce extreme emotions that exacerbate the situation. The team sees its coach under control and rational. Players know the coach is controlling the situation, not the other way around. They also may realize from the coach's reaction that he or she has supreme confidence in running the team. Controversial calls won't win or lose a match; the ability of the team to overcome questionable calls and continue to perform at a high level is what will decide the match. Our model coach doesn't whine or grovel for calls, and generally his or her team doesn't either.

So what does the model coach say to the officials? How does the model coach get a point across? Questioning what one sees and asking for clarification seems to get our model coach a calm response from the official. The coach also lets officials know when they have made a correct call and acknowledges agreement with the way officials viewed and called the play.

This coach-official relationship is ongoing. Experienced officials pride themselves on helping the game at each level grow, and the model coach takes every opportunity to aid the growth of the game. Talking with officials about the game is a priority for the model coach. Discussion allows the coach to learn from the point of view of a referee and the referee to learn from the point of view of the coach. In addition, it can be quite entertaining to realize the game can be seen from many distinct perspectives. The more honest the coach is in discussions with the referees, the more honestly referees seem to respond in dealing with the coach.

Finally, the coach-official relationship is important in forging improvement in the game. Input from both sides is needed to strengthen the game. Many underrate this relationship, but the model coach works hard to cultivate this informative conduit to the growth of the game.

Coach-Parent Relationship

At every level of the game, parents will be involved. It appears that the model coach has the confidence of the parents of the players. They seem not only to support but also to assist the coach. The coach seems to direct the assistance, somehow molding the parents into a team just as he or she did the players. How does the model coach accomplish this? What magic does the coach weave? Is it even possible for mere mortal coaches?

Coaches at different levels have different parental concerns. At the elementary or beginning level, parents may be concerned that their child is having fun. Winning and losing is not much of a concern.

At the high school level, participation concerns crop up as the lure of an athletic scholarship may drive the parents to ensure that college coaches will see their child.

The model coach communicates to the players the roles they will have. With this in mind, the model coach also communicates the roles the parents will have. Let's face it, negative dealings with parents generally stem from their perception that their child is not being treated well. Remember that the model coach has established that everyone will be treated equitably, but individuals may not be treated fairly. The coach is able to convey this message to the parents, and perhaps more important, the coach maintains consistency in this area with the team. Parents may not care about the team when their child is unhappy, but the model coach finds appropriate ways to allow the parent to voice concerns. Our coach listens and explains in terms of the development of the team and the player.

There is no question that some parents are too involved. The model coach, however, seems to have the patience of Job and the wisdom of Solomon and never constructs walls that add to the frustration of the parent. The model coach never ignores this parent but does filter input and uses what is useful. The model coach is firm and unwavering in dealing with those parents. The coach never compromises the philosophy or the basic tenets of the program, but instead communicates expectations to the players and parents.

The model coach helps educate the parents, not only in the game of volleyball but also in the ups and downs of an athlete's life. Parental pressure has received enough press in recent years—witness the stories about football player Todd Marinovich, an athlete pushed hard by his parents who later suffered burnout and was arrested on drug charges. Parents with lofty plans for their children as athletes may harm the child. Our model coach understands that players will have pressures from outside the game pushing and pulling them. The game itself will add pressure to the player. The coach can educate parents that tough times will be ahead for players and explain to parents that how the player handles adversity in athletics is just as important as how well he or she practices.

The best trait our model coach can have in this relationship is the ability to care for and treat players as if they were his or her own children. In the coach-parent relationship, at any level, parents want the best for their child. Our model coach understands their concern, and within the environment of fostering the team the coach provides a care for the individual that is evident to the parents.

Finally, although parents will always (and should always) raise concerns, the model coach takes the time to address matters in a professional manner. Our model coach makes this seem comfortable and always seems to placate the parents. The situation never escalates, and the player continues to improve. For many of us, this is the toughest situation as we attempt to create a team environment that may not be fair to some but is equitable to all. Taking a cue from our model coach, listening and communicating will not eliminate parental concerns, but it should provide them with an understanding of why and how decisions are made.

Living Up to the Responsibilities of a Model Coach

How can we, the merely mortal coaches, live up to such lofty expectations and great responsibilities? How will we know when we have mastered all that is required of us?

Maybe the answers to those questions lie in what we coaches preach to our team—effort! We ask them to do all the little things with enthusiasm and effort. We ask them to work hard at what they can control. We ask them to understand what we require of them and how their actions affect those around them. We ask them to be at their best when their best is needed. (OK, so those are Coach John Wooden's words, but the sentiment rings true.) We ask them to realize that their conduct and attitude always reflect on their teammates and team. We expect them to put forth the effort to do the best that they are capable of doing, no more, no less.

We expect them to do all of that over time. To gain in maturity, to gain in understanding, and to gain in appreciation of the game and the people around it are goals that we push them to attain and expect them to develop.

Ask any coach of any sport if any player ever stops learning the game. The answer will be that the learning never stops. It is that way with coaching too. The learning never stops.

How do we live up to the responsibilities of the model coach? We need to do it through sheer effort. We need to do it through an understanding of what is required of us. We need to want to do it.

A coach never knows when, where, or why former players will look back on their experiences with that coach, but every coach hopes that players, both current and former, will have learned something and appreciate the experience. So it is also that a coach never knows who will view him or her as a model coach. Will it be a player? An administrator? An official? A parent?

Approaching these relationships with the energy and dedication we give to our teams will significantly help us live up to the responsibilities of the model coach. Will we always react in a manner appropriate to the situation? Most times, yes. The time when we do not respond in the desired way offers an opportunity to learn and reflect. Hey, the model coach had to figure some things out the hard way!

Finally, the coach must be true to himself or herself. The coach must find what works for him or her. The coach should keep refining the various relationships by asking for feedback, listening to what others offer, and continuing to learn. Coaches can affect many people in a positive manner, and when we get right down to it, this is generally what hooked us into being coaches. Good luck and good coaching!

CHAPTER TWO

Establishing Principles and Setting Goals

Mike Hebert

I was sitting on the bench recently during a match. It was an important match, featuring live television, a crowd of over 5,000, and a lot on the line for both teams. In the middle of this intense match I suddenly hit the pause button in my mind. It was one of those strange molecular moments to which I am occasionally prone. Everything slows down for me, and right there, in the midst of an action-packed event, I can find myself wondering about some offbeat things. As the sights and sounds of the match receded into the background, I was struck with the incredible confluence of scenarios that were playing out in front of me.

- That player right there, hitting the ball, I wonder if I am living up to the promises I made to her during the recruiting process?
- And that referee, should I have said those things to her in game one?
- Look at all these event support people—the PA announcer, the sound guy, the band members, the ushers, the event manager, the equipment manager, the ball girls, Dick, the concessions guy, Liz, the TV producer, Tom, the radio play-by-play guy. Have I thanked them recently?
- Those walk-ons who are cheering at the end of the bench . . . am I giving them my best shot?
- All these fans . . . they came to watch my team play. What are they thinking? Are we playing hard enough? Will they come back for another match? I wish I could thank each of them personally for attending.
- I'd better watch myself tonight. Our guest coach sitting right behind me on the bench is a regent of the university.
- I wonder how our recruits are doing on their campus visit?

This type of thing doesn't occur all the time for me. But when it does, I am reminded of the fact that we coaches have to equip ourselves with a set of values and strategies for guiding our actions as we attempt to steer our programs toward success.

Goals and principles in coaching volleyball—where do they come from? It would be nice if everything were contained in a neat, precise outline available at the campus bookstore. But that's not how it works. Every coach has to earn his or her stripes in the coaching business. And it's not easy. In fact, acquiring the necessary Xs and Os is a simple task compared with the sometimes exasperating trial-and-error process required to piece together an effective coaching philosophy.

What is a coaching philosophy? I believe it comes from the values that serve as the foundation for the important decisions all coaches have to make, along with the leadership skills that serve as guidelines for a coach's goal-setting and goal-pursuing strategies. But where do these values and strategies come from?

First, we all carry into our coaching the accumulated experience of a lifetime. We develop our own code for what is right and wrong. We are patient, or we are impatient. We are tyrants in the gym, or we are benevolent and compassionate. We are arrogant, or we are diplomatic. We see the glass as half full or half empty. The bottom line is that our accumulated life experience imprints each of us with a particular, unique disposition. It is the starting point for each of us as we seek to develop a set of coaching principles and goals.

Second, we rely on the mentoring process. Mentoring provides a significant reservoir of ideas from which we select some of our most important coaching principles. Those who coached us during our formative years as athletes often leave lasting impressions. Later on we strive to observe the methods of highly successful colleagues, hoping to glean from them the concepts that have led to their high-level accomplishments. We go to clinics, read books, and view videos to study the master coaches. Our mentors, no matter how we access them, can save us from reinventing the wheel. They can provide us with proven, time-tested principles. Mentoring is an essential component in assembling a coaching philosophy.

But a third, and sometimes overlooked, source comes from what I call "defining moments" in our coaching lives—powerful moments that leave us with new and valuable insights. We rarely know in advance when or where they will occur. But their effect can be deep and lasting. I'll go so far as to say that most coaches, when asked at the end of a career to identify the most influential experiences in the development of their coaching philosophy, will refer to a series of defining moments.

The defining moments—what do they look like? And how do they weave their way into the effort to build a coaching philosophy? Allow me to lead you through some of the defining moments in my coaching career and demonstrate how those experiences helped me build a collection of principles and a strategy for pursuing goals. I ask you to understand that the following samples are only momentary snapshots of how some of my principles have evolved. I do not intend my experience to be a roadmap for everyone to follow. It merely provides groundwork for further, more sophisticated thinking on this important subject.

Respect the Process

The season had just ended. Like so many coaches of my generation I could no longer tolerate the lack of appreciation displayed by the modern athlete—appreciation for the game, appreciation for discipline, appreciation for the hard work of the many people who had pioneered the development of the women's college game.

I had begun to notice things. Little things. Thinking they were going undetected, players would occasionally roll their eyes when asked to try harder and practice longer. They complained more frequently about uniform style and shoe discomfort. Vans gave way to charter buses, commercial flights, and, in some cases, charter air travel. Still I noticed pockets of complaining, unappreciative behavior, clique formation, power tripping, turf protection, and a myriad of other forms of what I considered disrespectful behavior.

In response to each of these interactions I would act out the silent, internal dialogue with which so many of you are familiar because you have, at some point in your coaching lives, encountered the same emotions.

"How dare they bring that behavior into my gym? In the old days players bought their own shoes, wore hand-me-down uniforms, drove eight hours in crowded vans, felt pampered whenever the budget allowed for a sit-down meal, slept four to a room at the Motel 6, sold sandwiches and candy on campus to raise money, swept the floor and put up the nets before matches, and were stuck with unreasonable practice and lifting times because every men's sport had priority over women's volleyball in facility scheduling.

"Where is the respect for history? Where is the appreciation for the people who fought all those battles through the years so that these players could enjoy today's sparkling volleyball environment? I want every face to radiate appreciation. I want exaggerated thank-yous for the cool shoes and apparel that my hard work with a sponsor has provided. I want oohs and aahs as they walk into the lobbies of the nice hotels we stay in. I want expressions of gratitude when they order freely off the menu without having to stay under the $6.50 cap."

I wanted respect, and I wasn't getting it. I was angry and had reached the end of my rope. I had officially lost it. I hunkered down in my office with a stack of yellow legal pads (computers were not part of a volleyball coach's office arsenal in those days) and a supply of pencils. Nostrils flared, brow furrowed, beads of sweat on my forehead, I attacked the first legal pad with self-righteous vengeance. It took me over three hours. But I did it. I listed everything I could think of, every single thing about coaching today's athlete that had begun to tick me off.

The next day I hurried to read over my notes. They sounded great! I rewrote them into a list of 82 items (I called them atrocities), each one packing the solid punch of a coach who had had it with the attitude of today's athlete. "Today's athlete"—that became one of my favorite terms.

Phase two of my plan to save the sport of volleyball was about to unfold. As the self-proclaimed supreme ruler of the volleyball universe and protector of all historical volleyball purity, I decided it was time to lord over my subjects. I called a team meeting. I was going to blast the players with both barrels. I would finally have my moment to say the things that I had wanted to say for so long.

The meeting lasted over four hours. You can imagine how long it takes to deliver 82 items, complete with embellishments and accusations. Afterward, I felt great. I had held back nothing. I had been cleansed. At last, the air had been cleared. And there would be changes, huge changes! Certainly the players would return from the holiday break with a renewed attitude, elevated to new heights by the laserlike messages contained in my marathon rant.

Or so I thought.

The meeting was a bust. I was the only one who walked away feeling good. The assistant coaches were mortified. The players were in shock. What had happened to their easygoing, sincere, compassionately demanding leader and colleague? Comments among players went something like this:

"What in the hell was he talking about in the meeting?"

"Who is Flo Hyman?"

"Do you really think he wants us to clean the gym floor with a toothbrush?"

"Whoa . . . is this what a midlife crisis looks like?"

"Holy buckets, four and a half hours and no potty break!"

A few days passed. One of my assistant coaches finally mustered the courage to talk to me. She started with this: "You might want to tone things down a bit, like substituting something softer for the word *atrocity*." I encouraged her to keep talking. She went on to tell me that although I expressed some valuable insights during the meeting, they were unrecognizable by the time they reached the ears of my players. Then it hit me. I had stopped coaching. I had become a complainer. I was in the early stages of coaching burnout. So I did what all of us do when our behavior is shown to be out of line. I freaked out.

This was a defining moment in my coaching career. I had allowed the emotional magnets of frustration and job pressure to pull me away from my obligation as an educator and a coach. My response to the dilemma that I had created would be crucial. But what was I supposed to do? I had to win back my team and reclaim the level of respect that I had earned before my botched attempt to set things straight. Then, maybe I would be able to get my program back on track.

I went back to my notes. I began to sort out the legitimate messages that I wanted my team to hear and discarded the rest, which turned out to be emotional venting that had little pedagogical value. I boiled the 82 items down to 25. I reworded the points so that the players could hear them instead of being bludgeoned by them.

For example, "Atrocity number one involves the constant lying and half truths that I have to witness on a daily basis. Your sniveling attempts to stretch and hide the truth remind me of children trying to lie about sneaking cookies out of the jar. This immature crap will cease immediately," became "I will work hard to tell the truth in my interactions with teammates and coaches."

Eventually I trimmed the list of 25 items to 15. To this day I still use these 15 as an expression of some of the principles that I believe are important to team success. I have a title for this list. I call it "Respect the Process." I learned to believe that participating on a team is not a thing, but a process. The success of a team lies not in the material things that it acquires (fancy uniforms, beautiful locker rooms, slick charter airplanes, expensive meals, etc.) but in how successfully its participants interact, manage conflict, develop pride, cultivate a sense of discipline and loyalty, and commit to the pursuit of goals. In other words, good teams are, first and foremost, good at understanding and negotiating the process of living in an athletic team environment. This is why I label my list of 15 items "Respect the Process" (see page 19).

All of this came to me during a defining moment, during the hours, days, and weeks that followed the conversation with my assistant coach. I realized that I had lost track of the principles of teaching. I had blamed the players for my frustration level. I forgot that a good coach plays the hand that he or she is dealt, and that good coaching is measured by how one plays the hand, not by the quality of the cards that are dealt. A good teacher assesses the situation, sets goals for the group, creates sound pedagogical strategies that will lead to goal achievement, and all the while daily cultivates a positive environment that will accelerate the entire process.

I learned that, over time, a coach can break loose from these sound educational principles when personal frustration, unexpected failures in team performance, the presence of an "uncoachable" athlete on the roster, injuries to key players, irate parents, and other distractions team up to create a negative emotional spiral. And I learned that the correct response to this stage of coaching burnout is to retrench, to rededicate to the sound principles of coaching that had led to earlier successes, and never to forget that my players are students and I am their teacher. If they don't learn, it's not their fault. It's mine.

Clearing the Arteries

Team chemistry is an elusive thing. There are probably as many definitions for it as there are coaches. "Let's all pull on the same end of the rope" and "Let's have some fun out there" are examples of appeals to team members to play with chemistry. But what do we mean when we say these things? What are we asking our players to do? Well, here is what I think: team chemistry is the daily cultivation of common behaviors that maximize a team's ability to achieve their goals. In other words, the better the team chemistry, the better chance we have to reach our team goals.

The ingredients of chemistry can differ from team to team. But I suspect that an overlapping set of principles lies at the core of basic team chemistry. These principles have in common the goal of overcoming any psycho-

Respect the Process

University of Minnesota Volleyball

As a Gopher volleyball player . . .

1. I will work hard to tell the truth in my interactions with teammates and coaches.
2. I will learn how to set goals, live by them, and develop a lifestyle that will produce success on the court.
3. I will overcome the urge to complain, think negatively, backstab, take part in cliques, act selfishly, or to engage in any other unnecessary behavior that disrupts team chemistry.
4. I will maintain my academic life on a solid foundation throughout my career, never creating problems for the team because I failed to take care of my academic responsibilities.
5. I will be loyal to my teammates, to my coaches, and to my program. I will not air "dirty laundry" outside the team fabric.
6. I will become an ambassador of our program, going out of my way to make friends and boosters feel great about being around Minnesota volleyball.
7. I will learn the principles of positive reinforcement and apply them in practice and competition.
8. I will show frequent and genuine appreciation to those who work on our behalf (managers, administrators, support personnel, etc.).
9. I will comply with the acknowledgment rule at all times (using good listening, verbalization, and eye-contact skills).
10. I will operate with a high level of gratitude and respect for what has been provided for me in this program (e.g., keeping locker and team rooms clean, picking up after myself at practice, turning in equipment and apparel in acceptable fashion, never forgetting to bring handouts to meetings, keeping hotel rooms and busses neat during use, etc.), and I will do all of this with a sense of pride.
11. I will be accountable for all team requirements (e.g., completing tasks on time, being dependable, being on time, etc.), and I will do this with a sense of pride.
12. I will learn to anticipate upcoming responsibilities. I will not fall into the disappointing trap of hiding from issues, being the last to raise my voice when something needs to be taken care of.
13. I will learn to be aware of the effect of my mood swings on people around me and to keep these swings within a reasonable variance.
14. I will eliminate the use of obscenities during practice and competition.
15. I will accept the decisions of the coaching staff regarding playing time. I will support my teammates when I am not in a match.

logical obstacles that might keep a team from succeeding. These principles become the heart of the team, and they flow through the team's arteries to each player, coach, and staff member. They pump life into the team's mission. For a team to achieve its goals these arteries must remain clear.

Let me share an example, another defining moment.

I once had a team that was cruising along quite well. We were winning at a high level. But beneath the surface two issues were percolating that would soon begin to clog the team's artery system.

The first issue had its roots in the simple notion of communication on the court. All coaches are keenly aware of the need for teamwide verbal communication during practice and competition. This communication is vital to the ability of the team to clarify uncertain situations, declare intentions, elevate confidence levels, provide positive reinforcement to each other, rescue a player who makes a mistake, and so on.

But producing consistent and relevant communication requires energy. Some players are naturally better at it than others, or perhaps some work harder at it. And some players are naturally quiet and rely on the more outgoing players to supply all the energy. These players are either verbally challenged or lazy, and they exist on every roster.

Although we were winning, only two players consistently provided the energy required for an adequate verbal communication system. The other four players were selfishly relying on the two energy providers to shoulder the entire burden. This worked for a while. But about six weeks into the season, signs of frustration were beginning to appear. The energy providers were becoming increasingly impatient when a serve would drop between two of the silent types. Even worse, the energy providers were beginning to resent the fact that they had to carry the communication load. Their own performances were beginning to suffer, and they wanted help.

The second issue had to do with the division between those who were devoted exclusively to team goals and those who were stuck on selfish, individual agendas. The most common source of frustration was lack of playing time. This was not a problem unique to my team. Nevertheless, it had become a divisive issue for us. Some of the nonstarters had begun to openly display their frustration over lack of playing time, and their attitude was becoming an irritation for those who were committed to team goals.

Left unchecked, these two issues would turn a potentially successful season into an underachieving one. It was clear that we had to do something. I asked a consultant to sit in on a series of meetings with the team. He was a proven facilitator who specialized in values clarification and had a good track record in helping groups resolve conflicts and move forward. He guided us through some complex and sometimes difficult discussions. Here is what we learned.

- If we do not wish to remain the same, we must do things differently.

- The world of elite athletics creates a stressful environment, requiring that players and coaches operate in a stressful range of human interaction. It requires that all participants develop advanced communication and conflict-resolution skills. It requires the development of relationships strong enough to survive the stress.

- The absence of conflict does not mean that a team is doing well. The depth of conflicts is usually parallel with the depth of the relationships within the group.

- If a team doesn't have the ability to deal with conflict, it won't be able to deal with the stress of the season.

- All teams face the following challenge. When little things go wrong, the offended party takes a little step away from the group. When players repeat this response often enough, they pull apart from each other. Dealing with each of the little things is how groups achieve long-range success.

- Impulse control (frustration management) is the single most powerful quality for succeeding in a group. Players and coaches must learn how to manage themselves in the present and deal with the issue after the impulses have diminished.

- The rule of reciprocity must be in place. This rule states that if an individual wants to be critical of others, he or she must be willing to take it from others.

In our case we had a dilemma. Everyone wanted the team to be energetic on the court. But only two players had been providing energy on a consistent basis. Should their teammates trust that these two would never be sick or injured, never fatigued, never in a bad mood, and therefore rely on them to supply energy at all times? Or should we work on developing additional energy providers from among others on the team, even though they might not be naturals for the role?

The reality of this dilemma emerged during a brief exercise at one of the meetings. The facilitator asked the players, on the count of three, to point to the person who supplied the most energy and initiated the most communication on the court. "One . . . two . . . three." Every finger pointed in the direction of one player. When the facilitator asked the players to point to the teammate who was second in line as a supplier of energy and communication, all fingers again pointed at one player.

But when the facilitator asked the players to point to the person with the third-best skills in this area, not one player raised a finger to point to anyone. In this one moment, several things became clear. The top two energy providers quite obviously stood out from the others, and it was just as clear that there were no other energy providers.

This was, for our team, a defining moment. The players realized immediately that we needed a solution. They could no longer rely on luck. What if one or both of their energy titans were to become unavailable? Others would have to step up. From that day forward other players made a conscious effort to help out. None of them became nonstop talking machines. But their efforts were enough to render the issue sufficiently benign and allow the team to complete a highly successful season.

We also had to deal with the matter of playing time. Our chief concern was the distraction created by those who were not getting the amount of playing time they felt they deserved. This situation was nothing new. Distributing playing time is a problem for every coach of every team sport. But for some reason this particular episode became a defining moment for me. I suddenly understood why team goals and team values must always supersede individual goals. The players must make this commitment to each other. What would happen when things got tough? When unexpected losses occurred? When key players became injured? When the team faced adverse playing environments on the road? How were we going to survive these events without having made a total commitment to each other?

As the head coach it was my job to lay down the law. I had to clarify, for everyone in the program, why lack of playing time could never, ever become a reason for a player to become a distraction. I went to work on another list. I wanted to amplify the importance of team and to warn against the disruptions created by selfish, individual agendas. I went through several drafts and modifications. I resolved the matter in my mind. You may not understand every reference contained in the following document, but it will give you an idea of how I have learned to approach this matter.

Like you, I've faced numerous such episodes throughout my career and have seen how they can become roadblocks to the development of team chemistry. My response to each has been uniquely related to the circumstances of that particular moment and that particular team. But some generalizations have settled in over time as I accumulate more of these defining moments. Here are three of the more important ones:

- Team chemistry lies at the core of successful team performance.
- Every athlete brings to the table a uniquely different personality. It is impossible to cram everyone into one generic personality style. Each player deals with frustration differently, each player responds optimally to different motivational techniques, and each player sees a different path to resolving interpersonal conflicts. Every coach must tirelessly attempt to acquire the skills to identify these differences and to unify everyone around a common set of ground rules.
- Every player and staff member must learn and rehearse conflict-resolution skills on a regular basis. This is not always a popular team activity, but it is essential to team success.

Playing Time

University of Minnesota Volleyball

Playing time is a sensitive subject on any high-level volleyball team. I want you to be clear about my expectations and how I make my decisions.

1. You must learn to play one of the following roles:
   a. Stud
   b. Winner
   c. Stabilizer
2. You must display strong interpersonal skills.
   a. Be an energy producer.
   b. Resolve conflicts.
   c. Be a giver, not a taker.
3. You have to develop a strong skill base as measured by our statistical evaluation system.
4. You must display a commitment to team guidelines.
5. You must display a competitive attitude during practice and in competition.
6. You must display a commitment to strength training, conditioning, nutrition, and solid sleep and rest habits.
7. You will also be evaluated according to several "intangibles," such as your ability to inspire others, your ability to play well during critical moments in a match, your ability to be a "player," and so forth.

Clarifications

1. If you are not on the court during a match you might decide that you have read my mind and know my reasons for playing-time decisions without hearing them from me. Do not assume that you know. Many factors may be operating, such as limited substitution patterns, preferred matchups, or the quality of your practice performance leading up to the match. If you want clarification regarding your playing-time status, select a time apart from practice or competition and talk to me about my decisions.
2. I will attempt, whenever possible, to provide playing time for every athlete on the roster. But these opportunities cannot be guaranteed. And when they do or do not occur, my perception of when they should occur may not coincide with your perception.
3. Understand that above all, playing-time decisions are motivated by my obligation to produce a team that will defeat our opponent. I will always put the players on the floor who I think have the best chance to win.
4. It is likely that at some point you will disagree with my decisions. This is to be expected at this level of competition. Your job is to control your emotions and contribute to team chemistry.

I have learned that the process of cultivating the skills required to solve conflicts draws a team together, even if it never produces a total solution. Extracting a full commitment to the process is generally enough. Achieving full solutions to problems can often result. But the process itself is what keeps everyone committed to the maxim that team goals always supersede individual goals.

My way of making sure that we never lose sight of this process is to conduct regular "artery checkups." These might occur before or after practice, before or after competition, on a bus, in an airport lobby, or at a hotel meeting. But I provide many opportunities for players and staff to identify any blockages that might prevent those arteries from pumping valuable life to every corner of our team environment. If we find a blockage, we examine it, suggest a strategy for treating it, and work hard to minimize it. Keeping the arteries clear has become a staple in my list of coaching principles.

The Art of Goal Setting

I learned about the power of setting goals early in my career. The defining moment for me occurred at the conclusion of the EAIAW regional championships in 1976. I have written about this experience before in my 1990 book, also published by Human Kinetics, entitled *Insights and Strategies for Winning Volleyball* (pp. 108–109), so I'll do my best to provide the short version here.

I was coaching the women's volleyball team at the University of Pittsburgh. It was my first-ever coaching job. When I was first interviewed, I thought I was looking at coaching a men's team. I was wrong. There was no men's team. They wanted a coach for their women's team. I sensed a problem. I had never seen a women's volleyball match. I was unprepared for the challenge in every way. I had just completed a PhD in an unrelated field (philosophy) and had no formal training in physical education or motor learning. I had never taken a coaching class. All I knew about coaching was what I remembered from my high school and college coaches.

I took the job anyway because I needed the part-time income. When I first met with the team I was forced out of ignorance to ask questions like "Are we any good?" "How do you normally organize your practices?" and "Can anyone in the room set the ball?" I knew this was going to be a challenging experience.

For some reason, at that first meeting, I wondered aloud how many matches we might win. Silence gripped the room. I found out that the team had struggled to a poor record in 1975 and that none of the top players had returned. "We're not only going to qualify for the regionals," I blurted, "we're going to be in the top four!" To this day I cannot explain why I said that. I had never seen my team practice or compete. Nor had I seen any of our opponents. Why the regionals? Why the top four in the region? I don't know. It just came out.

The 1976 season unfolded methodically. Every day I would remind my players of our goals. If we practiced poorly I would say something like, "We can reach our goals only if we work harder to improve our passing." We won consistently and finished with a 25-3 regular-season record. We qualified for the regional championships as the eighth seed. We upset the number-one seed in the second round and earned the right to play in the semifinals.

We lost our semifinal match, but we had achieved our goals. We had qualified for the regional championships, and we had finished in the top four. The volleyball community was surprised by our performance. How could this mediocre team, using largely the players from the previous season, suddenly become a regional semifinalist? My answer is simple. I declared from the outset that we would achieve specific goals, and I relentlessly repeated those goals to motivate every aspect of our preparation before and during the season. I wasn't aware of it at the time. But I had discovered the center of the target. Goals, creating them and pursuing them, operate as a compass to guide coaches and players toward successful outcomes.

But there are some things about the goal-setting process that all coaches should know. First, you have to believe that how you think and how you feel affect your performance. Thinking and feeling—those belong to the domain of psychology. For those who believe that psychology plays a role in determining who wins and who loses, goals are an important part of the competitive process.

For example, consider these quotes taken from accounts of selected athletes as they explain how they achieved the upset, the unexpected victory.

"We simply believed that we could do it. We never stopped believing in ourselves."

"From day one we set our sights on beating them. Every day in practice we talked about how we couldn't wait to see the shock on their faces after we beat 'em."

"It all boils down to pride. You have to have the feeling. Without it you can't win."

"We were able to stay connected on the court. We've had great chemistry all year."

"It's all about respect. After what they did to us last season, we felt they didn't respect us as a team."

Belief, visualizing, pride, connectedness, chemistry, respect—this is the language of psychology, not technical execution.

My hunch is that all of you have attempted to set goals with varying levels of success. If you are one of those who have struggled with the process, consider these 10 reasons why you failed to achieve your goals.

1. Your goals were the wrong ones. You thought your team was a lot better than it really was. You had an unrealistic view of how good you were in relation to your opponents.

2. You didn't believe in the goals yourself, or maybe you lost faith along the way.

3. You were politically unsophisticated and failed to get your team leaders to buy into the goals.

4. You didn't trust yourself to know instinctively what would motivate your players.

5. You didn't know how to empower your players to pursue team goals. Maybe you're a control freak.

6. You didn't cultivate the proper environment so that your goals could grow. You allowed counterproductive thoughts and behaviors to get in the way.

7. You clarified your goals at the beginning of the season, but you forgot to reinforce them regularly.

8. You structured your goals in the wrong language for this team. You superimposed your preferences without listening to your players.

9. You assumed that the same things that motivate you would motivate your players.

Language of Goal Setting

Here is an example of what I am talking about, an episode that became another defining moment. One year my team suffered a difficult opening-night conference loss. The players became obsessed with winning the return matchup scheduled for the final weekend of the conference season. They created "the countdown." They dedicated themselves to winning every intervening match, thereby guaranteeing that they could do no worse than tie for the conference championship. With each win they would extend their hands into the center of the postmatch huddle and yell in unison, "15!" which became 14, 13, 12, and so on, all the way to 0. When the countdown reached 0 they were poised for the showdown. The countdown had taken on a life of its own. It became the ceremonial centerpiece of the team's vision for success. This simple act, counting backward to 0 as a group, was the perfect expression of this team's emotional approach to realizing their goals.

I have suggested this strategy for teams since then. In one case, a team decided that its goal would be to win 14 conference matches. They counted backward from 14 after each conference victory. The deliberate, methodical psychological process of the countdown was perfect for this team, and they reached their goal.

But I was in for yet another defining moment as I approached the next season. Addressing a roster filled with veterans from the previous year, I suggested that they continue with the countdown strategy. I was surprised to see the players rebel at this. The psychological epicenter of the team had shifted from the previous year. This team believed that the countdown was an admission that they were going to lose a certain number of conference matches. This was unacceptable for these players. They perceived it as a lack of belief in their ability to win. It provided an escape clause. They wanted to believe, and they wanted their coaching staff to believe, that they could win every one of their conference matches.

So they created their own goal, crafted in their own language. They dedicated themselves to going "1-0" before every match. This clever adaptation allowed them to eliminate the problem of agreeing to predetermined losses, which was terribly demotivating for them. And it allowed them to face each match with the same, repeatable optimistic outlook. Unlike the earlier teams, which had found clarity in the countdown structure, this team wanted the emotional freedom to go into every match with determination and, significantly, with no escape clause. They felt insulted and mistrusted by the former strategy and fired up, empowered, by the latter.

The lesson is that the coach must learn the language, the emotional triggers, for each team. Teams are not all the same.

But this is only one aspect of the goal-setting process. Consider the additional lessons I learned along the way. All have their roots in defining moments similar to the one described earlier.

Pushing the Edge

Team performance goals must have credibility. Players know when you are missing the mark. You can't shoot too low. You could lose the respect and trust of your team if they begin to feel that you do not believe in their potential. And you shouldn't set goals too high either. Players don't want to be naively propped up for success only to be embarrassed because their coach misread their competitive potential.

Instead, a coach must engage in a strategy that I call "pushing the edge." Before each season I review several factors before meeting with my team to set goals. I research the rosters of each opponent on our schedule. Which players have completed their eligibility? Who is returning? Who are their new recruits? How might these departures and additions affect the chemistry of that team? What appear to be the strengths and weaknesses of each opponent as they head into next season? Then I ask the same questions of my team.

I also superimpose over each team, including mine, a template of what a conference championship team looks like from a statistical point of view. I ask myself which teams are capable of, for example, keeping their hitting errors below a certain percentage, or passing and digging with sufficient efficiency, or keeping their serving-ace-to-error ratio within an acceptable range. I also assess the leadership and chemistry potential of each team. I evaluate each opponent with a fine-tooth comb, and I project two possible scenarios.

First, I consider what might happen to my team if everything went our way during the season. How many matches could we win if we were to remain injury free, if every official's call were to go in our favor, if we were to catch quality opponents having an off night, if the schedule were to unfold perfectly for us so that travel fatigue would be minimal, if my players were able to play their best in the biggest matches, and so on?

Second, I consider what could happen to my team if the opposite were to occur. How many matches could we win in spite of suffering key injuries, experiencing poor calls, trying to fend off the opponent's best effort night after night, drawing an unlucky travel schedule that might exhaust our players, and absorbing less than outstanding performances from our go-to players in key matches?

This analysis provides me with a range of what to expect. Let's say, for example, that if everything goes well for us we could finish with a record of 25-6, but the opposite scenario would leave us at 18-13. Where do I set my performance goals? Do I play it safe and convince the team they can win at least 16 matches to guarantee that we will have at least a .500 season? No. That would insult the team's self-esteem and demoralize them. Do I announce that the team will go undefeated? No. That might set the team up for failure.

Instead, I push the upper edge of the range I established through my painstaking evaluation. I walk my team through my thinking process at a team meeting. We discuss my conclusions. The team has the chance to provide input. We agree to set our goals at the upper edge of the projected range, or slightly beyond. This allows the team to rally around a performance goal developed through in-depth analysis. By setting the goal at the higher end of this range, or slightly beyond, the players know they cannot relax. In fact, they know that they must overachieve to reach this goal. But they also know that they have not been saddled with something overwhelming or impossible. Pushing the edge has become a way of life for me as I work with my team to establish goals each year.

Stages in Team Building

Another critical skill in the goal-setting process is to know when and how to apply an understanding of the sequential stages that occur in the evolution of a winning program. For many years I knew intuitively that goals could not be the same every year for every team. I knew that each team possessed a unique personality and motivational style. I also knew that each team was precariously perched on a unique rung on the ladder to success. It was my job to identify each team's rung and to apply my understanding of the realities of being at that rung as we developed our goals.

For example, a young team facing a schedule of veteran opponents will have different goals, use a different language, and respond to different motivational strategies than would, let's say, a team of older conference-hardened players who have been through it all and are poised to punctuate their careers with a final drive for success. A team seeking first-time success will operate in a different goal environment from a team defending a conference championship.

Fortunately for me, my early thoughts on this matter received an unexpected boost. I read Pat Riley's book *The Winner Within,* in which he describes in detail how to set and pursue goals. The process requires great skill and sensitivity in a coach. In fact, it is an art. A coach, much like a gardener, must cultivate each day the rich and healthy topsoil from which these goals can grow to fruition. The skills outlined earlier—using appropriate goal language, pushing the edge—are building blocks for becoming a master goal setter.

Conclusion

I left out a lot. Coaches confront many dilemmas that require us to develop a principle, clarify a value, or set a goal. Consider these examples:

- As collegiate coaches, should compassion for a student-athlete's legitimate difficulties, such as illness, poverty, or a disruptive home environment, override our professional obligation to follow every NCAA rule, no matter how obscure?

- If we understand the intent of a rule and find a way to do something legally that may violate the intent but not the actual rule, should we do it? Or do we take the high road and do what the intent of the rule expects from us?

- Your all-star left-side hitter is hurting during warm-ups before the match. The tendinitis in her left knee is acting up. The team doctor tells you that he can use a medication that will help her get through the match. But you know that the result could be the beginning of a cycle of pain and medication that could be damaging to the athlete. What do you do?

- You are working at a state university that requires the separation of church and state. Three of your athletes ask if they can use the team meeting room to discuss Bible study. You also have non-Christians on your roster. What do you tell those three athletes?

- An athlete calls you at home one night. She tells you that she is pregnant. But she also pleads with you to tell no one. A complex set of issues immediately confronts you. What do you do?

- What do you tell your team about the use of alcohol? Do you condone it? If not, how do you monitor your players? If you ask them to be responsible in its use, what are the limits of responsibility? Are your policies the same for those who are minors?

These are but a few of the kinds of dilemmas we face every day as coaches. As I said earlier, there is no manual that contains all the answers. We do have a national governing body, rulebooks, conference policies, and institutional guidelines that provide some answers. But overall, the situations we confront are not cut and dried. They demand on-the-spot judgments. We have an obligation as coaches to take as much care in the development of values and goals as we do with technical development. We can look to our mentors for some of this. But we also need to remain vigilant in recognizing defining moments as they unfold. If we listen carefully, they can tell us volumes about how to manage ourselves as professionals.

As my brief mental interlude on the bench began to wind down and the action of the match began to recapture my focus, I remember feeling reasonably secure in the fact that I had at least tried during my 25 years of coaching to create a foundation of principles and goals that would provide answers to the questions that raced through my mind that night. I knew that I had tried to live up to my recruiting promises. I felt that I had improved my conduct in dealing with officials. I was confident that the support people working for volleyball felt good about being around the program. I liked the way that walk-ons were enfranchised and made to feel as though they played an important role on the team. I sensed that the fans were being treated to an exciting, well-administered event and that, indeed, many would return for subsequent matches. I trusted myself and my staff to behave with dignity and class. I knew we would never give cause for a regent, or anyone else, to think poorly of us. And I knew that everyone in my program would treat the visiting recruits with genuine courtesy and warmth.

I felt good about things. I was at peace with the goals and values I had crafted. And given the minefield of distractions, temptations, and other challenges that coaches confront on a daily basis, that is about as good as it gets.

CHAPTER THREE

Finding Direction and Inspiration Amidst Ups and Downs

Jona Braden

The season has ended, and the team has gathered to put closure to what has transpired over the past few months. It is a time of reflection, capturing, remembering, and celebrating. How many times have we done this exercise as coaches? What are our conclusions about the season? Do winning and losing define it, or do we become more three dimensional in our thought process as we distance ourselves from the moments of victory and defeat? What do we value about the experience of athletics? How would we describe it, explain it? Before we go any further in this journey, we need to travel back in time and recall how the season began.

The beginning of a season is full of excitement, expectation, and energy. Much thought, preparation, and planning have been given to the makeup of the team, that is, young versus experienced, leadership possibilities, veteran setter versus rookie, physical capabilities, team chemistry, and so on. The coaching staff anticipates the return of the team, hoping for a physically fit, enthusiastic, and focused group of athletes. Their leadership in establishing a clear-cut perspective must occur from the beginning. Capturing the magical moment surrounding the team's arrival for preseason is crucial to helping players make the transition quickly.

I ponder many questions. How prepared and informed are the players before their arrival to preseason training? Have I impressed upon the players the necessity to be ready to go from day one? Have I shared enough detail about the upcoming season throughout the summer? Has the team been mindful of what they said they wanted to accomplish and taken ownership of that vision and purpose? Are they supporting, encouraging, and challenging each other to their best effort in all areas? Where is the leadership coming from? Do they know and understand what they need to accomplish during preseason? How much have they invested this summer in physical training, working on skills, thinking, dreaming, and talking about the upcoming season? How pinpointed is their focus?

You speculate about where you believe the players are and how they fit into a competitive team. You may be approaching the season with many veteran players, or you could have a roster filled with youth. Either way, a coach takes time to look at the strengths and weaknesses of each player and begins to formulate a plan for the team.

A team can accomplish a great plan only after they put it into action. Putting it on paper and posting it in the locker room or playbook is a start, but the question that needs to be answered is how this group of individuals will paint the picture. How will they fit together the talents and personalities to form an interdependent unit? A team is not something that we can write down, read, and then regurgitate. It is a dynamic idea that must have substance, purpose, and action pulling and pushing it forward. For this idea to grow synergistically, the players must drive it. As a coach, how will you steer the process without limiting the players' ownership or stifling their vision?

The 2000 season was unlike any that I have experienced as a coach or player. It was a season laced with more than its share of adversity, disappointment, frustration, setbacks, and failure. As I look back on the season, I am reminded that it was not easy. Much of the time it was downright hard. Oddly enough, the difficulties we faced did not seem overwhelming at the time. The adversity we met did not cause us to feel as if we could not persevere, the disappointments we weathered seemed to urge us to keep moving forward, and the frustrations that surfaced allowed us to let go of the nonproductive mind-set and encouraged us to gain strength from what we were enduring.

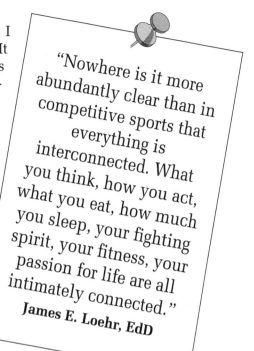

"Nowhere is it more abundantly clear than in competitive sports that everything is interconnected. What you think, how you act, what you eat, how much you sleep, your fighting spirit, your fitness, your passion for life are all intimately connected."
James E. Loehr, EdD

The most compelling and significant aspect of the season is that the team did not punt. Through it all the players kept fighting for the psychological air to keep moving forward. For the most part, they came to the gym every day with the attitude and intention of getting better. The questions kept coming: "What do we value? Is the win-loss record our primary criteria for defining a season?"

Keeping the Team on Track

Purpose always looks within to find itself, and then looks out. The athletes' efforts in challenging themselves to continue making improvements and having fun is why they keep coming back for more. By resolutely stepping into the practice arena every day and pushing their talent, the athletes will leave satisfied with how they faced the challenges and more confident because they've discovered more about who they are and what their team is all about. Being a part of sport is a process. Every day builds on to the next. Determining how to bring clarity and purpose to each day is an essential component to building and growing a team from the inside out. It is important to create an environment for success—one that encourages and supports players to come back to the gym every day with an enthusiasm for learning, with the humbleness and courage to try something new, with the discipline to maintain a solid work ethic, and with an understanding and respect for the process.

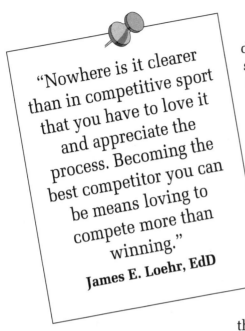

"Nowhere is it clearer than in competitive sport that you have to love it and appreciate the process. Becoming the best competitor you can be means loving to compete more than winning."

James E. Loehr, EdD

Involving yourself in sport must go deeper than what you see on the scoreboard. We all want to be crowned the champion, have the gold medal placed around our necks, and to have our hands held high declaring us the winner. The moment of glory when we step on the podium in recognition of our triumph is part of everyone's dream about sport. Is this truly what drives us each day of training and competition? If this is the only reason we step into the competitive arena, then how do we handle the many times that our performance does not put us in victory lane? I believe that competing goes deeper than that. Granted, we all love to win; that challenge is a huge component of sport. But is it the winning that speaks to our soul?

This season we were selected for a conference television match scheduled for our last weekend of play. As the season progressed, I forgot about the television opportunity. As I was preparing for the match, I received a telephone call from the sports commentator asking about my thoughts on the team and our upcoming opponent. Politely the commentator progressed through his list of questions. My instincts told me that I needed to put him at ease so that he did not worry about offending me with his interpretation of our season record and statistical data. Straight up, the current record did not give him the impression that we were a team to contend with, let alone appear on television. Without going into further detail, I shared what we had been accomplishing, learning, and experiencing as we progressed through the season, that we were maturing mentally, emotionally, and physically. I conveyed confidence in the competitive spirit of the players and noted that they continued to fight to the end, no matter what they were facing.

The vision and the mission statement of the team and program must be ingrained in the group's heart, mind, and soul. They must breathe it as their own and put it at the center of what they do every day. It is the language they speak, the message they live, and the imprint they will leave behind. It must be so clear and concise that each member understands how she fits into the creation. There must be wholeness in the spirit of the team, a faith that drives them forward. The mission must be what they stand for and believe in wholeheartedly. The emotional deposits they make with each other will reflect their trust. Their decisions will confirm what they value. Their actions will create a louder and deeper influence on the words they speak. The strength of their convictions lived out will be the glue that connects and binds the heart and soul of the group. Their shared dreams will foster joy and enthusiasm and keep the possibilities alive.

The televised match ended with our winning the match in four games against a team in the upper half of our conference who had beaten us in four games just 48 hours earlier at their place. The commentator approached me after the match with an exuberant, "This was a great match, this is a great story, and this is the best match that we produced all season." Who would have expected a team with a losing record going up against a program that was having one of its best seasons to come out the victor and give the audience a great performance?

It has been said, "In every experience there is a lesson. If you don't find the lesson, then there was no experience." In the episode of a season, the record does not define you. Winning does not define you. Losing does not define you. The experience of sport defines you by

- what you've given to the experience,
- what you've learned and how you've grown from the experience, and
- what you've become through the experience.

This validates the process.

The Game Within the Game

In sport the primary game is competition defined by winning and losing. Right? That is how we look at and evaluate sport. The emphasis is on winning the competition on the scoreboard. That's stimulating and gives purpose and reason for playing for the moment. But there is another game, an important game within the game. It's a game that, as a participant, we can always win.

For the sake of this premise let's recognize that competing against the opponent, winning or losing on the scoreboard, is full of things we cannot control—referees, the bounce of the ball, the environment, and so on. We'll call that game 1, and the game within the game we'll call game 2, which I define as the process or experience of sport. In game 2 everything is in your control because the contest is to be your best. The opponent is yourself, and the game is won or lost on a daily basis. Game 2 shows us that the primary reward in anything we set out to accomplish lies not so much in attaining the goal but in what we become and discover about ourselves by doing all that is necessary each day to attain the goal.

If we achieve the goal of game 1, we feel really good for the moment. We feel proud, and we should. But the feelings of success or failure, of winning or losing, are ephemeral—they fade over time. Game 2, on the other hand,

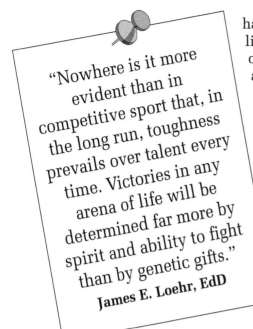

"Nowhere is it more evident than in competitive sport that, in the long run, toughness prevails over talent every time. Victories in any arena of life will be determined far more by spirit and ability to fight than by genetic gifts."

James E. Loehr, EdD

has substance and truly contributes to our lives. The process we go through in pursuit of game 2 and what we contribute to it make a lasting impression and give us something to draw from beyond the arena of sport. What lessons can we learn from the depth of this experience?

Part of this experience is courage—looking dead in the eye at the challenge in front of you, focusing on the moment at hand, and giving it your all to the end. Whether they have triumphed or have fallen short on the scoreboard, athletes know deep inside their hearts what they have given, what they have believed, what they have invested, where they have faltered, and how pleased they are in their effort. The glory of winning game 1 can carry an athlete only so far. How athletes experience sport, what they value and learn, is the harvest of what they planted during the process—the day-to-day pushing of their talent, the expectation of discovering more about themselves and each other, playing every day to win by doing all that is necessary to fulfill the shared vision and purpose. Throughout the journey, the means justify the end.

Assessing the process needs to be tangible and objective. Players need to understand the goal and the plan they will use to attain it. They should have a method of measurement to assess individual and team performance.

Principles of Play

We have established 11 "principles of play" as our yardstick. Each principle defines clearly what we expect individually and collectively. The principles are not subjective. Because everyone practices and plays from the same premise, the likelihood that players will become defensive over critique of their performance is reduced. Players are more open to receiving coaching that will help them improve their strengths and eliminate their weaknesses. In short, by using the principles of play, we avoid many potential obstacles to learning.

The exercise of establishing the principles of play involves the players in defining each principle. They establish criteria for why it is important, how it can be measured, and how they must demonstrate the principle to meet the expectation. For example, one of our principles of play states "*Protect* the attacker, *balance* the court, and *cover* the block." The language "protect, balance, and cover" speaks explicitly to the team. The cue words describe the expected action. One of our expectations is accepting the result of a point, letting go, and staying in the present. The principle that came out of this is "Play the next point." At the top of our list of principles of play is "Prepare for battle: mentally, emotionally, physically, and spiritually."

The principles of play are our compass. Although we hold ourselves accountable to this performance assessment, it is not rigid. The principles are a dynamic instrument in constant evaluation. If at any time the team wants to add a principle, delete one, or edit the language to meet increased expectations, they may do so.

Kentucky Volleyball Principles of Play

1. Prepare for battle: mentally, emotionally, physically, and spiritually.
2. Serve tough, aggressive = point opportunity
3. Protect the attacker. Balance the court and cover the block.
4. "Better the ball" with intention—precision.
5. Protect the floor at all times. Be instictive and fearless.
6. Prepare to attack. Be aggressive.
7. Communication is the key to timely and productive information.
8. Be alert and aware throughout the entire flow of play—proactive vs. reactive. Respect the process.
9. Remain connected and strong. Do not let go of each other. Be resilient.
10. Block with intent. Set a solid block, put hands on the ball, take an area away from attacker.
11. Play the next point!

Understanding Motivation

The most important question players or coaches can ask themselves is, "Why do I do what I do?" Over time, what motivates players becomes evident and instructive. Do they depend on the external environment and the result of sport? Or does their passion for the game provide the wind for their sails? Do they cherish and respect the opportunity to step onto the court with their teammates? Where is the experience of sport taking them? What lessons are they learning? What legacy will they leave behind? What story will they have to tell?

Coaches, too, must have a clear understanding of why they have chosen to teach this game. What makes their heart sing? How much patience do they bring to the process? Is your philosophy one that establishes a "way" of approaching sport that enhances the growth of young people across the spectrum of their lives? What legacy will it leave behind and what story will it tell?

A couple of seasons ago our team was on the bubble. We had grown much from the year before but were still looking for the consistency that would result in triumph more often than failure. We needed to win our last match to qualify for the conference tournament. Because the race was so close, a win would not only secure a spot in the tournament but also provide a better seed. We did not start well and went into the locker room down two games to zero. I reminded the players of what we had agreed on at the beginning of the season. I encouraged them to take a deep breath, to refocus their energy on being more productive in our execution, and to take it one point or side out at a time. Most important though, I asked them to believe in what they could do together by linking their hearts with a purposeful mind-set and staying the course until the last point. There was no question that our backs were against the wall, but the players affirmed that we needed everyone committed to the fight and that they could and would do what was necessary!

It's important to find a source of inspiration. Helen Keller has been a huge inspiration to me, and I share her story with my players at some point in their careers. All the odds were against this little girl. With no sight, no hearing, and no voice, she was trapped inside her body without any way of communicating her thoughts, fears, ideas, and dreams. Not until a certain teacher, Anne Sullivan, came along did her world begin to open up and permit her to discover that her circumstances imposed no limitations, that only great things lay ahead of her. Helen said, "I am only one, but I am one. I cannot do everything, but I can do something; and what I should do and can do, I will do." Coaches should encourage in players the self-talk of "I can" and "I will" because what they look for, what they expect to see, and what they believe is possible is what they are likely to discover. A phrase such as "I'm trying" does not provide clarity and the confident mind-set that pushes people to get better.

The team came together in the locker room, took a deep breath, looked each other in the eye in silence, grabbed hands in the center of the circle, and quietly said, "Together." A focused group stepped out on the court and executed with a fervent, fearless enthusiasm that they could muster only among themselves. They chipped away point for point, side out for side out, determined to pour everything out on the court, leaving nothing to spare. The fans witnessed a transformation right before their eyes, most likely leaving them with the same question that a sports writer asked me after our team won three straight games against the number-three seed in the conference tournament. He asked me, "What was said in the locker room, Coach, between games two and three?" With respect for our opponent, I quickly reflected on what had just transpired—a come-from-behind victory with our backs against the wall and much at stake (qualifying for conference tournament), our individuals rising to the challenge and answering the call. I smiled and said, "It is not what was said between games two and three that carried us to this moment, but what we started in March of 1998, when we began to plant the seeds, share the vision, steer the course, and encourage growth and ownership to occur from the inside out." From the beginning, in practice and in working each day to improve, we tried to impress on the players this thought: Today it is being decided, when a match is on the line in a difficult moment, whether you will rise up to meet it or shrink from it.

I felt that our victory was a defining moment, not because we had won the match but because the players demonstrated in the heat of competition what they had been learning day by day. They did it together, without fear of failing and without hesitation. That match is one of the most memorable moments of my career because the players rose up from within, and they knew it.

Now we all know that a great plan must provide flexibility, adaptability, and creativity. Limiting it to just what is written will not give the athletes a chance to make their mark on the blueprint, to bring forth a three-dimensional performance that they can accomplish together. Joining heads and hearts with hands firmly clasped together draws out the reality of what each person brings, the vulnerability and trust that develops when a dream is shared and pursued, and the humility and compassion that must be a common denominator in our day-to-day walk together.

Sport can be as unpredictable as the changing of the seasons. We can make a forecast, but circumstances occur that are out of our control—sickness, injury, change of heart, personal struggle, and so on. So what is the main objective? Teaching the Xs and Os? Putting together a tough schedule? Designing a complex offensive and defensive system? Yes, those may be the goals if you focus only on competing, but what about the life lessons that athletes can learn along the way? Those lessons can carry individuals through the challenges of life and allow them to pass on this collective masterpiece of effort, triumph, failure, disappointment, struggle, and thrill.

I received a letter from a former player a few months ago. "Hi coach, I finally got it. I was in the middle of giving birth to my first child. The doctor kept encouraging/asking me if I could push harder with each new contraction. It never dawned on me to quit, but to ask more of myself. So each time I felt

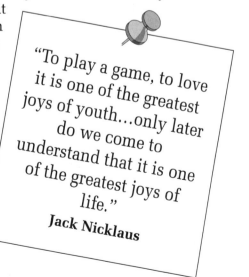

"To play a game, to love it is one of the greatest joys of youth...only later do we come to understand that it is one of the greatest joys of life."

Jack Nicklaus

a contraction, I bore down and pushed with everything that I had, invariably finding out that I had more to give to each 'new' contraction. That inner determination that I have only felt one other time in my life and that is when I competed in sport. I heard your voice in my head, resonating in my heart that the sky was the limit and it was up to me to find out how high I could truly climb. Well, I will leave out the gory details, but my daughter was born, and I received several stitches to prove it. My doctor asked my husband where I got my fight . . . he said without hesitation, she was an athlete in college . . . he went on to say, she often shares what it was like to compete and train at the college level, and what she carries in her heart from her athletics experience, but today is the first time I got to first hand share in the glory of her athletics moment in the birth of our daughter."

How do we define a season? How do we find direction and inspiration amidst the ups and downs of the competitive sports experience? I have learned that the process defines the success of an experience. In sport, as well as anything we do in life, the means, or the process—what we give on a daily basis, what we discover, and what we become—justifies the end. Life develops by what we demand of it, and at the center of the process is quality:

- The quality of our intentions and motivation to do what we do and continually clarifying that for ourselves—to learn to live, work, and play from the inside out.
- The quality of our work ethic, our responsibility to the talent we've been given, and our dedication to helping young people actualize theirs.
- The genuine and sincere quality in which we relate to others who are in the process with us, from which lasting relationships are formed—that is the greatest gift of sport.

The New Toughness Training for Sports, James E. Loehr, EdD.

PART II

Program Building and Management

CHAPTER FOUR

Seeking Excellence in a Program— Going for the Gold

Doug Beal

Developing a successful team is like constructing a building. It is a project with many different components, and it all begins with drawing the blueprints. You start with the outside appearance and move inward to how the structure will be supported. Next, you hear the hammering and sawing of the carpenters as they work toward the goal of creating a strong, durable, and long-lasting structure. The contractor is the picture of confidence, referring to the blueprints at various stages of construction and, based on translations of those hieroglyphs, directing the workers and ensuring that everything is on schedule. I have noticed that the process of constructing a building has this in common with the process of building a winning volleyball team: both require blueprints to ensure that the process is on track.

To have a successful program, you must be able to develop an overall plan or blueprint of the goal. You then do your best to break down that ideal image into building blocks useful for laying the foundation of a winning program. The plan for a successful team comprises five building blocks. The first building block is the formulation of goals. Goals are of three types: end goals, individual goals, and collective goals. The second building block is selecting a staff. When selecting a staff, I try to keep in mind that I want to provide these people with the freedom and flexibility to perform in the areas that I identified as their responsibilities. I want to maximize their strengths, just as we want to take advantage of players' strengths. The third building block is identifying players, with any luck, talented players. The fourth building block is placing responsibility on the players for the success of the program. The last building block is the system of training. You must develop a training system that produces positive changes in skills as well as team play or systems.

Formulating Goals

In the period when we were preparing for the 1984 Olympics, we structured a four-year plan. I believe that you work backward from the end objective, or the end goal, which for us was to play in the Olympic Games and be successful. I don't think that you ever say or are ever so specific with a big goal that you say, "We are going to win the gold medal" or "We are going to win the league championship" or "We are going to win the national championship." Rather you say, "What do we need to do to be in position to play for the gold medal, league championship, or national championship?" In working backward from this end goal, you have intermediate goals. These goals are like checkpoints to be sure that you are as far along as you want or need to be in the plan. Then you need to check on your so-called short-term goals, whether tactical issues or physical-preparation issues.

For us in that period of 1984, an important goal was to beat the Soviet Union. The Soviet men influenced the direction of volleyball, fielding a team that dominated international competition from 1977 through 1982. That team demonstrated an unbelievable ability to score points through the two easiest point-scoring skills, serving and blocking. The Soviets would defeat many opponents by barely having to touch the ball after the serve. They served numerous aces, and on those occasions when an opponent was able to mount an attack, the Soviets responded with an extraordinary number of stuff blocks. No team had beaten the Soviet Union for a long time. We felt that the Soviets were one of the teams we had to get above to be in a position to win the gold medal.

In a college program, you might have a season plan or, if you have a lot of continuity and experienced returning players, a multiseason plan. It depends on your situation. This plan is significant, and as the head coach, you will constantly hear your staff ask, "Where are we along this plan? Have we fallen behind, or are we a little ahead?" Wherever you are, by doing this evaluation, or roadside check, you are modifying the remainder of the plan. It would be unusual to be perfectly on track.

The second and third parts of goal setting are as important as the first. It is important to do goal setting with your players, both individually and collectively. I think you need to sit down with your players individually and talk about what they can do to contribute to the success of the team, what they can do to be the best player possible. Players need to have a role so that they have a sense of importance, which is important at any level of play. With this in mind you must play as many players as possible so that all gain the sense of contributing to the team effort. You can accomplish this by giving the six players on the floor different responsibilities. The main passers, for example, could be in charge of the formation of the serve receive or the options on how to receive. Middle blockers could be in charge of blocking decisions, read blocking, or setting up different formations. The back row could be in charge of defensive alignment. This building block is important because you have to teach your players that they have the ability to make the best decisions on the floor during matches. Sell your players on competing with themselves by constantly setting higher standards, pushing themselves to reach higher physical levels of accomplishment, and developing higher skill levels. These standards were an important part of our training for the 1984 team. We ran the same drills in every practice, so the athletes became familiar with the drills. With this in mind we wanted to have the players perform to a standard for success. Once they reached that standard, we kept raising it for each drill. To create this environment, your top players need to demand more of themselves instead of demanding more from their teammates. In volleyball, as in most team sports, it is easy to structure statistical objectives. The players can see and measure themselves against individual or team goals so that they can see graphically how they are performing.

Next, you sit down with the team collectively to set team goals. I think the issue here is having as many of the players as possible on the same page as you are. It's ideal if you can get them all to enunciate, buy into, verbalize, and commit themselves to the team goals. If you can somehow encourage the group, or manipulate them a bit, to state their goals, then the goals become powerful. When players define their goals, the motivation to achieve them is strong. We certainly did that in the early 1980s leading up to the Los Angeles Olympic Games. We spent a lot of time identifying individual and team goals. We conducted structured team meetings led by a group facilitator, or so-called sports psychologist. We tried to massage, manipulate, and direct the players' energies toward reasonable common goals that would build toward putting us in a position to win the gold metal.

Selecting Your Staff

The next building block is putting together a coaching staff. One person does not achieve excellence; a collective group of leaders attains it. I realize that most coaches don't have the luxury of a large staff, but I believe strongly in specialization. I think that you try hard to get the best people you can. Almost everyone who is qualified to be staff has some skills, and I think the head coach has a responsibility to match up the staff person with his or her strengths. Whether you have fully compensated assistant coaches, graduate assistants, volunteers, interested onlookers, or experts in some special aspect of your team or program, your use of staff and personnel can be critical to the success and growth of your team. Give your staff meaningful responsibilities but never abdicate accountability for the ultimate decisions regarding the team. Sometimes staff roles change, but role definition for the staff is just as important as role definition for the players.

Make sure that you are using your staff members in their areas of expertise. Give them responsibility, freedom, and flexibility but reserve the major decisions for yourself. In selecting your staff, seek people who complement your skills and strengths, filling in areas in which you may be weak or lack experience. You have to give them enough rope so that they have the flexibility and autonomy to be successful in their areas of responsibility. The balancing act is tough because in the end the head coach has to be responsible. You have to be accountable, and you must be knowledgeable about the areas that you delegate. Even if you're not an expert in those areas, you have to be familiar with the process that your staff is using to achieve their objectives and manage their areas.

Putting a staff together is like assembling the pieces of a jigsaw puzzle. Be patient. Look for different perspectives and points of view. If you can find people who challenge your ideas, who look in new directions, and who build on tactics that have become comfortable, your team will take a step beyond where it is now.

Identifying Strong Players

The third building block in this plan is to identify players, especially talented players. I don't think anyone wins unless the players are talented. Players are the limiting factor in most cases. Beyond identifying and recruiting the most talented players, I think you have to identify the strengths and weaknesses of individuals and then the team in a detailed, specific fashion.

I believe that in putting a team together you emphasize the players' strengths rather than spending extensive time on their weaknesses. In my mind at least, teams win because they do some things, usually relatively few things, very well, not because they do many things reasonably well. So if your team is a great serving team, or has the ability to handle the ball, or can be a great blocking team, or whatever, make that skill or system as overpowering as possible! I think you should spend a lot of time to become extremely good, as good as you can possibly be, in the areas where your team has natural strength or some individuals have natural strengths. Clearly, you can't ignore weak areas, particularly if they are critical to the success of your game or sport. We can't be outstanding at everything—we have limited time.

Prioritize your time to work on the team's strengths. You have only so many hours to train, whether with a national team, a junior club, high school, or college. Within these limitations you want to use your hours as productively as you possibly can. I think the better you can be at your strengths, the more productively you spend your time.

Make Players Responsible

One of the things I believe strongly about is putting responsibility on your players. In an excellent program you want to put some responsibility on your players for the success of the program. You want your players to be mature, to be accountable, and to understand that the success you are going to achieve is based on their abilities, their commitment, and their motivation. Certainly the coach plays a key role in establishing parameters for those behaviors, but I think it is easier to set limits if the players have a role in seeing how those rules, limitations, or guidelines lead to success. One of the things that we regularly preach to the players is that everything they do, whether on the volleyball court or off, has an effect on success or failure. How they prepare in the morning before training, how they eat, how much sleep they get, and how well they take care of themselves have a significant influence on how well they will train and, therefore, how effective they will be as players and how much improvement they will show. You want to eliminate the belief among players that what they do in practice is the only thing that is important. Everything they do is important. Being a great athlete and being part of a great team is a total lifestyle commitment. The more you can convince the players of that and the more they buy in to it, the more likely it is that you will be successful.

The last component to the plan is the training system. You have to develop a training system that creates stress and pressure in practice that mirrors what the players will encounter in competition. You have to put together the balance of training hours with physical preparation, scouting, videotape, and recovery time.

The practice session is the heart of a successful team. The structure of your practice, your drill development, and your training methods will all contribute significantly to building a great team.

Both you and your players must view practice as an opportunity to improve, to be your best, to develop all the skills that you will use during a game. Behavior changes constantly in practice. No one ever stays the same; players are either improving or forming wrong habits. It is simply not possible to perform many repetitions of some technical or tactical skill of the game and remain on a plateau in skill level. People go either up or down.

To ensure that your players are going up as much as possible, you must maximize the number of good opportunities for them to respond and execute the skills. Good opportunities to respond are characterized by effective feedback by the coach regarding performance. Exercises or drills should be

1. gamelike or game-specific, or
2. goal oriented with a clearly delineated objective that is progressively raised to allow for continued success and improvement.

Learning takes place in an environment of maximum meaningful contact. A practice session should include a minimum of standing around, a minimum of discussing, talking, and explaining, and a maximum of player contacts with the ball. The more contacts, the better the practice session. A typical 2+-hour practice session might look something like the following plan description. The beginning should be the warm-up period. A time for teaching ball-control skills follows, in which the entire team is involved and the ball is kept in play as long as possible. Your next phase might be a teaching phase during which you separate your team into smaller groups and work on an area of the offense or defense on more than one court. Following that you might have a combination drill that focuses on a particular weakness in your team that needs improvement. You might finish with one or two highly competitive team drills.

Keys for a Successful Practice

1. Never end a drill artificially. Teach your players to play every drill out, regardless of the drill's objective.

2. Create a competitive environment. Players can compete with themselves to raise a new standard for individual drills. That competitive element makes the players comfortable with winning, losing, and scoring points and it fosters a head-in-the-game attitude right up to the end.

3. Try not to talk too much. Coach effectively in a concise manner. Most coaches (including me) talk too much. When you coach, don't stop the exercise or drill unless it's absolutely necessary. Coach while the activity continues by talking directly to an individual or a small group. On those rare occasions when you must stop the entire activity and bring something to the attention of the team, do it quickly and succinctly. Then get back into action immediately.

4. Positive feedback elicits a better response than negative feedback. Praise when it's warranted; otherwise say nothing.

5. Give your drills names that your players will remember. The next time you do a specific drill, you won't need to waste time explaining it. Just name it and run it.

6. Make sure the players understand the objective of each drill. Tell them what they are trying to accomplish.

7. Adjust and modify the scoring system of a drill to increase the complexity of drills that your players particularly enjoy. Doing this will keep the drill effective. Move gradually from having your players accomplish a certain number of successful contacts, to a certain number of successful contacts out of the total number of efforts, to a completely competitive situation in which both sides of the net have an objective. One side wins, and the other side losses.

8. Give your players simple practice rules to follow consistently at every training session, perhaps nothing more than starting on time with a certain sequence of events, using a particular method of receiving instruction, and taking breaks at predetermined times. Rules of practice should provide structure and create a comfortable environment for your athletes.

9. Normally, practice is not the best environment in which to do physical training. You can accomplish that more effectively outside practice, when physical training can be the first priority.

10. Be sensitive to the moods and flow of a practice. If things simply aren't going well, it may be better to end practice prematurely than continue to practice poorly. On the other hand, abbreviating practice too often is not the way to develop a high-caliber team.

Training Your Players

Volleyball is an extremely difficult sport to prepare for physically. Our sport is neither aerobic nor purely anaerobic; it requires an unusual combination of the two energy systems. At the beginning, with a low-level team, with a new club, or with inexperienced players, the dividends from just playing volleyball will far outweigh dividends from lifting weights or performing other physical activities. Don't misunderstand me. I believe that physical preparation is an important element of success in volleyball. But this advantage is significant only for higher-level teams. For success at the lower level, skill is a much greater factor.

Don't push your players into physical training too soon. Teach them the game and get them to enjoy it. Keep them motivated and enthusiastic for play and practice. Physical training is a natural evolution that will become a benefit at the right point in their development. Let's talk in general terms about physical training, without regard to a specific program or type of physical training.

Never use your practice hours to wear down players with physical drills that principally measure their endurance and don't teach them the game or allow quality repetitions. Try to separate physical training spatially and temporally from practice time. Train physically early in the morning, later in the afternoon, or during the lunch or evening hours. I greatly prefer to have my players practice volleyball when they are fresh. If they must be tired let them be tired during physical training rather than during practice.

Monitor physical training closely. Coaches too often emphasize what happens in the practice gym, and they assign physical training to another staff member. That approach separates the coach from the process of physical preparation. To motivate your players to reach their physical goals and to maintain control of your team, you must be aware of the physical-training process and spend some time observing, monitoring, and controlling it.

New methods of physical preparation and conditioning appear every year—new types of weight-training programs or new ideas in jump training, running, or specific exercises. Certainly, it's important to keep up on this rapidly changing area, but I feel that almost any reasonable program will help your team if your athletes perform it consistently and with intensity. What you do is less important than how you do it.

Address the safety factor. Let your players know that you are concerned about both physical training and safety. Encourage group physical training. A player working out alone is more likely to become injured or derive less benefit than is a player working out in a group or with a partner.

Have the players keep records of everything they do so that they can see their progress. Improvement is a strong motivator. Consider posting records of certain aspects of the program so that competition among players can play a role in motivation and improvement.

Make sure that players consider conditioning and physical training part of their lifestyle. Players should continue some sort of program on a year-round basis. Physical training is rarely effective if athletes perform it sporadically. Although volume and intensity vary, the most productive programs continue throughout the year. Persuade your players to adopt your program as part of their daily regimen.

Regular testing of physical parameters can be extremely motivating, but don't overdo it. Test only once or twice during the year. The progress that players demonstrate in the few tests you conduct can motivate them to improve and reach their goals.

Recognize that players may expend considerable effort before they notice improvement, especially with a weight-training program (which I'll discuss in more detail in a moment). Begin slowly, progress gradually, and don't worry if it takes some time to make progress. A gradual week-to-week effort is essential for a safe and effective program.

Individualize the program as much as the team setting will allow. Competition is fine, but individual difference can be significant. Dividing the team into small groups may be the answer.

These days it's difficult to imagine reaching a high level in any sport without spending a lot of time in a weight room lifting and conditioning specifically for the particular sport. Strength gains can be substantial. Almost every top athlete in every sport knows the benefits of a weight-training program and understands the dedication, time, and intensity necessary to achieve goals. When people speak about the scientific improvements in athletic training in the past generation or two, they are talking principally about conditioning programs, specifically weight training. Volleyball is no exception. After your players have learned the skills and have discovered the joy of the game, instituting a weight-training program is essential. A correctly executed program will pay huge dividends. Your athletes will build a base of strength that allows them to benefit more from practice time in the gymnasium. They will deal better with the physical demands of the sport, protecting themselves from acute, traumatic, and long-term injuries and maintaining a peak level of performance over a longer period. The advantages held by the well-conditioned, strong athlete are too numerous and too obvious not to invest the hours in a weight room necessary to achieve them.

The last part of the plan is scouting. The importance of scouting your opponents varies in direct proportion to the ability of your team. Scouting is of almost no importance if your team is inexperienced, but it can be the difference between winning and losing if you're coaching at an elite level. If you're coaching an inexperienced team, don't be worried about your opponents; concern yourself with how your team plays. Your players should be able to make some adjustments to adapt to the opponents. Scouting tends to be more useful for preparing the coach and staff than for preparing the players.

The best way to scout your opponent is to do so on a rotation-by-rotation basis, charting your opponent's tendencies for side-out and point-scoring offense. You'll want to discover where to serve, which hitter their setter prefers to set to in each rotation, and the type of defense they play. These are the key considerations in preparing your game plan. Give your players only the information they can use. If they're not sophisticated or comfortable with scouting information, keep it to a minimum.

As you can see, developing a successful team is broken down into basic building blocks that almost every team can attain. It boils down to having a well thought out plan, the right staff to explain and project the ideas of the plan, and the right players to execute the plan. A successful team requires goal formation to reach the end goal, likes ours in 1984 to be competitive and successful in the Olympic Games. When you build a staff with qualified, talented, and responsible people and give them the freedom and flexibility to perform in their designated areas, your plan is on the right track. When you identify talented players and give them responsibility for the success of the team, the improvement of your team as a whole intensifies. When your players receive training that mirrors stressful situations during competition, they are better prepared to handle those moments of pressure. In addition, if you scout your opponent you discover tendencies, preferences, and defensive coverage that you can take to the players to help them prepare for the game. All these building blocks will help create a competitive and successful team that will bring home the gold.

CHAPTER FIVE

Marketing and Promoting Your Program

Terry Pettit

Every decision you make is a marketing decision. How does your secretary answer the phone? Is the voice level and tone consistent with the enthusiasm you have for your product?

When your players sign autographs after the match, do they look into the eyes of the fans they are interacting with or are they uninterested and eager to get out of the gym?

Is your volleyball camp named after you, or does it work to promote the volleyball program? Some coaches who take over unsuccessful programs make the misguided decision to promote themselves rather than the university that employs them. No volleyball coach has more credibility than the institution that he or she is working for.

Do your uniforms take on a different design every two years, or do you work to develop a consistent look that comes to reflect the stability of your program? Do you have a logo that becomes your brand?

Could other volleyball coaches name two positive characteristics of your program? When you talk about the team to the media, do you make yourself or the players the focus of attention? Do you educate the media about the goals of your program? Do you invite your athletic director or senior women's administrator to become emotionally involved in your program?

When you walk into a room can people sense the energy you have about the challenges you and your team are facing? Does your recruiting reflect your philosophy of volleyball, or is it more of a reaction to who you can get? Can each of your assistant coaches do at least one thing exceptionally well?

Do you spend your time building on the strengths of your players, or do you focus on trying to shore up their weaknesses? When you host a volleyball match is it just a competition, or do you stage it as an event? Do you spend your time wishing that someone else would promote your volleyball program for you, or do you embrace the concept that every decision that you make is an opportunity to market your product?

Marketing Volleyball Begins With the Coach

Our job description has changed. We need to spend more energy taking responsibility for putting people in the stands and less energy complaining because someone else in the athletic department won't do it.

We tend to think of marketing as a task for someone in the athletic department whose job it is to think up ideas to promote our events. We want advertisements in newspapers and spots on the evening news. We want our athletes on billboards and feature stories about our team above the fold in the sports section.

Although some of this may develop because a program is consistently successful, in the beginning the marketing of a volleyball program starts with the coach's enthusiasm for the sport. Who can better promote the program than the head volleyball coach? We have more passion about our sport than anyone. We stand to gain the most if we can attract consistent crowds. Initial marketing success is in direct proportion to a coach's willingness to share that enthusiasm in as many ways as possible. The coach and team must behave as if what they are doing is important before anyone else recognizes its significance. We often spend energy feeling sorry for what other people won't do for us rather than being enthusiastic about the things we can take charge of. So what can we take charge of?

Think of Your Volleyball Program as a Snickers Bar

The best thing about a Snickers candy bar is that you know what you're getting every time you buy one. If you love milk chocolate, a Snickers is great. If you love peanuts, Snickers has got 'em. Caramel? It's there every time. The absolute best thing about a Snickers bar (or a Hershey Bar, Milky Way, etc.) is that you get the same quality every time you buy one.

If you came off a 10-mile hike in Bangladesh and were fortunate enough to come upon a candy machine, how could you not pull the Snickers lever, especially if it were competing with several exotic candy bars that you had never seen before?

Even if Snickers wasn't your favorite candy bar, you would probably still pull the lever because you could bite into it knowing what it was going to taste like and being confident that it wouldn't introduce you to some form of mad cow disease. There is beauty in consistency. Although we are interested in the exotic we are fans of the predictable.

We follow the same inclination in our backing of exceptional athletic teams. We loved the Chicago Bulls not only because they won but also because they would impose their will on an opponent with exceptional defensive intensity. It didn't happen some of the time. It happened every time in every important game, usually five minutes into the second half.

The outstanding women's intercollegiate volleyball programs all have consistent identifiable qualities. These programs are as different and as identifiable as candy bars:

- Long Beach State is synonymous with technical ballhandling and an offense that has more rhythm than hip-hop does.
- For years Penn State was a team built around one exceptional offensive player while everyone else played great defense and didn't make attack errors.
- Nebraska volleyball is built around exceptional athletes who can block and transition off a gifted setter.

The point is this: what first comes to mind when you think of your team? If you don't know who you are or what you do consistently well, then you can't market the product. The key to marketing a sporting event is not having the most talent or the best insight into how to teach technical passing. The key is not even winning. (The Chicago Cubs are exhibit A.) The key is to know what you are selling and to provide that product night in and night out.

You do not have to be coaching one of the most talented teams to make this happen. Great effort, great serving, and great pursuit don't have anything to do with having a stable of top 50 recruits. One of the challenges that confront intercollegiate volleyball is not so much whether we can develop a core group of exceptional teams. We've already done that. Six schools have won all but two of the NCAA women's national championships. Our challenge is to have a pool of 100 programs that are consistently competitive and have developed identities even when they don't have exceptional talent.

Volleyball is not such a unique game that it is interesting in and of itself. There is nothing much worse than having to watch a volleyball match in which neither team has a clear idea of what its strengths are. It is absolutely one of the worst sports to watch unless the teams put forth great effort. Coaches frequently say that if they can get someone to come to a match, he or she will be a fan for life. The facts don't bear this out. We've all seen special one-night promotions that attract a couple thousand people who may never come again.

Whether or not they return depends on many things—the staging of the event, the competitiveness of the match, the enthusiasm of the coaches and players. But one of the principal factors that determine whether people return and become fans is their having the intangible feeling that they witnessed a group of young athletes risking everything in a kind of disciplined dance between athleticism and chaos. Spectators want to know that they are going to see the same kind of effort, the same commitment, and the same sense of purpose the next time they return to the arena. They want the last bite of the Snickers to taste as good as the first.

Season Tickets

In the early 1980s I decided to commit a large portion of my time one summer to selling season volleyball tickets. The athletic department wasn't convinced that volleyball would ever produce significant revenue, but I believed that we had a better chance of building a consistent fan base if we charged for matches and if we could sell a minimum of 1,000 season tickets.

If we don't place a value on our product then nobody else will. For a solid month I walked into stores, banks, hospitals, and factories selling season tickets for $10 and student tickets for $5. Frequently I sold them in groups of five to eight to personnel managers of various businesses, who would then make the tickets available to their employees. I also encouraged the athletic department to develop a family season ticket that would allow two parents and up to four children to come to volleyball matches for $20. The season-ticket campaign was successful. We sold over 1,200 season tickets, 150 of which were family season tickets. Although prices changed significantly over the years as volleyball became a tough ticket to come by, many of the original season-ticket holders are in still in the Coliseum for every home match.

I do not think that anyone else would have been as successful as I was in that initial season-ticket campaign. We didn't have an athletic marketing department at the time, and even if we had, no one else was as passionate about the product as I was. The price was right, and younger families did not have access to our sold-out football stadium.

Maybe some of our success was based on my naivete, but I believe most of it was because of my enthusiasm. When I go to the state fair, I always make a point of watching the people selling the ginshu knives and food choppers. I don't need either one, but they are so enthusiastic about the product they are selling that I can't help being drawn toward their energy. Nebraska volleyball is a product. The more people that watch Nebraska volleyball, the more that potential recruits want to play for Nebraska volleyball. It was in my best interest to do everything I possibly could to create an environment that people would want to keep coming back to. We had no ginshu knives, but we had athleticism that could slice a peach.

Ask a Favor

In the late 1980s I felt that to continue the development and interest in our program I needed the support of someone in the athletic department. I wasn't looking primarily for financial support. I believed that we were probably limited in our growth unless I could develop a relationship with an administrator who would feel some ownership in our program.

This task was not going to be easy. The athletic director had provided the financial support required by Title IX for our women's sports to be competitive, but he was emotionally tied to football. Our senior women's administrator was in the trenches fighting the daily battles over support that we now take for granted. In the early years following the enactment of Title IX, we were a split department, which meant that we usually had less talented and less experienced support people working on the women's side than on the men's side. The mission of most athletic directors was to prevent women's athletics from siphoning away too much money or resources. The mission of many senior women's administrators was to try to develop a program for women without alienating the men's athletic director, who still controlled the resources and probably had little enthusiasm for Title IX.

In 1986 Nebraska volleyball played for the national championship in the final match against the University of the Pacific. The match was on Pacific's home floor in Stockton, California, and the Tigers defeated the Huskers 3-0.

The match was significant for several reasons. It marked the first time that a non-West Coast team advanced to the finals. Two teams from the middle of the country, Nebraska and Texas, advanced to the Final Four. But the most startling fact to me was that despite our participation in the national championship match, no athletic director or senior women's administrator attended. No sports information personnel, no band, no cheerleaders, no representative from the University of Nebraska were at the match except, of course, the team and coaches.

I left the event knowing that we had the talent to compete at the highest level. I also knew that if we were going to be able to compete consistently for national championships, I needed to get someone on our administrative team emotionally committed to what we were trying to accomplish. We needed someone in administration to witness for Nebraska volleyball.

That person became Dr. Barbara Hibner, our senior women's administrator, who in time became an impassioned advocate for the program. The key to developing her as an advocate was asking her to do things for us that she had the power to make happen.

Have you ever noticed how almost everyone is eager to give you directions when you're lost? People want to help if they have the resources to do so and if they don't subject themselves to much risk. The most important thing in developing a relationship with an administrator is to ask for what you know they can give you. If you develop the relationship, and if the administrator believes in your consistency and commitment, in time you will be able to ask them for things that will require the person to take risks.

In the beginning I began to ask Dr. Hibner for small favors. Could she meet with the family of an incoming recruit? Would she help us create better work spaces for our staff? Could she help us with the plumbing in the locker-room showers? Would she help us find a sponsor to provide the funds to attract ranked opponents to our fall tournament?

Then in 1990 I asked her to accompany the team on an early season road trip to Hawaii. Four of the top-ranked teams in the country would be competing in the tournament, but what I wanted her to see and feel was the support that the University of Hawaii received from its fans. I wanted her to smell the atmosphere.

At first Dr. Hibner was hesitant to go on the trip, fearing that other administrators in the department might view it as a waste of money. Only after I asked Marilyn Moniz-Kaho'ohanohano, the women's senior administrator at Hawaii, to extend a personal invitation to Dr. Hibner did she agree, enthusiastically, to accompany the team.

I remember the day that she burst into my office exclaiming that the Hawaii senior women's administrator had invited her to the tournament. I knew that when she traveled to Hawaii and saw how important volleyball was to the local community, it would help her become an ally for the things that I was trying to accomplish at Nebraska. Athletic directors are competitive people. They want their teams to succeed, but they cannot help you fully until they become emotionally committed to your program. The first step in developing that kind of relationship is asking the person to whom you report to do you a favor. Remember that you should ask for something that you know is within the person's authority to do.

In Real Estate It's Location, in Volleyball It's the Arena

The three best fans' experiences that I've seen in college volleyball were at Klum Gym in Hawaii, Kenney Gym at the University of Illinois, and the Coliseum at the University of Nebraska. Klum and Kenney no longer host intercollegiate volleyball matches, but the Coliseum still serves as home for Nebraska. The three venues had several things in common.

First, the arenas were the home sites for teams that were having consistently successful seasons. Hawaii and Nebraska have been among the elite in college volleyball for the last 20 years, and Illinois was a national power for several years when it played at Kenney Gym. All three are older collegiate gyms that seat less than 5,000 people.

Klum and Kenney probably averaged just over 2,000. Nebraska's official attendance of 4,200 approached 5,000 before the consistent crowds attracted the attention of the fire marshal. In all three facilities the fans were almost on the court. In contrast most of the collegiate arenas built in the last 30 years, some of which can seat up to 20,000 people, place fans 60 feet or more from the action. When a volleyball team plays in such an arena, even when the event draws 2,000 or 3,000 people, the thousands of empty seats work against the feeling that the match is important.

Volleyball is played on a relatively small court—1,800 square feet compared with 5,000 square feet on a basketball court and 45,000 square feet on a football field. The problem on a volleyball court is not that you don't have enough people, but just the opposite. You have a lot people (six) in a relatively small area (900 square feet on one side of the net). To keep those people operating efficiently, intense and intimate communication must occur between the players, and sometimes between the coaching staff and the players, even as action is unfolding.

It is difficult to appreciate the speed of the game, the intensity of the players, and the amount of communication that takes place in every rally from a spot that is more than 20 rows from the arena floor. In sports that take place in large arenas, fans have to pay top dollar to get close to the action, and even then they may not get as close to the players as they can in a venue like the Coliseum.

The spectator who is close to the action has a chance to see how hard everyone is playing. The determination, the joy, and sometimes even the fear on the players' faces is noticeable. When you create a setting where the fans are close to the action, you are marketing not only volleyball but also certain values that have largely disappeared from professional sport and, to some degree, collegiate football and basketball. You are also developing an emotional connection between the players and the fans. The relationship that the fans have with the players is your most valuable commodity. If your arena does not create this kind of intimacy, you cannot create the special feeling that makes fans believe they are an integral part of a team's success.

One of the appealing aspects of volleyball is that it is the ultimate team sport. Every player must have every skill. The opponent determines to some extent which of our players is going to play the ball. Because of the net, players do not rely on brute force. Physical contact with the opponent does not occur, and to date we do not see the trash talking and self-promotion that permeates basketball and football. A well-staged volleyball match with two competitive teams in a small, intimate arena hearkens back to a time when sport was associated with terms like *teamwork* and *sacrifice* as opposed to the self-aggrandizement promoted on ESPN.

Some intercollegiate and high school programs that do not have the ideal site to stage a volleyball match in an intimate setting have found creative ways to solve the problem. Both Nebraska and Kansas State have older arenas in which the volleyball court runs across and perpendicular to the old basketball court. This configuration makes the space smaller and can create an enclosed arena, especially where a balcony is now present on three sides. The addition of permanent or portable bleachers then closes in the area.

Get a Band

Good lighting and good music are two elements that draw people into a room and make them want to stay: Well-staged events take advantage of both.

If I had to rate the most important thing about marketing volleyball beyond having a consistent product, it would be having a great band. A 30-piece orchestra isn't necessary. A 5-piece combo with an electric guitar and drums is great as long as the music they play invites participation by the fans. For years the members of the pep band at Nebraska received nothing but a T-shirt with the Nebraska volleyball logo. The players appreciated the music before the games as they warmed up, and the band entertained the fans during promotions between games two and three. If the team was sluggish and out of sync, the band would introduce a timely rendition of the fight song or "YMCA." The crowd would awaken, and soon afterward the Huskers would too.

In time, members of the pep band became the team's most enthusiastic supporters. They developed their own cheers and engaged in good-natured ribbing of opponents. The band didn't perform for the money because they weren't paid anything. They did it because it was cool. They did it because they felt as if they were part of something important, even before volleyball became important. In the beginning they did it because a coach invited them.

After a band, good lighting may be the next most important factor in creating the proper atmosphere for a great event. Lighting above the court that is significantly brighter than the lighting above the fans creates a feeling that something important is taking place. Great lighting creates the same sense of anticipation that a well-lit stage does for theater or a boxing ring. Institutions often spend a great deal of money renovating the gym floor and bleachers but discount the importance of lighting. Even old bleachers look good when fans cover them. A volleyball match becomes an event only when the lighting above it creates a stage that showcases the performers.

Involve the Players

For years the volleyball players at Nebraska have stayed after matches to sign autographs and interact with young fans. Before the match the players throw out small "autograph balls," which are also for sale at a souvenir stand run by the booster club.

After the match the players sit down on the team bench and patiently talk and interact with the young fans who come to see them. Some of the kids who came to the Coliseum to watch and get autographs when they were elementary-school students have gone on to play for the Huskers.

We teach the players to maintain eye contact and listen to the questions and comments from everyone who wants to talk with

them. The players do this even when the same people come back game after game, even when someone already has asked a dozen times for a player's autograph, even when we have lost a tough match and the players would rather be anywhere but sitting on the court where they just lost. Talking with fans after matches is one of the ways that the players can show appreciation for the support they receive in the Coliseum. It is one of the ways that we market Nebraska volleyball to families. It also helps us develop new fans and not become dependent on the people who already own season tickets. Marketing depends on developing relationships. The best marketing tool that we have is our performers (players) interacting on an intimate level with our consumers (fans).

Television, Radio, and the Internet

Nebraska volleyball has broadcast its home and away matches live on radio for over 10 years. In the beginning no radio station wanted to broadcast the matches, even though Nebraska volleyball was consistently drawing larger crowds than the high school football and basketball events that were being broadcast.

The primary reason for the lack of interest was laziness and lack of information. The stations already had sponsors for the high school boys events, and they didn't want to have to go out and sell ads for a women's event. They assumed that local stores, banks, insurance companies, and civic groups wouldn't want to sponsor athletic events featuring girls and women. They assumed that the owner of the local hardware store who sponsored the football games did so because he played football himself at one time.

What they failed to realize was that women bought most of the goods and services at those stores, gas stations, and banks. In addition, they failed to see that many of the men who had played high school football, basketball, and baseball were now raising young girls who wanted to play softball, soccer, and volleyball. In other words, the radio stations were operating with an inaccurate view of the business and athletic communities in Lincoln.

Our opportunity to get Nebraska volleyball on the radio came when one of the stations lost out in a process to broadcast Nebraska football and Nebraska men's basketball. At one time anyone willing to pay a rights fee to the university could broadcast its athletic events. The athletic department decided that it could make more money by selling the rights to one bidder, who could then create and market a network to stations throughout the state and region.

That decision, although positive for the bottom line of the University of Nebraska athletic department, meant that some stations that had carried Nebraska athletic events for decades now had no relationship with the university. Enter Nebraska volleyball and the opportunity for a station (and advertisers) to become associated with the university again and with a consistently successful product. The relationship has been so successful that in recent years more than one station has been interested in broadcasting games. Some fans bring radios to the match so that they can listen to the commentary of the regular play-by-play announcer. They also turn off the sound when Nebraska volleyball is on television so that they can hear the familiar voice of John Baylor on the radio.

Television is another story. One thing that volleyball coaches have in common is frustration with the limited amount of volleyball available on local, regional, and national television. People offer all sorts of reasons for the lack of visibility of the indoor game.

Some people say that a change in the rules that allows a more predictable duration for a match will increase the potential for televised volleyball. Others counter that baseball, tennis, and golf, all of which have carved out places in the television landscape, do not have a fixed duration. We should know soon enough whether a fixed duration is important as we move to rally scoring in the collegiate game.

What frustrate volleyball coaches are the amount of women's basketball currently on television and the lack of interest among advocates of women's sports in helping volleyball get the same kind of exposure.

My observation is that women's basketball was able to develop a presence on television for reasons that have nothing to do with the inherent appeal of the game. In dealing with the ramifications of Title IX, male athletic directors found it easier to support a sport they were familiar with. In the early days following Title IX, senior women's administrators supported women's volleyball more strongly than they do today. Those administrators soon learned that their male counterparts, who had all the power and money, were more likely to listen to an appeal for the funding and televising of a game they had played themselves rather than one they associated with picnics and intramurals.

The truth is that we have not had women's advocates on the national scene, like Donna Lopiano, former women's athletic director at the University of Texas, who are willing to fight for opportunities for volleyball.

Women's basketball is on national and regional television because when ABC or ESPN came calling, the conference offices negotiated packages that allowed for the inclusion of women's basketball. "If you want to televise Southeast Conference football," they said, "then you have to do x number of women's basketball games." Male athletic directors and male conference administrators made this decision, with the endorsement of the senior women's administrators who sometimes felt that unconditional support for one women's sport (basketball) was a start and better than nothing at all.

So what we are left with is the sporadic televising of some of the major conferences on regional networks and the local broadcasts of selected matches by public broadcasting networks or local cable operations. Even the national championship match has usually been broadcast on a taped-delayed basis. Semifinal matches are usually broadcast at a time that is convenient only for insomniacs and cat burglars.

Volleyball will not be consistently available on television until the head coaches at prominent Division I institutions take the responsibility for recruiting their senior women's administrators to the cause. A good start would be to invite the senior women's administrators to the Final Four, where we can wine and dine them and make our best case for why our sport deserves to be seen. If we can't evangelize and organize our own administrators and advocates, then we deserve what we get.

Another alternative is on the horizon. Many Division I schools are now carrying radio broadcasts of intercollegiate matches over the Internet. At times the technology is frustratingly slow and awkward, and listeners may have to upgrade software and make frequent downloads during a match to hear it to conclusion. But there is no doubt that the Internet is here to stay. Attempts have already been made to stream live video of volleyball matches on the Internet, and within five years it is likely that the technology will be available to a decent job. Right now the quality compares unfavorably with television. With Internet streaming one has the feeling that you are watching something taking place on a different planet where everyone moves like Charlie Chaplin or early 20th century ball players in movies from that era.

Volleyball will have another opportunity. Universities are continually looking for ways to generate income, and the opportunity to stream live broadcasts of events not now under contract to major networks will receive interest from athletic directors. I think that within the next five years several college and high school programs will be streaming their matches live to alumni and fans who may be paying subscriptions for the privilege.

In conclusion I would like to summarize what I believe are the 10 most important strategies to marketing volleyball.

1. The coach is the most important person in developing, implementing, and following through a marketing strategy.

2. Every decision a coach makes about the program has marketing implications.

3. You have to know what your product is before you can sell it.

4. The product must be consistently good.

5. You are marketing an event, not just a match. A band and great lighting are the most effective tools to bring this about.

6. Our biggest asset, the quality that sets our product apart from other athletic events, is the relationship we create between our players and the fans.

7. If it's worth something, you need to charge for it. The way to develop a consistent following is through season tickets as opposed to special promotions, which create only sporadic interest.

8. A coach's most important recruit is the administrator who becomes emotionally committed to the program.

9. On a national level we have to court the senior women's administrators to help us with our cause.

10. Marketing is a process. Every interaction, every decision is an opportunity to promote your product.

CHAPTER SIX

Developing a Successful College Program

John Dunning

As I approach the end of my third decade as a volleyball coach, I can look back and say that I would do things differently if I were given another chance to develop my first program. Thanks to my mentors, friends, peers, and the players I coached, I have had more than my share of opportunities to learn. I think I have learned enough to pass along some ideas I developed over the years to other coaches who have a passion for learning and for the sport.

My first program, a high school girls team, came into existence because of Title IX, a long overdue catalyst for the growth of women's sports. At that time I was spending my energy teaching and coaching another sport. Many new opportunities were available to young women, but few people were qualified to guide them. I had seen one volleyball game in my life and had never touched a ball, so when a few of the girls who had already played before asked if I would coach them, my response was to laugh and politely say no. But no other candidate came forward, and I soon had a new job.

Since then I have often told people that it scares me how little I knew when I began my journey into the uncharted territories of coaching women's volleyball. The ninth graders knew more than I did about the sport back in 1976. I could make a long list of the things I had never heard of then that I now feel are extremely important. Compiling such a list, however, would so exhaust me that I might never get to the point of thinking about what was important then and is still important now.

A Program for the Players

Although I didn't know it then and didn't realize it for years, the most important reasons for the success of that first high school program were with me on the first day of practice. As I look at successful programs I always find a key person or succession of key people upon which the programs were built. Those programs are all different, in part because of the differences in their leaders. Consequently, the uniqueness of those programs does not lie in how they teach or how they recruit, but primarily because of their distinctive qualities as leaders.

Because my personality and philosophy were fairly well set the first day I walked into the gym, many events were destined to happen in a certain way. I was just lucky that it worked for me; others are not so lucky. The key ingredient for me is that the programs I have been a part of have been run with the players in mind. I am sure that some of those players might feel that it didn't happen quite that way for them, but the outcome is not always easy to control. Our intent is and has always been to run our program with the mental and physical health of the players in mind.

As a 1st-year coach, I may have run my program that way only because it was a reflection of my personality. As a 25th-year coach, I run it that way because of a conscious decision to do so. During my career I am sure that I occasionally strayed from that path for various reasons. But I try to keep my focus, and I think that all coaches should do so. The two major aspects of this that I like to think about are physical health and mental health.

Physical health is something we wish for everyone. Yet in our desire to push athletes to a level of excellence or because of our fear of losing, we may not weigh the risks for them carefully enough. If we reach outside our normal circle to gather information about how hard to push or about how to instruct technically, we may be surprised with the opinion that we are putting athletes in dangerous situations.

For example, we have in our sport what some refer to as an epidemic of ACL injuries. Investigation has shown us that females are more prone to this type of injury than males. We can reduce this susceptibility not only by increasing the strength of the athletes but also by providing better technical instruction. Although we have asked athletes to attack with greater velocity and have increased the acrobatic nature of the game, we have not demanded that they learn how to land properly.

When we regularly teach this skill we see the frequency of this type of injury drop. Since we began to work hard on teaching proper landing technique, we have discovered some surprising secondary benefits as well. For example, as people work at landing in balance we find that after a while they begin to alter the location from which they jump. Athletes discover that if they jump from a bad place, they find it impossible to land well. They begin jumping from better places and find that they not only land better but also hit higher and feel less soreness in their shoulders and lower backs.

If we seek advice from other sources we may find that for the sake of our players' long-term physical health, it would be beneficial to alter the way we teach many skills. As we change our teaching methods to preserve our athletes' health, we may find that better performance accompanies the new techniques.

Mental health, certainly part of our responsibility as coaches, is no less important. As our sport has developed and become more significant, the pressure to succeed has increased. If a program is to succeed with the best interests of the athlete in mind, the coach needs to research the best ways to help the athlete. Each coach chooses his or her style, but all must be responsible for their part in the athlete's mental well-being. More often than not, better performance will result if coaches provide a learning environment that helps each athlete develop self-esteem.

As the sport of volleyball has matured we have seen increases in how much and how intensely we play the game. As this occurs, the love we all have for the game can fade away. I believe that we should work at helping our athletes retain the love of the game.

Although there may be many other aspects to this, these are just a few ideas I think about when I am considering the health of players in my program.

Personality and Philosophy

As a first-year coach I started with the values that I learned from my parents, my wife, and other people who have affected me. I brought those values to the court then and continue to do so now. In life generally, and in a coach's life in particular, we face constant pressure to sacrifice long-term goals for short-term success. Issues cross my desk every day that require me to make decisions that could solve a problem, help attract a recruit, or increase our chances of winning that night. Every time I choose to reach down for a quick fix or compromise a value, I risk the long-term health of my program. Some may feel lucky if no one learns of their dubious dealings, but it is fair to assume that every time someone finds out, the program will be hurt. Consistency in applying our values is one of the hardest things to do in life. Significant risks are involved when we stray from our values, no matter what the circumstances may be.

Our program is always out there for the volleyball world to judge. The assessments may not always be fair, but they are nevertheless part of our lives. I want people to view my program as honest, but if we are successful in terms of winning some will wish to see us suffer problems. If I do something that allows others to interpret what we do in a negative way, the outcome may be unfair and it may hurt. If I make a mistake with the recruiting rules and do not step forward and deal with the error, then others will hold the program accountable. If I offer an athlete a scholarship and she accepts, then as an adult I must honor that agreement. No matter what the circumstances, if I fail to uphold my end of the agreement, people will judge my action critically and the program will suffer. If I talk to a young athlete and her parents about the values they would expect we would live by in our program, I would hope that they would mention a few of the following— fairness, positive nature, good work ethic, accountability, honesty. If it is not in my nature to live by a particular positive value, then I must be great at something else or I will have difficulties running the program.

Some programs find themselves in the situation of having greater resources than their competition. If their reputation is impeccable, we will forever be chasing them unless they falter for some reason. Other programs are successful beyond what their resources should allow because their reputation is so good. Because most of us have adequate resources, the real success of a program depends on its reputation and resourcefulness.

Program Growth

In my first year I am certain I did not understand much about the game, about running a program, or about how decisive my values were in determining the success of the program. Since that time I have learned many things, but one that stands out is one that I would not have predicted to be significant. I now believe that our program is never static. It is either improving, or it is not. Some of the reasons for this are within our control, and some are not. Some are easy to understand, and some are not.

I must concern myself with two things to help my program go forward. First, I must have plans to add constantly to the program. We have made a commitment to do something new or special every year. Sometimes events occur that have helped us improve quite easily. For example, several years ago we decided that to protect the health of our athletes and to give our facility the appearance of a real volleyball arena, we would buy a new floor.

We started a fundraiser that continued for five years. The financial gain and community involvement were so great that it was worth the hundreds of hours of work we devoted to it each year. Another year we took the team on a foreign tour. The trip was so successful that we will no doubt go every four years, but the fundraising for this event is a huge undertaking. Significant planning and much hard work will be involved with each new project, but we have no choice if we want to improve.

Second, we now take significant steps to watch for anything that might detract from the program. In the past I failed to see signs of problems, ignored the signs, or avoided dealing with them. The longer problems exist, especially problems between people, the greater the chance that the problems will grow and cause serious damage. We have all heard about programs in which a coach has ended up leaving or players have left. Some of the departures may have been unavoidable, but I am sure that if problems had been caught early or dealt with in a different way, these situations would have ended better.

Academics

During the first decade of my career I was a junior development coach and a high school coach. I look back and realize that I was lucky and probably took the academic side of life for granted. I coached one team in which 8 of the 11 girls were enrolled in either trigonometry or calculus. At the end of the year the team GPA was 3.8. I was blessed to have coached many intelligent and successful student-athletes. In college, academics is definitely a different part of life for the student-athlete and their coaches. Institutions and athletic departments take this aspect of their job seriously, but in the end the responsibility lies with the coaching staff. In the end the volleyball program will suffer if students have problems with academics. We believe that more time should be spent on academic planning. More students get off track because of poor planning than because of poor performance.

Academics is the first thing I would choose in the draft if I could pick the way to start a program. Coaching at a great academic institution may be the only guaranteed way to have a chance with any recruit. But once we find a place to start a program, we must come to know the program well. We need to understand our program so that we can help our athletes be successful. Knowing our program will also help us get an idea of whom it will appeal to in recruiting.

The second thing I would hope for in the draft is to be part of an athletic program that has a terrific all-sports tradition. If the name of a program received favorable mention in the media for any favorable reason, all programs benefit. Recruits grow up wanting to go to schools they have heard of, and athletes want to be around other successful athletes. If I can help any program at my school, I will, if only because it will help my program as well.

If you weren't dealt those cards, then you must maximize what you have. If you are in a great location you can use it to your advantage. Great location can come in the form of being part of a wonderful community, having easy access to long-distance travel connections, enjoying a pleasant climate, or having lots of good competition nearby. Being part of an excellent conference usually means good competition and possibly good exposure, but it can also mean that you have a tough climb to be successful. A generous budget is another asset that can help you in many ways. If you have a long list of resources, your job may be to manage those resources well. If the list has some weak spots, may need to work some extra hours and become resourceful. On the following pages I have organized some ideas that I used to help raise the level of our program above the resources we started with.

Tradition

The best place to start is with tradition in your own program. The volleyball world has difficulty being excited about anything that took place more than a year ago. We regularly have to remind everyone who we are. We have to establish traditions or events through which they can view our program. If we can do more and convince them that these traditions display greatness, we really have a chance. A big-attraction tournament, a special fundraising event, a great community outreach, a poster-signing night, the team banquet, or an alumnae game are examples of long-running events on our calendar that attract attention because they have become traditions. These events are important enough that I would even take risks to start them. Although one must invest a great deal of time, resources, and attention to start traditions, the potential return is great.

Summer Camps

The individual who came up with the idea of summer camps supplied volleyball coaches with an excellent opportunity. How could we ever persuade the NCAA to allow both incoming freshmen and potential recruits of all ages to come to our campus for four or five days? We have the opportunity to teach them, watch them, and show them what a great place we have. This is a big recruiting advantage. Summer camps are also a great way to let people in your community get a little closer to the athletes and the program. Also, the program, coaches, and players' friends and peers have an opportunity to make extra money.

Running camps so that you can take advantage of all the exciting opportunities is not easy. The camp must be organized in a professional way if it is to be successful. The brochures, the reservations, the e-mail, the phone calls, the travel plans, the employment paperwork, the budget, the check-in and check-out of the dorms, the menu, the air conditioning, and the equipment all must be handled well. The coaching staff must be excellent, the teaching methods should be well thought out, and the staff and player manuals must be prized possessions. Like anything this big, risks are involved. The benefits can be remarkable, but a mediocre camp can hurt your program.

The key to our success in running camps is that from the start we limited enrollment, trained the staff, and organized the camp to maximize the focus on volleyball. We have two types of camps. One has a player-to-coach ratio of 7 to 1, and the other has a ratio of 4 to 1. Anyone paying money for service wants as much personal attention as possible, so we try to provide it. If the instruction is not consistent and the quality of the coaches is uneven, troubles begin to brew on day one. We provide the coaches with a handbook and require them to use our structure and language. We may lose some coaches because they cannot express themselves freely, but I have more concern for the players' experience than for the coaches' ego. We hope that players walk away with a personal volleyball experience, not quality time away from their parents.

For me there is one troubling part of volleyball camps—responsibility for the players when they are not in the gym. We could use a simple mathematical operation to calculate the liability involved, but it would be too frightening to interpret. We try to reduce the problems by taking supervision seriously. We hold ourselves accountable for the safety and whereabouts of the campers at all times. We make our camp rules clear, and then we enforce them.

The best advertising we could ever dream of is a before-and-after tape. We tape the campers in skill areas on the first day and again on the last day. The players take the tape home when they leave, so that while they are excited about camp they and their parents can immediately look at the difference our camp makes.

Recruiting

Probably nothing is more important to a program than the success of its recruiting efforts. The most important part of recruiting is the people and how they are perceived. Any action that compromises the long-term integrity of the program will be regretted. It is easy to be uninformed or misinformed about NCAA rules, but any misapplication of the rules will cast a shadow over the program. A decision that negatively affects the well-being of a recruit or is perceived to do so can damage the reputation of the program. Coaches must tread lightly and intelligently in the recruiting world.

Recruiting well requires organization, trust, a system, lots of hard work, a network of contacts, the ability to build relationships, an understanding of the current needs, a good eye for talent and character, good communication skills, and a good program. Every program will package these ingredients differently, but good values and solid effort will bring success. The only real rule we live by is to avoid risking the future when wrestling with the present.

Competitive Setting

Because I truly love volleyball, nothing excites me more than one particular match my team played at Nebraska. The arena was full, the band and cheerleaders were fabulous, the facility is first class, the event was run professionally, and the fans were loyal and loud. The community had a real connection with the program. The players were in volleyball heaven, and any recruits who attended surely decided to be Huskers on the spot.

All of us can improve the facility in which we host our events. The most important quality of an arena is that it should feel like home. When we welcome visitors with open arms, opponents immediately understand that they are the visitors. The setting should express the team's identity with decorations, identifiable traditions, and loyal people. The team should feel the pride of the hometown on its home court.

Any volleyball match can become an entertaining event. I try to be consistently involved with the promotion of events and game management. We start with the idea that if we expect people to enjoy a match only if it is a good one, no one will come back if we ever lose or if we win easily. Those situations are not exciting by themselves, so we work hard to create an atmosphere that is interactive and enjoyable. We attempt to include kids in the fun. If we can attract young people, then we attract their parents. We need to make it enjoyable for both. Fans, media, and players appreciate every bit of pride we put into making our arena and our events outstanding.

What Do Players Like?

If I were to listen in on a conversation between one of my players and a recruit, I hope that the player would talk about our team, the last match we won, dorm living at school. Those are the basics. I asked some of the players what they liked and what the recruits liked. We all have limited resources to dedicate to these items, but here is part of the list:

1. We arrange to launder their workout clothes.
2. The foreign tour is something they will never forget.
3. Someone is always available to help or just listen.
4. We supply them with good equipment that they are proud of.
5. We have a pleasant locker room that is home for the group.
6. They like the tradition, the feeling they are part of something big.
7. They like it when we help in the community.
8. They love it that the focus is on the team, not individuals.
9. They love one-on-one attention in meetings, on the court, anytime.
10. They love to play in our arena.
11. Good trainers and strength trainers make their life better.
12. They like playing a good schedule and seeing different places.

Players like these aspects of our program when they are at school, and they remember them when they are gone. I am sure that our equipment manager, our trainer, and our office manager—great people who made a difference in the quality of the players' lives—will hear from the players more often than I will. As in any organization the people are the most important ingredient.

People Make the Program

The best piece of advice I ever received about my job was to make a quick list of all the people with whom I would regularly work. Either those people would develop loyalty to my program or they wouldn't. I then worked at finding out how they went about their jobs and how our jobs intertwined. Most of the people I worked with wanted to help our program in whatever way they could as long as there was good communication and respect. I coached at Pacific for a long time, and after 16 years I was still working with some of the same people. One of the things that kept us together was that they knew I cared about them. For that to occur I must find ways to show it. If we ever get to the point of taking each other for granted, then we could easily have problems.

Our facilities people are the best anyone could find. Their jobs are hectic and involve so many details that I can't imagine how they remain calm and in control. I know that the more organized I am and the fewer surprises I spring on them, the happier they are. If I need help, they can usually rescue me. If they think I am operating in a way that shows my respect for them, then they are on our team.

I really need to think about my interactions with people with whom I am in frequent contact because we affect each other so much. I work closely with our office manager and assistant coaches every day. We have all decided to invest a big part of our lives in this program. Part of my job is to define job descriptions and structure them in ways so that all of us have value. If our assistant coaches' only role in the gym is to toss balls or shag balls, they will soon tire of their role at practice. If I become bogged down with my job or take for granted that each person understands or is satisfied with his or her role, problems can arise. It all starts with holding myself accountable and trying to establish an atmosphere that is conducive to enjoying life and pursuing greatness at the same time.

Alums

We all need to make more time for the athletes who have given so much to our programs. The least I should do is write them each year, call them on their birthdays, and send them regular newsletters. We also send them a calendar that lists our matches and special dates, with the alumnae match highlighted. What a great day that is! We have a big booster barbecue for fans, players, alumnae, and all the families. We make up a special T-shirt that the alums use as a uniform and later cherish as a work-out garment. We try hard to include alumnae in our program as long as they want to participate, because it is the right thing to do and they can make our program better. If their experience is enjoyable while they are in the program and we make them feel welcome when they are finished playing, then they will be in the program forever. They should be our most effective supporters and recruiters.

Team Versus the Individual

No piece of the puzzle is more important than the issue of the team versus the individual. I believe that this question has become more difficult and more important each year. Many influences work against the idea that the team comes first. As a coach, I have to talk it, believe it, and live it. And that is just the first step. One of our players helped me to learn a great lesson in this area. She was aware that another player on our team had some serious problems and that I was trying to help her. I am sure she respected me for wanting to help the other player, but she tried to let me know that sacrificing the team for any one person was not the right choice. I didn't listen to her because I thought what I was doing was right. I was wrong! It took me a while to figure it out, but the importance of the team is at the core of what I now preach as a coach. We start with the premise that we care for our players, but they must see it before they believe it. We make sure that they know that we really don't care who plays or who receives awards. We put on the court the group of people who do the most to help each other play the best. We have to be consistent with our actions and language to get everyone to think and talk in terms of the team.

Once the players begin to understand the priority of the team over the individual, we turn our attention to everyone who interacts with us. Family, friends, roommates, and people in the media all mean well but talk about events in a way that is oriented toward the individual. Awards banquets are a great part of tradition, but if we are not careful they can turn into individual celebrations, not team celebrations. We mean well with all our publications, but they can inadvertently focus on individual endeavors. I am committed to having the idea of the team remain at the core of my coaching philosophy.

Teaching Life Skills

At the core of our program philosophy is the idea that our teaching methods and coaching style must go along with our commitment to teaching life skills. As a father of two college students I have seen in my daughters the same thing I see in my players of the same age. In some ways they are mature, but they are still working at developing who they are and where they are going. They want to learn and improve, but they already know a lot. Therefore, they are stubborn when asked to learn. They have to perform and learn at the same time, but we all know that when we change things, our performance sometimes declines. How confusing for them!

I owe it to them to continue learning to coach the sport better. Exciting things are happening around us; we work to embrace change so that we can continue to advance our methods. Perhaps our greatest task is to understand how our methods and style work together. If you must convey a message that is tough for the players to hear (like being critical of them in some way), don't deliver it in a heavy-handed way. Their response may disappoint you. But if your message and delivery are too soft, the players may not hear and understand it. We have to find a way that works yet helps them find their way. We cannot hold their hands the whole way, but we still need to provide some guidance. College is the last step before life.

Last Thoughts

My father once gave me a hint about life in the business world. He felt that a good manager, coach, or leader should be able to leave for a time and return to a smoothly running operation. If our program is to be the best, it must endure time and troubles. It must be solid enough to remain on track even if good people leave or outstanding players graduate.

One of the people I have always looked to for guidance tells me that greatness comes not from doing great things but from always doing basic things well. This maxim is true on the court and in all areas of the program. If I can get many things in the plus column and work hard to eliminate things in the minus column, then the stature of the program will grow.

I feel as if I am a juggler and have many balls in the air. I am not going to drop a ball and allow my program to suffer because I care that much about the game and the program. We started with two balls in the air and slowly added more when we knew we could keep them aloft. If the program is to continue to prosper it will need to grow. As we work to help it grow we must keep an eye on the foundation. If the foundation we have developed is solid we will enjoy success in whatever way we define it.

CHAPTER SEVEN

Developing a Successful High School Program

Dave Shondell

The achievement of a high school volleyball program can be evaluated in many ways. Championships, win-loss record, and team improvement are some of the measuring sticks we might use. Certainly, providing a positive experience for each student-athlete is the primary objective. There are many ways to reach this goal. At Central High School in Muncie, Indiana, we have built our program on the premise that we will be the best high school program in the state. Having this goal does not mean that we expect our team to win the state championship every year, an accomplishment that may not always be obtainable. But our program will always provide a tremendous opportunity for each athlete to develop as a player, grow as an individual, and experience the best athletic environment possible.

High school sport teams can no longer count on athletic departments to furnish the necessary means to operate a first-class operation. Instead, the coaching staff, in cooperation with the booster club and athletic department, has the responsibility to ensure that the program has all the ingredients it needs to succeed. At Central we embrace a family atmosphere in which our players' parents are the backbone of the volleyball program. The team's success depends on the support of our booster club, which is predominantly made up of parents. The head coach must communicate effectively with the parent group and inspire them to realize their importance in creating the optimal environment for each player.

The amount of time involved in developing and maintaining a high school program is immense. The coach needs to understand the magnitude of the task before accepting the job of building a successful high school program. I have taken over two lackluster high school programs in my career and have used the available resources to guide each school to an elite level. I am going to describe many factors required to develop such programs. Some of the suggestions may not be practicable for a particular school, but I believe that a coach who implements the core of these ideas will develop a strong volleyball program.

Determining the Vision of Your Program

The most important factor in building a quality program is getting your team to establish a vision of how the program should be. It is essential to dream big. You should have two visionary goals—an initial vision of how the program will be now, for the upcoming season, and a second vision of how the program will be after reaching full fruition. The coach cannot mandate the vision. The players must develop it with the leadership of the coaching staff. The role of the coach is to allow the team to shoot high but to avoid establishing objectives that are unrealistically high or too low. Our team meets early in the preseason to establish a vision for the upcoming season. We sketch the vision during individual meetings in the previous winter and through team meetings in the spring and summer. When training sessions begin in early August, the team must narrow its focus and determine specific goals. Along with shaping the vision, the team determines how they will reach that destination. The team creates a blueprint that outlines the rules and guidelines for the season, which will serve as a compass to lead the team to their goal, or vision. We post the team's objectives and strategies to reach their goals in the locker room where each player can review the items before each practice.

Emulating superior programs with which your coaches and players are familiar can be effective. Instead of resenting the achievements of the best program in the area or state, use that school as a model and a measuring stick. Study the outstanding programs in the state and learn why they are successful. Choose the ideas that can work for you and help your team to reach new heights. The vision must be a shared belief. All players must have the vision in mind in everything they do. If your players don't understand the purpose of the long, grueling hours of practice during the preseason, they will not put forth maximum effort. If players do not understand the reason for spending tough hours in the weight room, they will not apply themselves in the manner necessary to reach their utmost strength. Coaches must constantly remind the players of the ultimate goal. The coach should meet with the parents and the athletic administration to encourage their identification with the proposal as well.

Establishing a Training Emphasis for the Season

High school coaches need to develop a team system around the abilities of their athletes. Each year, the strengths and weaknesses of your team will be different, and the coaching staff must become familiar with the abilities of next year's team. Hardly a day passes that I don't write lineups on a napkin or notepaper for next year's team. You need to know your horses. In other words, you must be familiar with the talent available, and design a training strategy and lineups well before the first day of practice.

Many years ago I heard former USA national team coach Taras Liskevych say, "There are a thousand ways to skin a cat." His reference was to the idea that there are many ways to win volleyball matches and each coach must use the available talent to design a system that will give his or her team the best chance to win. Some teams are tall but cannot control the ball, whereas other teams are small and cannot block or attack well. Find a way to put your best athletes on the floor and then design a system to emphasize their strengths. A few years ago I had a team without a true outside hitter. This is unusual because high school teams normally lack middle attackers. In preseason we emphasized developing the skills necessary to play the left-side hitting position. Each practice incorporated drills to develop passing, defense, hitting, and movement skills. The team never boasted two great outside hitters, but those players performed their roles well enough to allow our team to be extremely successful. The next year our emphasis was much different.

With two practices per day before the start of school, you might conduct 40 to 50 percent of your team's practices before your first match. It is essential that you understand what skills to stress so that you can create an effective plan of action before the start of training. Take advantage of the many hours of practice time before the season. A coach cannot wait until after the first few matches to determine what areas need attention.

Task of the Coaching Staff

The strength of a coaching staff is a huge factor in the success of a high school program. Certainly, the talent of the athletes is a critical ingredient. But competent coaching can develop quality players every year. Developing a productive coaching staff is a challenging, but significant, job. Most large schools provide salaries for a varsity coach, junior varsity coach, and freshman coach. Having three coaches for a large number of athletes makes the responsibilities of training the players difficult, but it can be done. Our program at Central is fortunate to have additional coaches who volunteer or work for minimal pay. Your players should receive as many ball contacts in each practice as possible. Using several coaches allows you to implement this philosophy and consistently conduct quality practice sessions. I have not always had this luxury. When I began coaching at Central I did not have an assistant coach until two weeks into the season. I was fortunate to hire a former high school player of mine who was a student at a nearby college. She understood my system and realized what we had to do to transform the program at Central. Although inexperienced as a coach, she learned quickly and did a thorough job in helping me establish the work ethic necessary to start the building process. Even with only two coaches, the program direction changed significantly.

The most important characteristic to develop in your coaching staff is loyalty. I have been fortunate to hire coaches of great character who have been extremely loyal to our program. Each coach must be committed to the vision of the program. The coaching staff must have confidence and trust in each other. I involve my coaches to a great degree in all operations of our team. Each coach has specific roles in practice that gives him or her an identity. This system enhances the personal pride the coaches have in their respective products. It is sensible to find coaches who have expertise in areas of the game in which you are less knowledgeable. Find coaches who possess personality qualities that are different from yours as well. A well-rounded coaching staff can more effectively meet the demands of a high school team.

The varsity team at Central has four full- or part-time coaches. When the junior varsity coach is available, five coaches are sometimes involved. This number of coaches on one team is probably above the norm, but I believe it is usually possible to attain additional coaches. Even coaches with limited experience can be productive when given proper training. During practice and matches, each coach has specific areas of responsibility. For example, assistant coach A is our ball-control coach. In high school volleyball, no area of the game is more important. She works with passing and defense. Coach A is often responsible for determining what drills to use during the segment of practice time designated for ball-control skills. She works before and after practice with players who need extra attention on ball-control skills. During matches her focus is on our defense and passing. Coach A has the authority to make defensive changes during a match.

Assistant coach B is responsible for net skills, such as attacking and blocking. Coach B often structures and directs blocking and attacking drills. During match play coach B observes block positioning and technique, and charts attackers to determine what is working.

Coach C is the setting coach. Her focus is always on the setter. Certainly, the setter-hitter relationship is part of her concern, so she also works with hitters on their location or timing to the setter. Having a coach responsible for the setter is a real bonus. I prefer to have a female coach who can work with the setter and discuss the emotional aspects of the position as well as the technical ones. Obviously, this coach should have a strong setting background. Coach C also works closely with the setter during matches. She trains the setter before the match and talks with her during time-outs and between games. Coach C also completes an evaluation form for the setter after each match. This tool helps the setter understand what improvements she needs to make and compliments her for skills well performed.

When able to attend the varsity practice, coach D helps run drills. He is also in charge of the majority of program organization. Each team needs a coach skilled in administering the program to relieve the head coach from most of the off-the-court responsibilities. Coach D also coordinates the statistical and managerial crews. Each coach will focus on his or her respective areas during practice. If we are involved in team offense or defense, all coaches concentrate on their particular tasks. These descriptions are a small part of the responsibilities of each coach. With this system, coaches take ownership of their roles and become more accountable and better coaches.

Off-Season Training

What occurs during the nine months outside the high school season is crucial to the enrichment of each player and the program. At Central we have a three-pronged plan that has proved beneficial over time. We encourage our players to participate in physical conditioning, individual training sessions, and club volleyball.

Of the three off-season opportunities, quality club volleyball training is the most valuable. Nearly 90 percent of our 40 players, freshmen through seniors, play club volleyball. Most girls train three to four days a week from January through June. Therefore, nearly all our players are engaged in skill development for 10 months of the year. This is important because the number of effective skill repetitions a player performs throughout the year determines skill level. Many of our athletes play on elite club teams who compete for national championships. The experience of playing in high-profile matches offers our players an advantage when competing in similar situations during the high school season. We are fortunate to have a quality junior club in our area. The high school coach is responsible for helping to provide good off-season club opportunities. Without the effort of the high school coaches in the Muncie area, a club program in which local girls can participate would not exist. In Indiana, a simple formula seems to operate: teams exposed to worthy club training and competent high school coaching are the most successful. If you do not have good club volleyball opportunities in your area, I encourage you to join other local high school coaches to organize a junior development club. Club volleyball is a vital ingredient to building your high school program.

A strength and fitness program is essential to establishing a winning organization. Your athletes will seldom be the most athletic in the area. A quality strength and fitness program will help your team close the gap between themselves and others who may be naturally more talented. The weight-training philosophy at Central has changed throughout the years. Initially, we trained diligently in a makeshift weight room at our practice facility. I feel that weight training as a team is the ideal method. Because athletes are involved in so many activities, however, it became increasingly difficult to assemble the team for the designated workout times. During the past couple of years, we moved our strength and fitness training to the local YMCA, which recently built a wonderful fitness area that provides our athletes with everything they need. Our players can use machine weights or free weights. Stationary exercise machines and workout classes are available to them. The YMCA staff has been helpful in mapping out specific programs for each of our girls. Most important, the YMCA offers convenient hours that allow our busy athletes to work out when it fits into their schedule. I have discovered that this approach works well during the off-season. As a coach, however, I must continually motivate the players to stay on their training schedule. During the season, the team begins training together. They have flexibility during the off-season, but we bring them back together when the official practice season begins.

The Indiana High School Athletic Association recently altered its rules to allow coaches to work with their high school athletes out-of-season. The new rule permits coaches to work with two athletes at a time, for two hours each day. Although we feel our players are receiving plenty of training throughout the year, in some situations our staff feels that players need extra attention. We establish a summer schedule for the selected players, often scheduling our setter and middle hitters together to improve timing and familiarity of middle attacking. As our staff evaluates the upcoming season, we determine specific areas that need attention, and we focus on those skills during the sessions.

Developing a Feeder System

Unlike sports in which youngsters develop skills on their own, girls rarely grow up peppering the volleyball in the backyard or setting the ball off the garage door. Instead, the head coach is responsible for making sure that the program's future players are receiving necessary training to play high school volleyball. Without the supervision of the varsity coach, elementary and middle school players seldom receive productive training. The initial, or continued, success of a team depends largely on the fundamental training received by upcoming players. The head coach must show a real interest in the young players in the district. To develop a perennial winner at the high school level, the head coach must be involved with the middle school program. He or she must help determine who will be the coaches in the sixth, seventh, and eighth grades. Varsity coaches should spend time with those coaches to describe the preferred offensive and defensive systems and demonstrate the desired fundamental skill techniques. Volleyball coaches at the middle school level often lack confidence in their abilities. Most are inexperienced coaches who appreciate the guidance of a more knowledgeable coach. By conveying information in the proper fashion, the varsity coach can help create an environment at the middle school level that will pay large dividends for the varsity program down the road. The varsity coach will be hard pressed to spend a great amount of time at middle school practices, but periodic appearances at practices and matches will demonstrate interest in the coaches and players. Coaches should encourage players to participate in a variety of sports and activities. Requiring the middle school or high school athlete to specialize in one sport is not necessary. The athlete can develop compatible skills while pursuing different activities.

Although the middle school season is important to skill development, the six- to eight-week training period is minimal in comparison with a five-month club season. High school coaches who run a club program for their middle school players will quickly see the benefits of putting forth the extra effort. I have worked with 12- and 14-year-old teams for the past eight years. The relationships that a coach can build while working with these club teams creates better coach-player understanding as players progress through the system. Each player will learn the priorities of the coach's philosophy at an early age, helping them to focus on the preferred aspects as the training continues. When a coach works with players in the younger age divisions, a bond develops between player and coach that is seldom matched when the same relationship begins later in high school. The benefits of running a club program for future players revolve around their believing in the vision of the program. Each player learns early that there is a plan for her future.

Summer Volleycamp

A great way to promote the sport to young players is to conduct a summer camp. This is a successful tool in teaching fundamental skills, providing a positive and enjoyable experience for the kids, and creating long-lasting relationships between coaches, current players, and future players. At Central, we hold our camp in June, soon after the final day of school. This schedule allows us to recruit potential campers through communications while they are still in school. Our coaches travel to the elementary schools and middle schools in our district to meet with classes and pass out the registration forms. The camp is open to girls completing grades one through eight, and our camp attendance consistently reaches the 100 mark.

All our high school coaches participate, but more important, all our high school players work as court coaches. The high school players serve as excellent role models for the young aspiring athletes and usually perform their camp coaching duties well. Former Central players, many of whom are playing college volleyball, also return to help with the camp. The camp runs for three hours per day on Monday through Friday. The focus for the first three days is fundamental skill training. It is important that the campers learn proper technique because they may not have received quality coaching at the elementary or middle school level. We spend most of the first three days in partner drills that emphasize maximum contacts and appropriate technique. We introduce team play on the fourth day and organize teams for the Friday tournament. Before tournament play begins on Friday, we review individual skills. The coaches and players enjoy an exciting day of volleyball, and the campers and high school players who serve as camp team coaches quickly develop a bond.

Many traditions have been established at the camp. The high school girls bring in treats for their team on Friday to celebrate the final day of camp, and campers sign each other's camp T-shirts. Last year, the names of nearly 20 camp sponsors appeared on the back of the shirts. The camp fee is only $25. We feel it is important to keep the camp fee affordable so that everyone can attend, and we provide scholarships for any camper who cannot afford to participate. We make it a priority to involve all interested girls in the camp.

Role of Booster Clubs

Our volleyball program provides more for our athletes than the programs of other sports at our school provide for their athletes. To build a quality program, you must help the athletes feel important, or elite. You can accomplish this task in many ways. A well-organized booster club can have a huge effect in what your program can offer. Seven years ago, we moved into a wonderful playing facility with a great athletic tradition. But the locker rooms, coaches' offices, and other aspects of the facility were inadequate and outdated. Since establishing residency in the Muncie Fieldhouse, these items have consistently been upgraded. We have recently made improvements to our locker room, including painting the walls and hanging motivational signs. The mothers supply the players with daily necessities in the locker room and help make the antiquated dressing area more female friendly.

We recently transformed an old classroom adjacent to the gym into a meeting room. We bought 18 padded chairs with "Bearcat Volleyball" printed on each backrest and six long folding tables. We hung banners with "Bearcat Volleyball" embroidered on each. We have a large banner hanging in the room that honors our state championship teams. The room has a large-screen television, video player, and 40 feet of dry-erase board with various volleyball court diagrams printed on each. We recently bought a piece of Bearcat purple carpet for the room to add spirit. The team uses this room on a daily basis for team building, viewing videos of our team and opponents, match preparation, and more. We believe it is important for the players to feel good about their home court and the related accommodations. Our booster club makes possible these types of improvements.

At the conclusion of the season, our volleyball program has a banquet in addition to the school honor program. More than 150 people attend the ceremony, held at the finest banquet hall in town. The booster club decorates the hall, makes all arrangements, and pays for the meal of each player, coach, and special guest. This first-class banquet finishes our season in a memorable fashion and is another way of making the athletes feel appreciated.

The generosity of our booster club makes possible several other advantages:

- The team is outfitted in the best uniforms and accessories available.
- Practice gear is supplied for each player, including T-shirts and shorts.
- Each senior receives recognition, including a large plaque and flowers, during her final home match.

- An attractive color poster with the home schedule showcases the senior players.
- For longer road trips the team rides in a chartered bus rather than the school-provided bus.
- Some nonsalaried coaches receive a financial stipend for their efforts.
- A media guide offers pictures, player profiles, schedules, records, history, honors, and so on.
- Sandwiches and fruit are available before road trips.
- Players and coaches receive partial funding for state championship and runner-up rings.
- Large state championship and runner-up team pictures hang in the lobby.

The booster club is able to assist our program by organizing various fundraising activities:

- The booster club earns over $2,000 annually by selling ads for the athletic department all-sports program.
- Booster club members pay $15 for an annual membership. Their names appear in the volleyball program. Membership exceeds 175 each year.
- The boosters sell Muncie Central Volleyball T-shirts, the same shirts that the players use in practice. Each player is responsible for selling five. The volleyball program makes $5 per shirt.
- The booster club organizes the athletic department fall golf outing, earning over $1,000 each year. They sell ads that are printed in bold color on the ball stops at the end of the court. The booster club normally sells over $1,500 in sponsorship.
- Game-ball raffles earn $25 to $50 per match. Local businesses sponsor the ball for $50, and a local junior club donates the balls.
- The booster club sells concessions at all home matches. Depending on the strength of the home schedule, profit from concessions is between $1,000 and $2,000.

Playing Environment

You should consider many factors in creating the environment in which your team will compete. Your team needs to play challenging opponents. Our program has reached a point where we want to play the most competitive schedule in the state. Our schedule normally includes 4 or 5 of the country's top 20 teams and 15 to 20 highly ranked teams in Indiana. Of our 33 regular-season matches, nearly 70 percent pit us against teams ranked in the top 10 of their class (Indiana has a four-class system). The schedule includes travel to tournaments early in the season to advance team chemistry. We participate in the Mishawaka Invitational, which includes an overnight stay, during the second weekend of the season. Of the eight teams in the field, three or four are perennial state powers. By traveling to northern Indiana the night before the event, eating meals together, spending the night at a comfortable motel, and competing well (usually) in the tournament, our team has an excellent opportunity to improve group dynamics.

Knowing when to travel is important. It is essential to stay close to home late in the season. Long bus trips in the weeks before state tournament play can add to the fatigue of playing a tough schedule. We schedule more matches at home than on the road. It can be beneficial to encourage opponents to visit your home venue each year. We have three or four schools that enjoy competing at our place annually. Because we have enjoyed success at the state level, we can find teams who will contract matches at Central each year. Although playing strong teams regularly is important, your schedule should include a few opponents that will cause less stress to you and your team. You should provide playing opportunities for all players. Those who work hard in practice and make a commitment to your program deserve playing time. Scheduling periodic moderate competition allows you to reward each player with court time.

Making home matches entertaining is important for many reasons. As mentioned earlier, we attempt to make the players in our program feel special. Organizing an enjoyable and exciting home-match environment will motivate kids to play in your program. High school basketball is big in Indiana. Our goal is to offer a better show for home matches than the local schools provide for basketball. We start by scheduling high-level teams in our gym. Most fans will not take the time or pay the price to attend a match that they do not expect to be competitive. Like most college programs, we use lively music to generate enthusiasm. One of the most critical jobs performed during the preseason is designing the pregame music for our warm-up. Fans hear a definite difference in the music when our team is hitting as opposed to when the visiting team takes the court. The performance of the announcer can also keep fans interested in the game.

The one obvious problem with high school volleyball is the lengthy delays involved. We use a three-ball system to keep the game moving quickly. Effective match management can minimize prolonged substitution exchanges or the wait for a ball that has rolled under the bleachers. Providing contests for the fans after game one of the varsity match and inviting special guests to each home match can improve the size and energy of your crowd. Try to develop good rapport with your football team. Having 30 to 40 football players in the crowd each night adds to your home-court advantage.

Summary

Developing a productive high school volleyball program is challenging and rewarding. To become one of the best programs in your state, coaches, players, and parents will have to put forth tremendous effort. The coach must successfully manage many factors to reach the elite level. Each coach will operate in a different way. I hope you can use some of the ideas I discussed in this chapter to help you along the way. Good luck.

CHAPTER EIGHT

Developing a Successful Junior Club Program

Tom Pingel

Each year hundreds of new junior volleyball clubs pop up across the country. The reasons that bring about their existence are numerous. In general, there are two types of clubs—clubs that appear first in a geographic area and those that start up in an area where at least one other club operates or spins off from the original. The type of club you are starting drives much of your start-up procedure.

Starting a New Club

Suppose you have recognized the need for a junior club in your area. Whether you are a volleyball coach wishing to strengthen the level of play in your area, or a parent hoping to provide better opportunities for your area athletes, or both, one of the biggest tasks that lies in front of you is educating the parents, coaches, and administrators in your area that a junior volleyball club is the way to go. Granted, with each passing year, accumulated history points to facts that will assist you in making your point. Nevertheless, some people will be hesitant to make the commitment necessary to be successful. Club administrators must commit time, effort, support, and a desire to provide consistent services to the participants. Club coaches must commit time and effort.

School administrators must commit support and possibly facilities. School coaches must commit support and possibly their services as club coaches. Parents must commit time, support, money, and possibly their services to ensure success of the club. The athletes must commit their time, effort, and desire to improve and learn.

If no club exists in your area and the whole concept is foreign to those you are presenting it to, you will surely want to obtain information on club volleyball for your area and nationwide. The primary two sources for information are the USA Volleyball (USAV) national office and the local region of USAV. Visit the USA Volleyball Web site (**www.usavolleyball.org**) to find information on all aspects of the national governing body for volleyball in the country. The "Regions" section of the site defines the USAV regions and provides contact information. Contact the person in your region to learn the procedure for registering your club and athletes.

Starting a New Club Where Others Already Exist

Regardless of your intent, when you start a club in an area where a club or clubs already exist, they will view your new club, at least initially, as a competitor. I recommend that you be completely up front with the other clubs about your plan for age groups, level of competitiveness, and sources for obtaining coaches and athletes. Clubs often form because existing clubs are simply overwhelmed with athletes and can't accommodate everyone. Athletes with nowhere to go end up banding together to form a club. The other common reason for establishing a new club is that coaches, parents, or athletes are unhappy with their former club and want to go a different direction. Regardless of the reason for the spin-off, the various clubs should try to coexist in harmony so that everyone involved has a positive overall experience.

My recommendation is not to actively recruit coaches or athletes already participating in area clubs. If these people contact you about being part of your new club, however, you can ethically nullify all territorial courtesies.

Having patience, maintaining a firm work ethic, and keeping true to your reasons for beginning the club will pay dividends. A quality organization will recruit for itself.

Before the Season Begins for a New Club

Before entering into your first year as a club, a new director should have a couple important things in place. First, you must set up the business. Regardless whether your club is projecting to offer one team or several teams over numerous age groups, I strongly recommend that you incorporate within your home state. Typically, incorporation is a relatively simple process that you can accomplish in a few hours without having to hire legal help. You should also set up a separate checking account. By establishing clear lines for the organization, you calm the fears of those who may question the finances of the club and protect your personal assets from the operations of the club.

One of the questions you may have is whether to apply for state and federal not-for-profit status. A couple of misconceptions exist regarding "not for profit" status. First, "not for profit" does not mean an organization can't make money. It simply means that the group must apply money made to conducting the business. Second, a club need not be a not-for-profit club. In some instances, being not-for-profit may be essential for obtaining facilities or gaining grants that go toward conducting club operations. In other cases, the effort the club must put forth to obtain and retain nonprofit status may not be worth it. Obtaining not-for-profit status can be a process that lasts months or years. If becoming a not-for-profit club is the way for you to go, I recommend that you find a lawyer who has experience applying for this status with sport organizations.

Depending on the type of corporation you ultimately decide to form, you may be required to form a board of directors. Boards can be helpful in the formation, promotion, and activation of a new or existing club. Boards can also create a level of bureaucracy that slows the decision-making process and even inhibits growth. A recommended board-member list would include all factions—administrative staff, coaching staff (at least one, but preferably more than one that would represent different age groups), a nonstaff college coach, a nonstaff high school coach, a parent of a former club participant (if applicable), and a parent of a current participant. Too often, the board of a club is heavily laden with parents of current participants. Decisions tainted by perceived or real levels of self-interest can cause serious damage to the reputation of a club and its ability to operate effectively.

Obtaining appropriate insurance should be a priority before the first information meeting occurs, let alone before the first day players enter the gym. Registering with USA Volleyball or the Amateur Athletic Union (AAU) will provide your organization with varying levels of insurance to cover certain activities. Obtain up-to-date information from the organization you intend to register the club with and be sure that all your activities are properly covered.

Learn the rules. Contact the high school association for your state to learn what restrictions they have about athlete participation. Research the rules about participation by staff of member high schools and know the restrictions on whom they can coach and during what time of the year they can coach. Check to see whether participation is restricted during certain parts of the calendar year. Contact the NCAA to learn the rules regarding the participation of college coaches and the rules governing the recruiting process of your athletes. Know NCAA and state restrictions regarding the acceptance by athletes of financial assistance to pay for club expenses. Know the restrictions on whether an athlete can accept tournament awards. Learn the rules governing the member organization with whom you choose to register (USAV or AAU). It is not the responsibility of the various organizations to educate you. It is your job to become knowledgeable about the rules.

Set your club philosophy. In general, there are three types of clubs:

1. A club can be interested in being highly competitive in both their local area and nationally. This club strives to make every effort to win events and prepare athletes for moving on to the college ranks with scholarships. Typically, these clubs travel extensively and therefore have high participation fees. The season will often run for seven to nine months.

2. A club may strive to prepare its participants to be better volleyball players for their school team. Travel is limited, and fees are modest. The season will last only a few months.

3. A club can be large enough to provide teams that fit into both philosophical areas.

Decide on the type of club you plan to have for the year and don't stray from it for at least that year. You may need to rethink the club's philosophy each year, but changing the plan during the season is a recipe for failure.

Identify your target market. Once you decide on a philosophy, the next move is to identify the market that will make up the basis for the club and tailor the club to meet the needs of the market. Is the target market primarily kids from one school or school district? One city? Or are the kids from many schools and age groups? Will members be coming from many miles away to participate? Identifying the needs of the target market and the methods the club uses to meet those needs will be reflected in the fee structure, the scheduling of practice sessions and competitions, the roster size and makeup, and the level of coaching.

Create a club Web site. Depending on the projected size and philosophy of your club, a Web site may be essential to distributing information to your club members and to promoting your club and its participants. Many college coaches rely on club Web sites to obtain information about prospective recruits, such as the teams they are playing on, the team's schedule, and the coach's name and contact information. Web sites also provide a means for club sponsors to attain improved exposure. For a relatively small investment, a club can provide a clean, attractive, and informative Web site. A note of caution is that although you may put athlete profiles on your Web site for the benefit of college recruiters, you should not include individual photos, phone numbers, or other personal information. If college coaches need this information, they should contact you as the club director or the team coach. You will thus be able to monitor who is gaining access to this information. If you commit to having a Web site, you must keep the information current. Otherwise, the site highlights your club's lack of organization rather than its efficiency and businesslike approach.

Decide on a membership organization. Most clubs and competitions are sanctioned by either USA Volleyball or the Amateur Athletic Union (AAU). You should determine which organization is the primary sanctioning body for the majority of clubs and tournaments in your area. Then contact the local office for that organization and request a registration packet for the upcoming season.

Starting Your Season

Each year before the first day in the gym rolls around, both new and established clubs must complete several administrative duties. The club must prepare preseason printed material, including fliers for prospective participants that introduce the club and inform them of club activities for the year. These activities should include at least one informational meeting open to athletes, parents, coaches, and anyone interested in learning about the club. At this meeting more extensive information can be distributed, including club philosophy, try-out schedule, fee schedule, competition schedule, and so on. This task would also include updating the information on the club Web site if applicable.

The club must set financial schedules for the year. One of the most important decisions typically made by new as well as existing clubs is setting the fee structure and payment schedule for participants. Will the club set a fee structure that spreads fee payments over an expanded period to make things more affordable for participants? Or will the club bill the participants for the entire fee early in the season? Although more affordable, the first option allows less commitment by the participants and adds to administrative and collection problems. The latter gives the club more working cash at the beginning of the season, locks the participants into a commitment, and reduces the headache of collecting fees. It also drives away prospective participants because of the financial hit. Again, evaluating the market is critical. Getting a workable mix may be the solution. One suggestion is to spread the fees over a workable length of time but load the first payment to ensure commitment. This method is typical because the club needs cash at the beginning of the season for USAV or AAU registration, uniforms, equipment purchase, and deposits on early season facilities and tournaments.

Many clubs incorporate into their fees a certain amount for tournament expenses. Others bill for events as they occur. Inexperienced clubs may opt to bill on a per event basis to permit more accurate accounting of the expenses. Experienced clubs can rely on history regarding the expenses needed for participation in various events. Of course, when an organization spreads out its billing, it runs the risk of being unable to collect the fees in a timely manner, or at all. Uncollected fees are the number-one reason why clubs dissolve.

Staff salaries, both coaching and administrative, will also play into determining a fee schedule. Typically, a club will promise coaching fees to a coach before the start of the season. Again, the going rate as well as the coach's level of expertise and responsibility will determine the workable amount of a coach's pay for a season. Administrative pay may be harder to pin down. A common problem is to underestimate the level of administrative work needed to start a club, maintain its finances, enter teams into events, and so on. Fortunately, participant numbers drive much of this work. More participants and more teams mean more administrative work. Setting up an administrative fee based on the number of participants may be the best approach for a new club. Existing clubs will have experience in knowing the level of the work load through the year as well as how much compensation will be required to produce a quality product in a timely manner.

The policy for paying coaches' expenses during travel should also be in place. Typically, coaches will receive reimbursement for their travel to competitions and hotel expenses, when applicable. Meals for coaches while at competitions may or may not be reimbursed. Covering this expense can be done on a per diem basis or by submission of receipts. If the club does not provide some sort of payment for travel, the compensation that coaches receive for their services is diminished.

Will your club conduct any fundraising activities during the seasons? If so, how will the club distribute the proceeds from the fundraiser? In other words, will all proceeds go to the club, or will a specific team or seller retain a portion of the revenue to apply toward his or her club expenses?

You must, of course, line up your staff, both a coaching staff and an administrative staff. Try to have these people in place before the information meeting so that you can introduce them at the meeting. Lack of quality coaches is one of the two main logistical problems in running a club. Attracting enough coaches is not the problem. Getting quality coaches is the problem. College coaches and players, high school coaches, intermediate school coaches, adult players, and parents with volleyball or coaching experience with other sports are all candidates. Most USAV regions have coaching education courses of varying degrees that can provide training for your staff going into the season. Most USAV regions require that coaches earn a minimum level of certification to participate as registered coaches in sanctioned competitions. You should exercise due diligence in performing background checks on prospective coaches.

Conduct a staff meeting before the club information meeting. At this meeting, the staff will complete and return the necessary paper work. You should spell out and discuss staff procedures, requirements, and guidelines. You may want to discuss coaching assignments.

All staff members should complete a staff application form that includes references, past and current employers, and coaching experience (volleyball and otherwise). Ask the candidates if they have ever been convicted of a felony or had their driving privileges suspended. (This is important if you ever ask your coaches to drive team members to and from competitions or training sessions.) Include some wording to the effect that you reserve the right to do a background check on all staff members of the club.

Policies should be in place regarding appropriate behavior of staff members during club activities, including training, tournaments, and trips.

When making your staff assignments, avoid putting your top coaches exclusively with the older teams. Instead, assign them to the top teams of all age groups to ensure a cohesive progression for the athletes of the club. To assist with the mentoring of less experienced coaches, assign them as assistants to the top coaches and, if their schedules allow, as head coaches of developmental teams. Will your coaches be required to write up practice plans, or will the club provide them? Will the club use a consistent technical system, or will each coach incorporate his or her own system? Many clubs identify a master coach who makes many of these decisions. This person may coach a top team within the club or may serve only as the master coach, or coaches' coach.

Before training begins you must line up your practice facilities. Securing ample quality training facilities is the other chief logistical problem in running a club. Schools, churches, recreational facilities, private gyms, and National Guard armories are the primary places that may be able to provide facilities. Often your staff or parents of athletes are the best resources in finding these facilities. Allow them to make the original contact to inquire about the potential of using the facility. After the initial contact you should try to meet with the organization's highest ranking official who deals with facilities. At this meeting you need to obtain answers to several questions:

- What is the rental rate, and what does it cover?

- If applicable, is the rental rate lower for not-for-profit organizations?
- How is the rent to be paid? What is the payment schedule? Will the facility consider volleyball equipment (balls, nets, etc.) as a means of payment? You may be able to obtain equipment at a better price than a school can. Donating used or new volleyballs to the school's program can be a huge goodwill gesture. If the facility net system is substandard, buying and installing a new system in exchange for facility rent benefits both the school and your club.
- What equipment does the facility provide? Poles, nets, balls, carts, or other items?
- Does the facility offer a grace period before and after your scheduled training session to allow for equipment setup and teardown?
- Does a facility employee set up and take down the equipment, or can the club do this?
- Do other groups use the gym before, after, or while you are there?
- How are cancellations handled because of weather, a conflict on their end, or a conflict on your end?
- In case of emergency, whom do you contact and how?
- Is a custodian on duty? What is his or her name? Where will the custodian be located while you are using the facility?
- If applicable, is it possible to store club equipment (balls, nets, first aid kits, etc.) at the facility? Is the storage area secure?

After reaching an agreement, I recommend finding the head custodian who will be on duty while your team is there. Introduce yourself and explain your club's impending facility usage. Begin a relationship. Find out how you can minimize the work that your club's use of the facility will cause the custodial staff. Typically, you will have only limited contact with the facility administrator after the initial meeting. The facility custodian will be your new primary contact, so try to have this person be a friend of the program. Be sure that your coaches are aware of the importance of this relationship and do their part to ensure that it remains positive. Make no mistake—if the custodian doesn't want you in the facility, your days are probably numbered.

Other than the obvious safety issues associated with a facility, any facility that you are considering should meet three minimum requirements:

1. A safe, forgiving playing surface. Wood, plastic tile, or a synthetic floor covering is best. Avoid carpet, concrete, tiled concrete, or any abrasive type of flooring.
2. Easily accessible rest rooms. Typically, showers are not necessary, but an accessible rest room is necessary.

3. An accessible telephone. A pay phone is OK for emergencies, but it must be readily available. Of course, a cell phone would meet this need as well.

Have a tentative plan for the season. Before going into the first information meeting, have some written or prepared answers to the following frequently asked questions:

- When and where will tryouts be conducted?
- What is the philosophy and method of team selection?
- How many players will be on each team?
- Once the initial teams are set, will they remain in place for the year, or will players move up and down?
- When and where will practices be conducted?
- How many times a week will a team practice?
- What is the club's policy if participants miss practices or tournaments for extracurricular activities?
- In how many tournaments will a team play?
- When and where will the tournaments be held?
- What is the policy regarding playing time?
- Are participants on their own for arranging transportation to tournaments, or will the club coordinate transportation?

Set up the competition schedules for the year. Depending on the area in which you live, travel distance will vary. Competitive opportunities can range from half-day and one-day events to multiday events ranging from two to seven days. In many areas, cooperative competitions or leagues exist in which teams commit to participate in all scheduled events. Leagues are a good way to establish a consistent schedule without having to worry about entering numerous events. Leagues, however, can be costly and joining one may commit a team to more competitions than they wish to participate in.

The adage "You get what you pay for" applies to most tournaments. Some events may offer a relatively low entry fee but do not provide referees (teams ref themselves), conduct the matches at lesser facilities, and offer minimal or no awards. At top-end events, a team can expect high-quality facilities, administration, officiating, and awards. Of course, this comes at a price that could approach $200 or more for each day of the event! When considering an event, evaluate what it offers for the entry fee—especially a minimum match guarantee and the provision of refs.

When entering the season, a reasonable plan is to have a tentative schedule in place with a certain number of definite events in which a team will participate. Then provide the team with a list of optional tournaments and decide as a group whether they want to participate. Be sure to include a date of commitment for the optional events so that the club administration can enter the team into the event before the entry deadline.

Tournament Travel During the Season

Obviously, a team can easily travel to tournaments that are within a couple of hours of home. Loading a team into several family cars and vans is the typical mode of travel. If the event destination is more distant than a couple of hours, the team must decide whether it is prudent to travel the day before or simply save money and leave early on the day of the event. The start time and importance of the event may weigh into the decision.

For travel to a tournament that is more than a simple drive, the team may choose to take a major road trip involving a drive of a day or two. Or they may choose to fly. Group rates can often be secured for lower airfares, but the arrangement requires more administration and coordination. I have found in these cases that we came up with nearly as many different travel scenarios as there were participants. On some trips a parent took the lead as the travel coordinator and lined up flights and hotels for the team. On other trips the club administrators secured the hotel, but the individuals were on their own to line up travel arrangements. For some participants this arrangement can be awkward. You must be sure that all participants have a plan for their travel. If they don't have a plan, you must provide one for them.

Athletes flying to an event should always pack their team and personal essentials in a carry-on bag in case a checked bag is lost or delayed in transit. Team essentials include everything they need to play in the competition—uniforms, shoes, socks, kneepads, contact lenses, and so on.

Once at the tournament, you must supervise the activities of the participants. The reputation of a club is on display both on and off the court. Teams should have strict policies on hotel behavior. Team curfews should be installed and enforced. Those responsible should take measures to ensure that participants keep hotel rooms in acceptable condition during the stay and leave them that way on check out. Many teams pack coolers with drinks and food for the day. Many events or facilities have rules restricting food, drink, and coolers, especially at major events conducted in convention centers. Respecting these rules enhances the club's relationship with the events and other clubs.

Coach-Player-Parent Conflict

Unfortunately, conflict and unhappiness among participants are inevitable in team sports. You must expect and plan for these situations. The planning involves having a system in place to deal with complaints, concerns, and conflict. Depending on the size of the club, it may be necessary for a number of administrative layers to be in place to deal with problems. The initial line of problem solving is the team coach. The final line is the club director or board of directors. Between these entities may be a number of additional layers as needed. The club director often provides the final level of dealing with problems by holding a meeting involving the coach, the parent or parents, and the athlete. All three participants are critical to the success of the meeting. The conflict is often simply a result of a lack of communication between coach and athlete, coach and parent, or athlete and parent. Bringing all three "players" together will often clarify the situation and make a solution easier to identify.

As in any youth sport activity, dealing with parent conflicts can be the most frustrating and time-consuming part of club volleyball. Part of being a coach of a team involves dealing with a certain level of parent conflict. In most instances, the coach is the primary source of a parent's unhappiness. Good coach-parent communication can smooth this problem without further incident. At some point, however, a club director must step in to allow the coach to do the job he or she has been hired to do—coach volleyball. Because the parent usually pays a fee for an athlete to participate in the club, he or she should expect a certain level of performance by the club and the coach. When a parent's expectations exceed the product received, a conflict occurs. At times, the parent's expectations are unrealistic. At that point, the club must decide whether continued participation by the athlete is warranted. In some unfortunate situations a parent may occasionally affect the status of an athlete in an organization. Clubs must expect a level of behavior not only from its athletes but from the athletes' parents as well. Parents should be viewed as members of the club.

Specific rules regarding parent participation during training sessions, matches, and off times at events should be published and addressed at the preseason information meeting.

A Successful Club

What makes for a successful volleyball club? Is it operating within the club philosophy outlined before the season began? Taking into account the philosophy, evaluation can center on participation, competitive success, and the overall experiences gained by the club's participants (athletes, parents, coaches, and administrators).

The success of a team can be evaluated by whether they reached their competitive goals. A surefire method to rate the success of a team and the effort of a coach is to look at how many athletes from the initial roster do not finish out the year. Although extenuating circumstances such as injuries may cause some athletes not to complete the season, the level of participation will indicate the general tenor of the experience of the teams.

The club's success is a compilation of the sum of the success of its various teams. Another measure of success often can't be completely evaluated until registration begins the next season. Registration levels should increase from year to year. Satisfied customers will tell their friends. Word of mouth is a great advertisement. A quality organization will recruit for itself.

The future and ongoing success of the club depends not only on the strength of the club but also on the strength of the school programs that feed into it. An athlete who is being pushed and trained to be the best possible volleyball player whenever he or she is on the court, within either the club or the school program, has the best chance to reach maximum potential. If either the club or the school program is substandard, the player loses training time in returning to the performance level of the previous season. A seamless transition from one program to the next will maximize the training progress for the athlete. Efficient transition is a product of cooperative efforts between the club and the school program. The two programs should not be in competition. An adversarial relationship will hamper the success of both.

The overall strength of the clubs in your area and the existence of good working relationships among them maximize the competitive success and enhance the overall experience of the clubs and their teams. Too often the two strongest clubs in an area refuse to interact competitively and logistically. Because of this lack of interaction, the teams spend more money and travel farther than necessary to obtain a solid competitive experience.

A team gets the most out of its competitive experience when the majority of its matches are against teams of a similar or slightly better competitive level. Blowouts—as inevitable as they are—do little to improve a team.

Conclusion

Most teams end the season with a loss. Therefore, it is essential to keep the entire club experience in perspective. The chances of a given club producing a future Olympian are slim. The chances of producing a college player are significantly better, but still not assured. That said, at the end of the season broaden the scope of your evaluation and look at the friendships that the participants made, both inside and outside the club. Consider the many experiences shared by the players during travel, training, competitions, and beyond. If you feel that the participants learn only to pass, set, attack, or block better, look at the way the athletes and their parents interact during their school season. The real goal of a club is to provide on- and off-court experiences that help the athlete become a better volleyball player and a better person.

PART III

Innovative and Effective Practice Sessions

CHAPTER NINE

Planning Creative and Productive Practices

Russ Rose

What does it take to create the type of volleyball team that fans love, that younger players crave to be a part of, and that coaches fear to compete against at the end of the season?

Before we reach the heart of this chapter we should recognize that the most important aspect of developing a team is to have players who are physically and technically talented, possess a hunger to learn, and are excited and committed to be part of the team. Several levels of play exist, whether we are looking at male versus female, high school versus college, or a team at the top of a conference versus a team striving to get to the top of the conference. The performance and development of players at all levels depends significantly on the productivity and effectiveness of practice.

How many times have you witnessed a coach call a time-out or make a substitution at a crucial time of the match and assumed that decision turned the tide of the match? Fans and boosters often wonder what we say as a staff to turn the team around at a key moment. I believe wholeheartedly that the game belongs to the players. The coaches are mainly responsible for preparing the players through meaningful practices and exposure to drills that advance their development. In my 23 years at Penn State we have traveled the full distance, from instilling a work ethic and pride in inexperienced players to working with and recruiting some of the top players in the country. With outstanding experience and talent we were able to address team concerns at a much faster rate than we could in other years, when we needed to start at the true beginning and focus on the most basic of fundamentals and movement patterns.

The purpose of this chapter is to share some ideas we developed at Penn State regarding the organization, execution, and evaluation of practice. My hope is that you will look at how you can affect some of the outcomes for your program based on what we have encountered along the way.

Planning Your Practice Schedule

In the college environment we are restricted in the number of hours per week we can practice (20), and we must provide the players one day off per week. In contrast, some high school and club coaches can schedule practice and open gym as often as they can obtain facilities. I like to break the collegiate season down into five small working units—preseason, early competitive, conference first half, conference second half, and postseason (see table 9.1). Note that although you should emphasize different areas at different points of the season, you must continue to practice the key fundamentals of volleyball that are highly correlated with performance.

The postseason offers additional benefits because, in my experience, at the conclusion of the regular season most players have a higher atten-

— TABLE 9.1—

Three-Hour Practice

	Pre-season (2 wks)	Early competitive (3 wks)	Conference first half (5 wks)	Conference second half (5 wks)	Post-season (2-3 wks)
Warm-up	20	20	15	15	15
Blocking movement patterns (with or without ball)	15	15	20	20	20
Ball-handling (partner or groups of 3-4)	20	15	15	15	10
Serve/pass/ defense drills	35	30	25	25	25
Team drills (serve receive, transition, coverage)	25	30	30	30	30
Daily theme (offense, defense, competitive spirit)	45	35	30	30	50
Wash drills	10	25	35	35	20
Cool-down	10	10	10	10	10

tion span and the excitement associated with the tournament to examine the areas that they need to work on. Note as well that a number of factors cross over into the various working units of the season and the off-season, and that other chapters in this book will address topics related to physical conditioning. To be well prepared, I establish and incorporate a yearly training cycle for players who have aspirations of playing beyond college. Those players are always keeping us coaches on our toes. My experience reveals that the top teams in the country at both the high school and collegiate levels are the ones in which the players strive to be their best and dedicate themselves year-round to reaching their goals.

The preparation phase of developing your plan requires careful execution. I prefer to look at the number of days available and then determine the times and areas of focus that we will address in the available practice opportunities.

The selection of drills is a key to having a meaningful practice. Your drills should simulate game situations. Drills should always emphasize the correct use of the court and ballhandling sequences that occur during a game. Drills that require players to pass a serve or attack, set that passed ball, and then attack it will reinforce the necessary sequences required in a game. The carryover effect and the benefits gained by having players perform adjacent to their teammates also reinforces the behaviors that coaches are looking to develop, such as communication and allowing the primary ball handlers to take as many contacts as possible.

My approach is to emphasize the importance of active learning, so I don't feel it is necessary to introduce hundreds of drills to keep players stimulated. In my thinking, players can learn the requirements of the drills and, following a brief introduction, proceed to being active as opposed to spending time listening to the coach talk. Once you establish tradition in your program and have experienced players who have bought into your system, the process of introducing drills becomes extremely efficient. I expect my older players not only to explain drills to the younger players but also to show them the intensity and focus required to sustain a high level of competitiveness in every drill. Once we enter the competitive season, I adjust the drills to focus on the areas that need improvement.

In the preseason, when we are permitted to practice two or three times a day, I like to provide ample time for the players to learn the foundational behaviors and skills on which we have built the program. From a physical standpoint, we like to run as many drills as possible at game speed. If we are doing a hitting drill, we may choose to have the ball initiated from a serve or a down ball. This allows our hitters to gain experience focusing on something before they actually have to swing at the ball. Although I believe that in some instructional settings it is necessary to break down the skill into its basic elements, I want my attackers to pass and hit, dig and hit, block and hit, or cover and hit. I like the idea of including conditioning in the drill as opposed to ending the practice with exercises to fatigue the players. How players perform at the end of an extended rally or game often decides the outcome. We try to simulate this effect by the continuous initiation of balls rather than performing sprints at the end of practice. Learning, especially physical or active learning, is specific to the practice situation. If our team runs sprints at the end of practice, they will improve their ability to run sprints. But if our players compete in a challenging six-on-six drill at the end of a tough practice, those behaviors may transfer to success in a long five-game match. I keep hearing in the back of my mind what a player said to me in my first year of coaching: "You can't run the ball over the net, so what's with all the running?"

Developing Your Team

Other desired behaviors fall into a practice attitude that asks players to recognize the value of calling the ball and playing at 100 percent effort as much as possible. The development of the core values of your team occurs in practice on a daily basis. All players must acknowledge what the acceptable and unacceptable behaviors are going to be in the development of the team. A simple example of what I have subscribed to in my tenure at Penn State is that if a player doesn't go for a ball or plays a ball with one hand that she should have controlled with two, the player is out of the drill. The players now out of the drill police the drill better than the staff can because they know that they will be going into the drill at the occurrence of undisciplined play. The staff takes no time from the drill to talk to the player or players about the error, and therefore the drill continues until completion. If we find that several players are experiencing the same difficulty in a drill, we evaluate the drill and assess whether we are attempting to advance faster tactically than we can perform technically. Our preseason enables us to see the level of conditioning of the players, evaluate the technical capabilities of the team, and predict what our areas of strength and weakness will be. The preseason allows the staff opportunities to teach the players the skills, refine their teaching, and emphasize the cues that they feel are fundamental to learning the various skills.

In the development of our team and in preparation for the competitive season or the conference schedule, we attempt to assess where we are today. We then look at where we need to be for the stretch run for our conference championships or the NCAA tournament. The staff of an experienced team that returns a number of players from the previous year can move much faster to the important team-related skills. New teams have to travel at a safe speed and must avoid attempting to master more than they can handle. The patience necessary comes with experience and keeping a clear view of what you need and when it is critical to be at your best. An additional benefit that experienced players can provide is communicating what is happening with the players and performing with the necessary energy level. This transfer of information requires trust and maturity, and is critical for the development of the team. Coaches and players have to maintain the lines of communication to allow the necessary transfer of learning.

During the long college season, coaches and players should recognize the demands on the university student. During some periods the pressures of academic work catch up with the players, and the staff must adjust practice time, intensity, and duration. Coaches need to familiarize themselves with the academic calendar and recognize the effect that school has on their players.

College programs are limited by the NCAA to no longer than 4 hours of practice daily, but I have found that most quality work occurs in periods of 2-1/2 to 3 hours. I have always planned the practices and am willing to throw a drill out the window if the players are struggling with it or they are forcing me to struggle with watching it. Some drills take time for players to understand the tempo required, and some drills are established for the players to communicate at a high level. Therefore, in planning a practice, it is critical to recognize the learning curve associated with new drills and provide ample time for instruction and questions and answers.

We initiate practice with some movement drills or basic one-on-one or two-on-two short court games to increase circulation and reinforce primary ball handling. Then the players go through a variety of static stretches designed to maintain proper range of motion. I then like to see the players blocking and moving along the net correctly as well as demonstrating some of the movements appropriate to transition to get them comfortable with the demands at the net and the need to move quickly from defense to offense. Some of these drills incorporate a ball while others are focusing on the necessary movement over ball contacts.

The next area of emphasis pinpoints the individual ballhandling skills of the players and normally ends in a heated game of pepper. I prefer to have players contacting the ball specific to the positions they might play in a game so that they develop a feel for the ball and the necessary spatial orientation to their assigned position or positions. For example, if I have a player who plays in the left back on defense, I want that player to do most of her work from that position. In my opinion, players need to specialize in one back-row area but be familiar and comfortable in the others because game situations and substitution may force a player to play across the back line.

I like to schedule serving and passing as part of every practice because I am convinced that these skills transfer to a team's ability to side out and score, regardless of the level of play. Emphasizing the proper sequence of passing a hard serve pays dividends for both players. Servers and passers should perform their respective skills in a competitive environment. We often attach a score to our serving and passing drills to provide pressure situations.

At the end of this segment of practice we address the theme for the day. I normally fall into a specific pattern when we enter the conference portion of the season. On Mondays we normally address the areas of concern that we feel the weekend matches exposed. Combined with an analysis of the weekend stats, we determine what we should try to improve on in the practice session. On Tuesday we focus on team and individual defense and work the players hard because they have time to regain their focus and recoup their energy by the weekend. We want to focus on the areas where we were coming up short defensively. Wednesday is normally a day for offense. We spend a great deal of time on serve reception and transition with a minor emphasis on wash drills and other drills that require players to compete with and against each other. Thursday is when we introduce information on the upcoming opponent and try to solidify all areas from ballhandling to team serve-reception and transition. We try to end with some rally score games and reinforce some of the patterns that we expect to see over the weekend. Friday and Saturday are our competition days, and we take Sunday off. Your schedule may be different from ours, so you may have to adjust your sequence of practice sessions. Regardless of your playing schedule, I highly recommend that you develop an organized weekly plan for your team.

Making the Most of Practices

Every staff is different. Many coaches are the entire staff, responsible for everything from facility setup to drill control. The normal college staff has three paid coaches and may have volunteers, former players, and managers. It becomes an administrative task to assign responsibilities to everyone. At Penn State I know I will have two assistants, and we address the various tasks on a drill-by-drill basis. I think coaches need to possess basic ballhandling skills so that all of the staff can train the players rather than having the players depend on only one coach for their development.

I am not a big fan of the various training tools on the market, but I do recommend having wooden coaching boxes for the players and coaches to use in training various skills. For example, I think players get a much better feel for hand placement in blocking if they have the proper position that a box can provide. Certainly, coaches can attack balls more effectively from a standing position on the box than they can from jumping all the time. Digging balls from a coach on a box is not game specific, but it does allow the players to understand the need to be low and active.

Players need to know and acknowledge the area of expertise of each staff member and to feel comfortable in exchanging their thoughts and concerns with each of the staff. Rather than being the center of attention and running all the drills, I like to have my assistants run demanding drills and initiate balls for various team drills while I watch the sequence of events to evaluate the entire environment. When I had no staff, no managers, and an abundance of energy, I had the chance to establish my practice persona, but I certainly welcomed the arrival of other people who have the energy and enthusiasm to keep the practices moving. Many teams think that the coaches are responsible for providing the energy necessary to keep the practices fun and alive, but I have always felt that this is one of the players' main areas of accountability.

I have always believed that you are going to play like you practice. Therefore, it is important that someone focus on the energy expenditure you expect to see in practice. I feel the head coach is best suited to handle this area, but others on the staff may have the ability to play good guy or bad guy on different days of the week. It has been my experience that the makeup of the team and the meshing of their various personalities has a large effect on how players approach practice and how much fun they have during practice. I try to recruit players who want to work hard and have fun in the process, so I am always looking for players who exhibit character and for players who *are* characters. At the college level, we are able to recruit our players. I often look for players with a certain energy and attitude, knowing that practice requires individuals who can make my life entertaining as well as rewarding in a competitive sense. In conducting tryouts at the high school level, coaches should recognize that they need to generate certain characteristics in practice to assist in solidifying the team.

In my opinion, the excitement necessary to compete at the highest levels comes from within the player. Coaches can try to massage the team psyche by scheduling drills in practice that the players enjoy. Therefore, energy always increases at the disclosure of the next drill, but I like to remind the players that they need to have the same passion for every drill because the game demands passion, focus, and a willingness to commit to the team. I feel that coaches too often continue to provide the drill that the players like. Eventually the novelty of the drill wears off, and the players then approach it with a sense of boredom. I hope to make practice challenging, but I also want the players to have fun. I believe that the coach is responsible for the environment the players work in. You need to look forward to practice, as this is where your impact is going to be established.

CHAPTER TEN

Using New and Proven Teaching Techniques

Mary Jo Peppler

Every team you coach will be a different version of what you and your players view as the sum of their perfection. A sports experience is a living canvas. Other than the painting of your life, the work you do with your teams is probably as important as anything you will ever do. As a coach, you keep getting fresh chances to paint more beautifully. You can hone your skills and artistry, team after team. Coaching is not something you can learn quickly. Like anything truly important, it is a skill you develop through a lifetime.

Many years ago I had the privilege of being part of the Gold Medal Clinic staff. For several years I traveled nationwide conducting 12-hour programs on one of my passions: how to coach volleyball. Although the travel was annoying, the clinics were wonderful. Coaches who worked at all levels of coaching attended the clinics, and they were there to learn something. They were motivated. I usually had the opportunity to work with another clinician, so each weekend was an opportunity to participate in a modified think tank. To add icing on the cake, our demonstrators were collegiate teams, so I was able to try my ideas, old and new, on some of the brightest volleyball players in the country. Each gym I walked into was different. I soon learned that teams reflected their coach in subtle and often surprising ways.

In the five different decades that I have been able to coach, I have tried and rejected many ideas. Not a year goes by without my doing some fine-tuning to my coaching style. At every moment I would like to be able to say that I am a better coach than I was yesterday. What I can share with you here is what I am today. Tomorrow may be different. But today, what follows are some of my favorite ideas.

Your Team Will Wear Your Attention

I remember doing a defensive clinic in the Midwest when one coach asked, "How do you get players to try for the ball like that?" Indeed, this team never let a ball hit the ground without joining it. My response was, "Why don't you ask their (collegiate) coach? She is the one who made this happen." She was sitting at the top of the bleachers, and all eyes turned to her. She replied, "Ask the players." So I did. They replied, "If the ball hits the ground, she makes us roll. After a while, we just made ourselves roll because we knew we would have to anyway."

This lesson is one of the most valuable a coach can learn. Behaviorists call it the feedback loop. I call it knowing what is of value to you. By working with so many different teams, I learned a lot about what is important to coaches. Some made their players stand in a line when talking to them, some organized their shagging impeccably, some teams talked, some teams tried. I found that in some gyms, teams were focused, others were competitive, some were moody, and some tiptoed around dominating attitudes.

How teams talked to the coach, talked to each other, and solved their problems all reflected their coach's values. Some teams invested their egos in defense, some in hitting, and others didn't seem to notice when they repeatedly failed.

I am sure that no coach starts out every practice saying, "Let's reinforce the players every time they fail today." Yet coaches continuously send messages, through exclusion as well as inclusion, about what is acceptable in the environment of the team. Through the privilege of being able to work with top teams in their own environments, I have learned that when you direct your attention and invest your consciousness, your environment will follow that lead.

My advice to you as a coach, experienced or inexperienced, is to continue to rework your values, your goals, and your mission statement. Periodically observe your own coaching to see what you never allow to slide and what drives you crazy. What never goes unnoticed in the feedback loop is what you value the most. What drives you crazy is what you have not attended to in your feedback loop. For instance, maybe you never allow your players to say, "I can't," but you let their internal dialogue go unchecked. The beauty of experience in coaching is that you have time to train yourself to monitor multiple factors. More elements enter the feedback loop. The team becomes more consistent, behavior settles in, and as a result the learning environment becomes more supportive.

Energy Follows Intention

I think that it is impossible to talk about playing sports without discussing energy. Energy is available to us everywhere. What prevents us from being able to have energy or to use energy is stagnation. Movement creates energy. Success and failure is all about how we mobilize and direct the energy that we can access. Focused intention creates success. Players must learn the skill of locking their intentions to their goals. One way to reach goals is to master self-talk, the most basic skill of energy mastery. Because emotions lock beliefs into the body, coaches must teach young athletes to talk to themselves constructively. Don't be misled—self-talk is a skill.

Here is what I tell my athletes: "Emotionally engage your positive experiences and intellectually engage your negative experiences." Emotionally engaging the positives locks the experience into the body, where the athlete can easily translate it into confidence and self-esteem. The player can do this by either internal or external interpretation. "Even though we were discouraged and could have quit, we kept fighting. We (or you) are a team with great courage." People want to believe the best about themselves. They want to be convinced that they are good. It is an easy sell.

Conversely, when players get into a negative, self-criticizing loop, they are engaging those emotions into their bodies. When this occurs, players can easily develop low self-esteem, fear, and failure. The energy building blocks are already gathered. They too are subject to interpretation. "I suck." "We're losers!" "We always lose the close games."

I think that the coach needs to become personally responsible for the individual's self-talk in the early going. Players should recognize the importance of their internal climate. A coach can guide players in two primary ways—first, by interrupting the player's self-dialogue when the head drops, the body slumps, and the energy wanes, and second, by example. I have seen many players use negative self-talk as a defense mechanism to keep the coach from abusing them. Please do not participate in this type of coaching. If you are asking your players to engage their errors intellectually, then you must also do so. The coach who responds emotionally to failure or mistakes sets a strong example. Mistakes happen for a reason. Sort through it.

Locking the Intention

Once players get a grasp on their internal talk, then they are ready to begin learning the skill of locking their intentions. Until you can control your thoughts, you are probably not going to be successful holding on to a thought with unwavering attention.

Winning in sport is usually not logical. We often have to do something that we haven't yet done. We have to fabricate evidence along the way that supports our dream. We have to discard evidence that does not support our dream. This task also requires skill. Some call it optimism. Some talk about the glass being half empty or half full. Whatever its name, locking the intention is a precise ability.

When we consistently pass a ball to a target, we have demonstrated the ability to lock intention. Before contacting the ball, the successful player will create a consciousness stream from contact to the target. This precedes the player's contacting the ball. The most successful players not only create the consciousness stream but also program the result of the contact. For example, a player is getting ready to receive a serve. She identifies herself as the passer, moves to the ball, and just before contact visualizes the pathway of the intended pass. This is the intention of targeting.

Another player jumps to hit the ball. She doesn't really know where she is going to hit it; she just wants to hit it hard and terminate it. This is the intention of results.

Ideally, we can train players to mobilize full intentions. The passer not only passes the ball to the target but also feels connected to the intention of the team. The player also plans to get a side out. Anyone who has played on a team performing at its peak knows the feeling of team intention. Getting blocked and knowing that your teammates will cover you, jumping to block, turning around knowing that your teammate will get a dig, or feeling the team's passing pattern set against the server are all examples of locked team intent.

These things happen as a matter of course in sport. But having control of one's thoughts allows an athlete to fill his or her head with intention rather than useless, distracting self-talk that is often overflowing with negative emotions. This clear-thinking champion emerges quickly.

Movement Creates Energy

Energy is always available to us. It is in everything. The ball, the court, the net, and the poles are all made up of energy. I personally do not think that a person can be tired. All dysfunction is a product of stagnant energy. Anything in your life that is stuck prevents you from being able to use the full complement of energy. Every part of your life can prevent you from receiving energy, including your physical body (lack of flexibility), your physical environment (messy closets), your emotions (negative or fearful thoughts), and even your spirituality (lack of connection with a higher power).

From the sport perspective, movement creates energy. If it is stuck, move it. You can lock on an idea about how you are going to win, you can limit your ability to work hard, you can be anxious about your bench and afraid to substitute, or you can have unresolved issues that are locking up energy. Every time you unlock energy, more is available for you to use. When you master your self-talk and intention, you can use that energy to get what you want. It seems rather simple.

I don't like to have many rules because I personally do not like them (they lack energy), and I don't like to expend energy monitoring and disciplining the infractions. But I do like one rule: If it brings us together, it is the right thing to do. If it separates us, it is the wrong thing to do.

Volleyball is an intense team sport, partly because the team is in close quarters. In no other sport do so many athletes play in such close proximity. If someone said, "Make up a ball game that you can play on a 30-foot-by-60-foot surface and put 12 players there," it would be hard to imagine the physical sport we have created. Teamwork is paramount. How we interact with the opponent is also structured and interdependent. Everyone starts this experience with individual ideas and goals. A closely contested volleyball match is a beautiful weaving of human consciousness.

The rule of doing only what brings us together is not simply nice or idealistic. The energetic weaving of a volleyball team is imperative to the experience. Without this weaving, there is no experience. When you sign up, like the Borg on Star Trek, "You must comply." Understand the choice you have made to play volleyball. You may want to consider other sports. The rule is more than a rule. It is the essence of the sport.

Learning Theory

In one Gold Medal Clinic I had the joyful experience of working with Laurel Kessel as the other clinician. During her presentation, she outlined some of Carl McGowan's information on learning theory. Carl didn't invent this information. Indeed, it has been available for decades. What Carl has done, however, is to gather it and make it available to the volleyball community. Laurel's presentation was my first exposure to learning theory. The lights went on.

The best way for me to help you grasp this concept is to relate the following story. In my first year of coaching at Kentucky, Marilyn Nolan and I had inherited a physical team. They engaged one particular skill—hitting. They did not care much about any other skill. Because Marilyn and I had read all the coaching manuals, we knew that winning correlated highly with passing, so we went to work. We did individual passing, group passing, team passing. We set varying criteria for the drills. We gave them many opportunities to demonstrate their prowess in competitive drills.

Nothing. Nada. Zilch! Our team could not pass. We spent 60 to 70 percent of our practice time passing. We initiated all our drills with a pass. We were passing challenged. One day I planned a whole practice with alternatives to passing. Still nothing.

After many clinics and countless conversations with coaches, I found that our experience was not atypical. Time spent on a skill in practice does not necessarily translate to results in the desired area. Thus, when I listened to a presentation on block versus random training, not only did the lights go on, but I still have electrical burns.

Here is how it goes. You use block training to teach a skill. If you can get a repetition once every seven seconds, optimal learning takes place. Block training, however, puts the information learned into short-term memory. Thus, our players experience amnesia when you revisit the same skill at the next practice or in a game.

Random training is what happens when you play a game, when you have no control of anything that is happening. Here is what is scarier than any horror movie—random training. Random training (you know, all that slop that happens when you scrimmage) goes into your long-term memory. Now that's scary!

My coaching life has never been the same.

Now what? I'll give you the short version. I created core drills that simulate various random parts of the game.

An example of a core drill would be the 3 versus 3 (or 4 versus 4) 10-foot game. This drill has all the elements of random training. Almost anything can happen. Confining the game to the 10-foot, or three-meter, area enhances the demands on transition and communication. Thus it is a core drill for setter training and transition. Now, if I run this drill in practice, I will most likely get slop. And, more important, I will be putting slop into long-term memory so that it will show up at the next practice and the next match. Are you with me?

Fortunately, I will need some specific behaviors from players to turn this slop into something resembling volleyball. For instance, I can use block training to establish bases and postures, to identify routes, to recognize when to run the routes (cueing), to discipline hand control during routes, to identify when and what players should communicate, and so forth. I can train these items in block training drills. I call these drills training intervals. In these intervals I establish word cues that describe the desired behavior and train them to the team. For instance, when I call "base," players go to a position on the court and stand in a specific posture. Then I call "shift" (on defense) or "pull" (for hitters to come off the net). During this block, or interval, training, I can stylize their movements to suit my idea of skills. I can take my time.

As soon as I have players trained to word cues, and the players have learned the correct postures, positions, and routes, I insert the players back into the core drill. Now my challenge is to lead cue the players in the random, or core, drill. Lead cueing is talking the player into the proper response before the need for the behavior. Remember that the cue must be succinct and the player must have the ability to respond to it (established through block training). You must also cue the player at the proper time for the behavior. Now the players cannot fail because you are leading them into proper behaviors and responses rather than responding to what they have done wrong (reaction cue).

Now I have some control over what is happening. I train the specific behaviors I want in the block training, give them word cues that they can respond to, put them back into the core (random) drill, and cue them so that they cannot fail. During practice I pop back and forth between block and random training. The random training dictates what the block training will consist of because I can see what is not working. The random training anchors my block training cues and puts the work I have done into long-term memory. Yippee! Now I love random drills because they are no longer slop.

So there you have it, three of my favorite coaching gems—your team will wear your attention, energy follows intention, and my favorite piece of learning theory, block versus random training. I hope something here will spark a light, connect something anew, or give you a new approach. May the sacred trust you have been given to shape and lead others give you joy and inspiration.

CHAPTER ELEVEN

Making Drills More Beneficial

Bill Neville

We were having difficulty reacting to the sets in our opponents' fast-tempo offenses. Our players executed our read-and-react blocking scheme as if they were lumbering through *Gray's Anatomy.* We weren't ingesting anything. We had a problem. So, in one of those final-thoughts-before-falling-asleep episodes that everyone has on occasion, I came up with the solution, or what seemed to be the solution—the Seven-Contact Drill. The offense could have up to seven contacts, forcing the block to track the sets and finally react to the attack. The drill had all the elements of a great drill, including a descending scoring system, premium points for stuff blocks, and excellent teachable moments. I fell to sleep anticipating the introduction of this superb drill. Of course, you have never seen the Seven-Contact Drill in print or presented in a clinic, and there is a reason for that. It was pathetic. Right idea. Solid on paper. But ridiculous on the court interpreted by human beings.

Simply put, a drill is an organized solution to a problem. Some of these problems are generic to the sport, such as ball control, attack timing, or footwork. Others are specific to a tactical or systematic situation where the application of basic skills is insufficient.

The coach must be able to identify priority needs of his or her team, analyze the key points of attention, and design methods to strengthen those needs accordingly. It is important to be a creative thinker and have sound knowledge of motor learning and guiding principles.

For example, *sophistication is earned.* They must go through stages of skill development (Maslow would love this). Players must understand that they need to master the fundamentals before they learn advanced skills. In some instances health is at stake. Poor floor defensive skills can lead to bone-jarring injuries. Poor attack approaches can damage shoulders.

Another guiding principle is to *attempt tactically only what you can execute technically.* We coaches can become carried away. At times we devise drills that require a skill level beyond that of our players. The violation of this principle is likely at the root of the demise of the Seven-Contact Drill (and it was custom-made for the 1984 USA men's team that won the gold medal).

The Purpose of Drills

Drills are the organized units of a practice. Each drill should enhance the goals of any given practice. Further, the drills should be progressive so that every drill embellishes the next. In this way players will understand the objectives of each drill and its relationship to playing the game.

Through the course of the season the competitive results of the team will greatly influence practice and drill design. In my early coaching career I had the opportunity to coach the Canadian men's team through the 1976 Montreal Olympics. We were young and not quite ready for the top 10 teams in the world. But as a young, idealistic, immortal-feeling coach I believed we could defeat the best in the world. (Remember that we earn sophistication.) After a disheartening loss to Czechoslovakia, the Montreal press corps was on me like a summer day in New Orleans. When asked what the problem was, I responded, "When you lose there are a thousand questions. When you win, you answer them all."

Neither side of that response is accurate, but it seems that way. Effective practice and drill design enable us to provide answers to questions. But be wary: If your team is losing, don't wallow in despair. Learn to identify real questions and prioritize them. Be able to recognize the questions you can answer considering your personnel and time allotment for training. If you are winning, enjoy the euphoria but never assume that you have the answer to every question. Examine the situation dispassionately, ferret out pertinent questions, prioritize them, and design effective answers.

To put it simply, coaches function in a problem-solution world. Our careers ride on our ability to identify and prioritize problems and generate solutions.

Considering the Athlete of Today

Years ago when I was coaching the Canadian men's national team, I had the opportunity to rub shoulders with the most renowned coaches in the world. In conversation with the Romanian coach I learned that they had only 11 drills. Eleven drills? Yes. In designing his practice he would select two to five drills based on the goals for that day. Bizarre, I thought. His method made practice design simple but banal. Over time, how dull. How would the players stay motivated?

At this point I began to formulate the opinion that players make drills successful. The effort that players give to any activity determines success or failure. It is the coach's responsibility to trigger the players' efforts to ensure success and resulting benefits. The reason I knew the Seven-Contact Drill wouldn't yield the desired results is that I trusted the players to give it the maximum effort to make it work. When a coach has the confidence in his or her players to attempt anything without prejudice, the freedom of creativity to find solutions greatly increases.

I also mused on the need to be aware of, and be sensitive to, cultural differences even within a common society. To remain effective, coaches must study historical imprints that influence current trends and resultant behaviors in today's athletes. An in-depth study of the contemporary athlete is worth the time that a coach devotes to it. Effective practice and drill design will spring from the coach's sensitivity to what motivates a given group of athletes.

Macroplanning and Microplanning

To be beneficial, drills must be designed and implemented within the grand scheme of total team preparation. You must start with a yearly plan based on analysis of players' skill and motivational levels, training facilities, equipment, time available, opponents and what it will take to beat them, and coaching staff. You must prioritize these factors based on your team's needs. Remember that we deal in solving problems or, if you prefer, overcoming challenges. Don't waste time sniveling about what you don't have or what the opponents do have. You don't want your athletes to whimper. You want to imbue them with a "can do" attitude. Let's look at the general considerations in a macroplan and how they affect practice design:

- Preseason
- Early competitive season
- Midcompetitive season
- Late competitive season
- Postseason playoffs
- Off-season

Preseason

Every team has some form of preseason, usually determined by a governing body that typically regulates the exact numbers of days and, in some cases, the number of hours. You must determine how you will use the allotted time to benefit your team, considering the potential limitations listed on the next page. The drills should reflect the priority needs of your team in this critical time of preparing for competition.

Early Competitive Season

This is the time to establish successful routines to prepare for matches, dial in lineups and substitution patterns, determine player roles, and establish the level of tactical sophistication. Evaluation of the practicality of plans on paper will influence design and adjustments in the next phase.

Midcompetitive Season

Your team is now hitting a certain stride. Its competitive personality has formed. You have a clearer understanding of how individuals will come through in various situations. You understand how opponents are attacking you. Strengths and weaknesses are becoming evident. What does and does not work in practices and drills is clearer.

Limiting Factors

Several potential limitations can influence how you design your practices and drills:

- Your facility may house only one court, and you have 36 players.
- You have just six balls, two of them dog-eared, and you have 36 players.
- You have no assistant coach.
- Several bulbs are burned out, and the rest generate less light than the lamp Abraham Lincoln read by in his cabin at night.
- A climbing rope hangs from the beams above. The monkey-fist is hauled up with a thin, frayed cord just waiting for an errant ball to snap it and send the fist hurtling down to deliver a knockout punch.
- You have a ball container only a forklift could move.
- Sharp steel racks attached to the wall, designed to hold some long-forgotten apparatus, now serve as implements to puncture balls and flesh.
- Your poles are embedded in truck tires filled with concrete.

The first thing you must do is make sure that your facility and equipment are safe and functional. You must decide what you can influence and what is out of reach. Here's a basic list of what you should have:

- Enough balls, ideally the brand and quality of ball you will use in conference play. All should be inflated to the same pressure. Two balls for each player will provide enough balls to keep drills flowing.
- Ball containers on wheels, preferably high enough so that you don't have to bend too far down to get a ball. If you are bending to get balls out of a low-slung bucket, you will feel it.
- Good net setup with floor-inserted, clean poles with the minimum number of flanges, hooks, and other laceration-producing accoutrements. A good net, at the correct height, tight top and bottom, with well-fitted antennae.
- A hazard-free playing area. Eliminate or pad anything potentially harmful to your athletes when they are pursuing the ball.

You may not be able to influence or control some things—number of assistant coaches, number of courts, ceiling height, how many days and hours you can train, and so on. Decide what you can do to maximize your training environment and work around the rest.

Late Competitive Season

Whether this is a period of making adjustments or staying the course depends on results of the previous matches. Be aware of the thousand questions if you are losing or having all the answers if you are winning. Neither side of that thinking is accurate. Stay rational. Fatigue and injuries may become factors. Personality conflicts among players may emerge. As with any group or family unit, individuals become tired of each other. Introducing fresh activities or new drills may be beneficial. The fitness level of the players will likely be declining because of shorter practice time, limited playing time for some players, fatigue, and attention to tactical play. I heard many years ago of a study conducted in the Soviet Union. The study indicated that approximately two-thirds of the way through a competitive season a solid week of preseason training intensity could bring fitness back to optimal levels and rekindle the motivational fires for the stretch run. Although unsubstantiated, the suggestion is worth consideration.

Postseason Playoffs

If your outfit has made it into the championship playoffs, motivation will be high. Drills and activities that reinforce the feelings of success are in order. Short, crisp, high-energy drills will probably be effective. Focus on the skills and tactics that are team strengths. Emphasize the tools that will give you the best chance to succeed and devote less attention to weaknesses. If your team did not make the playoffs, this is a time for evaluation, reflection, and rest.

Off-Season

Use this time for skill, strength, and power development. Teach mechanics and related details. Competing against oneself, to improve personally, is the order of the day. This developmental phase is based on prioritization of team needs that develop from the previous competitive season and the players' roles.

Problem? Solution!

Basically, problem solving best describes beneficial drill design. The key is to be able to identify and prioritize the problems. For example, if your team has weak ball handling skills, virtually nullifying any chance of getting into an attack, you must focus your practice attention on ballhandling. But wait! Which ball handling skills are deficient? Are all players afflicted? If you have outstanding serve receivers but setters who set like commercial sprinklers and could randomly irrigate an arid half-section, you must concentrate your drills on improving setting. If the reverse is true, then focus on the skills of serve receive. You will gain maximum benefit from identifying specific needs. Prioritize them with the ultimate goal of working on those areas that will make your team more competitive.

For example, my team is young, with erratic ball handling skills. Although the problems are individualized, the coaches have determined that the most dramatic improvements for this team will result from improved ball handling. We have further identified that serve receive, free-ball and down-ball passing, out-of-system setting, and floor defense all need significant work. Based on the premise that we won't be able to attack effectively without consistent ball handling, we must master those fundamentals. Next, we took each skill and identified deficiencies that we must improve. Finally, we put together a teaching plan to achieve the skills necessary to compete effectively. Taking into consideration our list of limitations and assets, we designed the activities with an ongoing evaluation and grading system to ensure we achieved the best results.

Drill Categories

Drills can be categorized into three main groups:

• Coach-centered drills are those that a coach controls directly. Examples include (1) coach-on-one (or more), a defensive drill in which the coach repeatedly hits balls at one or more players and (2) player goes and coach throws, a common hitting drill in which players are in line, a coach tosses balls to a designated area, and players approach and hit.

• Coach-initiated drills are those in which a coach starts the action at a predetermined point and the players react and play out the rally to its natural conclusion. An example is Jousting, in which one or more blockers face each other across the net. There may be one or more back-row players behind each set of blockers. The coach initiates the action by tossing the ball so that it comes down on top of the net. The players jump and joust and play out the resulting rally. Other examples include Queen or King of the Court, Deep-Court Exchange, and any number of team drills in which the coach starts the action in a particular situation and the players play out the ensuing rally.

• Player-centered drills are those initiated by the players. The coach indicates the parameters, lays out the evaluation plan, and sets up any other design features, but the players create all the action. The ultimate player-centered drill, of course, is playing a match.

Grouping of Drills

Drills can be single-task or multitask activities. To make drills beneficial, plan drills appropriate to your goals. For example, if the goal is to teach mechanics of a skill, then a single-task drill may be best. To develop skills that players can apply to the game and its unfolding situation, multitask drills are better. You should introduce gamelike activities concurrently with mechanics instruction so that the players clearly understand the skills and how they relate to the game. This coupling is critical to motivation. Learning occurs when there is a need to know. The players must be motivated to learn the basics by understanding why they need to know.

Most drills can be generally grouped by how they are organized. Adaptations to fit individual and team situational needs can be part of the organizational scheme. Table 11.1 presents examples of drill groups.

TABLE 11.1

Group	Task	Scoring	Adaptations
1. 1 ball, 1 player	Single	Time or reps	FAP, OHP mechanics
2. 1 ball, 2 players	Single	Time or reps	FAP, OHP, Def mechanics
3. 2 balls, 3 players (triads)	Single or double	Time or reps	FAP, OHP, Def mechanics
4. Shuttles	Single or double	Time or reps	FAP, OHP, Def mechanics
5. Rotation (stations)	Single or multiple	Time or reps	All skills
6. Waves (3-player waves)	Multiple	Time or score	All skills
7. Team	Multiple	Time, score, or reps	All skills

Key: FAP = forearm pass; OHP = overhead pass; Def = defensive skills

Name Your Favorite Drills

You will use some drills repeatedly. Be sure to give your drills memorable names so your players can immediately picture the organization, feel the tempo, and understand the goals. Best use of time is important in a practice session. Players' knowledge of the drills makes practice perfect. You and your team will become familiar and comfortable with specific drills. You should be able to adapt a certain drill to predetermined priority goals. By identifying a drill by its category and organizational grouping, you can quickly put it to good use. Early in your team's training you must teach your players how to practice. Ultimately, you should not have to spend much time teaching your team the rudiments of drill mechanics. You can focus instead on the skill and tactical goals of a drill. For example, if you say to your team, "The next drill is the Diamond Drill" (a coach-initiated, rotation-station drill organized in the shape of a diamond), your players immediately picture the organization in their minds. You say, "The focus of the drill is on the following keys. At passing and setting stations, *arrive* at the point of contact before the ball in *balance*. At hitting stations, be *available* so that you can make a full *accelerating approach* to the point of attack. Blockers must *front* the hitter." Your players understand what they must focus on at each station. "You have 15 minutes as a team to execute 50 perfect repetitions." The scoring system will dictate the intensity level.

Measuring Drills

The way you measure a drill will determine the mind-set of the players. You can measure or score a drill in many ways. The block of time available for any given practice will heavily influence how you measure. For example, if you set a specific time for each drill you can hit your practice time on the money. But time may not be the best way to gain the desired results. You decide that your players need to extend their focus, so you choose to measure it by requiring them to perform a given number of perfect executions in a row. If they miss, they start over. Theoretically, the drill could go on forever. I still have two or three players and a couple of teams working on an "in-a-row" drill that I designed 15 years ago. Seriously, these types of drills can yield excellent results, but working toward an unrealistic number goal can compromise a tightly planned practice.

The way you measure a drill has as much, if not more, influence on the results of a drill as the organization does. Table 11.2 shows some examples of measurement systems. You can combine several scoring systems. There are others and, quite likely, many that haven't been invented yet.

Summary

Drills are the foundation of individual and team training. Several elements contribute to the design of beneficial drills. Have a plan governed by principles to guide your decisions. You must have a working knowledge of motor-learning principles. The learning process will become more efficient by the clear understanding of keys, chunking information, naming of drills, and timely feedback describing desired behaviors. Your players must understand the purposes of drills and how they relate to the execution and enjoyment of the game. To attain the greatest benefits for your team and program, the players must have a base level of general athletic skill and the potential to execute the activities you design.

TABLE 11.2

Measurement	Intensity	Purpose
Time	Low-medium (M, P) High (P)	Define keys; teach exact execution; practice time control.
Number of reps	Low-medium (M, P) High (P)	Focus on execution of each contact.
Number of reps in a row	High (M, P)	Executing under pressure.
Side-out scoring	Low-high (M)	Tactical application of technique, control of emotional ebb and flow.
Point per play	Low-high (M)	Sustained concentration; tactical application of technique, game tempo, control.
Premium points	Medium-high (M, P)	Emphasis on specific skills or tactics within a drill or game.
Wash points	Medium-high (M, P)	Incorporates most or all of above purposes.
Bongo	High (M, P)	Most emphasis on tempo, control of emotional ebb and flow, situation tactics.

Key: M = mental; P = physical

Finally, we must all remember that we are playing a game, at every level, designed for the enjoyment of those who play, watch, and coach. Volleyball is competitive, which means that it involves winning and losing, achievement and setbacks, frustration and satisfaction. How we deal with these fascinating elements of sport will determine the quality of the life lessons we provide for our charges. Drills are daily segments of the total experience.

CHAPTER TWELVE

Conditioning for High Performance

John Cook

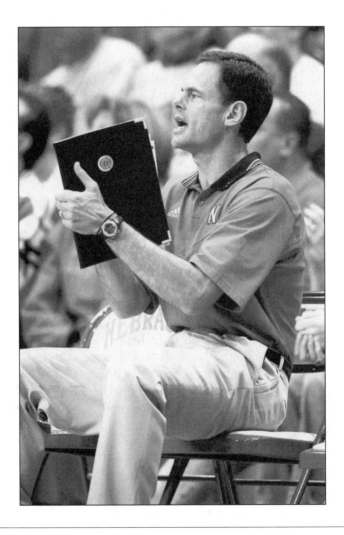

In 1990 I was hired as an assistant coach for the USA men's national team. Our first task was to design a program that would increase strength and prevent the injuries that were common on a team in which several of the athletes were in their early to mid-thirties.

We sought out the best people in the United States to help us with our challenge of keeping the team strong and healthy as they pushed toward winning a gold medal. We assembled a team of three advisors with diverse backgrounds and expertise: Boyd Epley, head strength coach at the University of Nebraska; Rick Butler, director of the Sports Performance and Research Institute; and Pete Egoscue, founder of the Egoscue method. We put together a program that involved increasing strength, flexibility, and endurance and preventing chronic overuse injuries.

Meeting the challenge of the men's team in 1990 was the beginning of a program and a philosophy that we have refined over the last 10 years. The results are medals, championships, and most important, healthy athletes who play volleyball pain free. I do not proclaim to be a strength coach or expert on strength and conditioning. I do know athletes who can move and are functional. The purpose of this chapter is to explore a program and a way of thinking about conditioning volleyball players. The concepts presented apply to all athletes, from my 10-year-old daughter to national team members. The exercises and drills presented are not a scientific prescription for your team, but more of a way of thinking about how coaches should condition their athletes. I will not be able to prescribe reps and weights in this chapter; determining those parameters is the art of coaching and a challenge that awaits you.

The first concept a coach needs to understand is hydration. Most of your athletes are dehydrated. They load up on pop and juice (sugar water). Water is essential for survival. A person can live without food for 30 days but without water for only about 72 hours. The human body as a machine depends on water to function. Hydrate your athletes with water for optimal performance.

The second concept is posture. I will use the terms *functional* and *dysfunctional* to describe athletes. A functional athlete moves to the right or left with equal efficiency, jumps off both legs equally, and coordinates the work of the two sides of the body. A dysfunctional athlete favors one side over the other, has one leg stronger than the other, and rotated or uneven hips, causing shoulders, knees, and other joints to be out of alignment. If a dysfunctional athlete trains hard with poor posture and imbalances, he or she is training dysfunctionally. This kind of training causes overuse injuries. An example of this is a volleyball player who constantly jumps off the left leg and lands on the left leg. Which hip will become weak and out of alignment? As coaches we will train athletes to hit hundreds of slides off that left leg or hit outside and land on that left leg hundreds of times. Over time imbalance develops between the two hips and sides of the body. As the athlete continues, overuse injuries will occur, and now you are coaching an athlete who is in pain, cannot do what you ask him or her to do, and may eventually wear out one of the hips and require a hip replacement.

Besides being subject to our training methods, players sit in class all day, ride in a car for an hour each way to attend a two-hour practice, and then go home and watch television or sit at a computer all night. They spend all this time in flexion and poor posture. Volleyball requires dynamic movement in extension (hitting, blocking, extending on defense). Include dehydration and a fast-food meal that provides inadequate nutrition, and the result is an athlete who will not be able to perform at the highest level. Dysfunction steals the athlete's talent. Add to that the repetitive drills and movements that we train on the court, and you as a coach are contributing to the dysfunction of your players.

Furthermore, we add knee and ankle braces, sleeves, back braces, and so on to help these athletes with pain, but the equipment limits their movement and increases their dysfunction. I have had the opportunity to travel all over the world with the sport of volleyball. Most countries that have great volleyball teams cannot afford ankle braces, the latest $125 shoes from Nike, trainers, and stem machines. Countries like Cuba, Russia, and China do not even have ice machines. How do they produce the world-class athletes who dominate volleyball?

Their world creates functional athletes. Athletes in these countries do not grow up with cars, computers, Nintendo, and elaborate equipment. Bicycling, walking, and cross-training are a part of their daily way of life. These athletes do not often find pop machines selling Mountain Dew.

Our bodies are designed to move, run, reach, and gather, but our lifestyle takes all that away. Examples of function and posture can be viewed daily—runway models, soldiers, gymnasts, dancers, and children. Can you imagine a downhill ski racer with a weak right hip? Most volleyball players have a hip disparity on one side. Watch children move at recess. The reason they cannot sit still is because they are doing what is natural—climbing trees, playing chase, twirling hula hoops, jumping over logs, and so on. Active children are functional. They do not have pain, sprains, or impingement problems. Our world and our training take away our function.

The previous examples will help the reader understand the principles behind the program. The first step is to put function back into our bodies. Here is an example of a dysfunctional exercise. We ask an athlete to bench press 200 pounds. Let's assume that the athlete is right-handed and is stronger on the right side than the left. As the athlete executes the bench press, the right side is doing 60 percent of the work and the left side is doing 40 percent. The athlete is now training dysfunctionally. Unless the athlete is 50-50, the bench-press exercise will add to the dysfunction of the athlete. Now, have that athlete hit and serve volleyballs with the right hand for two hours per day, and we train additional imbalance. Scenarios like this are why we have to put function back into our athletes!

Core Stretches for Functional Posture

Athletes must perform the following exercises exactly as prescribed and in sequence on a daily basis. I will give you starting repetitions, and you will need to adjust from there depending on time, your athletes, and how important function is to your program. Your athletes will try to compensate with their bodies, assuming they are dysfunctional. Watch your best athletes do the exercises compared with the weakest, and you will see why attention to detail is important.

ARM CIRCLES

With feet forward, use good posture and a golfer's grip. Perform tight arm circles with the arms straight and shoulder blades squeezed together. Start with 25 forward and 25 with palms up.

ELBOW CURLS

Use a golfer's grip, hold fists to the temples, squeeze the shoulder blades back, and then bring the elbows forward. Do this exercise on a two count. Maintain good posture, like a runway model. Start with 15 reps.

OVERHEAD STRETCH

Interlock the hands with the palms facing up. Raise the hands above the head, turn the palms toward the sky, and push. Inhale with five deep, slow breaths.

HEEL DROP WITH SHOULDER SQUEEZES

Stand on a raised surface so that the heels can drop over the edge. Hold the position and squeeze the shoulder blades together. Two sets of 15 will wake up the shoulders and improve posture.

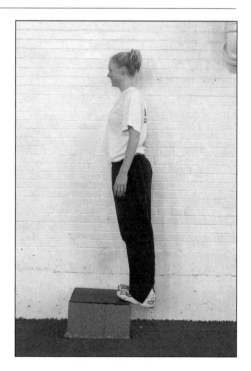

ASSISTED HIP LIFT

Hip and knee angles are 90 degrees. Take the right foot and place it on top of the left quad. Push the right knee toward the wall using the muscles in the right leg. We usually do this exercise for 40 seconds per side. You will notice that your athletes usually have one side tighter than the other. Although the butt and hips should stay on the ground, players will try to raise one hip off the ground to compensate for their dysfunction.

SPREAD-FOOT FORWARD BEND

Start with the feet spread, knees locked, and quads flexed (you will have to remind them to stay flexed). Interlock the thumbs and push the palms to the floor. Hold for 20 seconds, move the palms to the right foot, but keep the fingers pointed straight ahead. Hold for 20 seconds and move the palms to the left foot and back to the middle. The quads stay flexed the whole time! Bring the palms back to the middle and watch how much lower the palms will be to the floor. The first time athletes do this drill their legs may start shaking.

CATS AND DOGS

Begin on your hands and knees with your hands directly under the shoulders and your knees directly under the hips. Make sure the knees are shoulder-width apart. Smoothly round up the back and curl the head under; then smoothly sway the back and raise the head. We usually do 10 of these with a "cat and dog" counting as one.

KNEELING GROIN

Place one foot out in front of the other with the knee bent. Place interlocked hands on the front knee. Lunge forward, but don't let the knee go forward of the ankle. Feel in the groin. Switch legs. Notice how the back is in good posture position. Hold for 40 seconds on each side.

UPPER SPINAL FLOOR TWIST

We perform this one for 40 seconds on each side.

CATS AND DOGS

Repeat this exercise, again performing it 10 times.

DOWNWARD DOG

Start in the position you used for cats and dogs. Push up and flex the quads, keeping the back flat. Athletes will want to round the shoulders, and their legs will shake. A functional athlete should be able to have palms and feet flat on the ground. See how easily a 10-year-old can do this one. Our freshmen at Nebraska cannot do this when they arrive, but a week later they can. Work to hold this position for one minute.

AIR BENCH

Lean against a wall and bend your knees as if sitting on a bench. Your feet should be shoulder-width apart and away from wall to make a 90-degree angle with your knees (feet are over knees). Hands should be clasped behind the head. You should not be able to see your toes. Press the lower and middle of your back to the wall to feel the quadriceps working. If knee pain occurs, raise hips slightly up the wall. Work toward holding this position for two to four minutes. Your legs will shake the first time you do this one.

INCHWORMS

This exercise requires you to imitate an inchworm. Follow the photos and remember good posture (flat back). We usually will do six-inch worms. Start with figure a and walk your hands out until you reach the position of figure b. Keeping your hands stationary, walk your feet back up to a standing position (figure c).

a

b

c

HURDLES

We spend about two minutes going over and under hurdles to promote hip flexibility.

Landing Program

DROP JUMP

Purpose

To learn how to land. To strengthen the legs and hips.

Procedure

1. Stand with feet parallel about hip-width apart.

2. Step off the box, landing on the balls of the feet.

3. Flex the knees and hips and hold for a five-second count.

4. Relax the legs and immediately get on the box for the next repetition.

5. Do five repetitions.

Key Point

1. Start with box only 2 feet high and gradually work to greater heights as strength increases. It is not necessary to use boxes higher than 3+ feet.

VERTICAL JUMP

Purpose

To learn how to land. To develop explosive power.

Procedure

1. Stand with feet parallel about hip-width apart.

2. Use a counter movement by dipping four to six inches before you jump.

3. Swing both arms straight up and reach as high as possible.

Key Point

1. Do not take any steps before jumping.

TUCK JUMP

Purpose

To learn how to land. To develop explosive power and to prepare the body for more intense power drills.

Procedure

1. Stand with feet parallel about hip-width apart.

2. Use a counter movement by dipping four to six inches before you jump.

3. Bring the knees up to the chest as high as possible.

4. Land as softly as possible and hold the landing position for five seconds before doing the next repetition.

5. Do five repetitions.

Key Points

1. Do not take any steps before jumping.

2. Can hold hand palms down at chest height and attempt to touch palms with knees.

3. Visualize landing like a shock absorber.

180-DEGREE JUMP

Purpose

To learn how to land. To develop explosive power and prepare the body for more intense power drills.

Procedure

1. Stand with feet parallel about hip-width apart.

2. Use a counter movement by dipping four to six inches.

3. Explosively jump up by simultaneously swinging the arms forward and extending the legs.

4. While in the air rotate 180 degrees.

5. After contact, hold the landing for two seconds and rotate 180 degrees in the opposite direction.

6. Do five repetitions.

Key Points

1. Jump with both feet.

2. Rotate while in the air.

3. Land softly (like a feather) on both feet and hold for two seconds.

BROAD JUMP AND VERTICAL JUMP

Purpose

To learn how to land. To develop explosive power and prepare the body for more intense power drills.

Procedure

1. Stand with feet parallel about hip-width apart.

2. Swing the arms backward and bend at the knees and hips.

3. Explosively jump up and forward (at a 45-degree angle) by simultaneously swinging the arms forward and extending the legs.

4. While in the air pull the knees up toward the body.

5. Jump as far as possible.

6. Land as softly as possible and hold the landing position for five seconds.

7. Perform three broad jumps (up and forward) and then do a vertical jump.

8. Do five repetitions.

Key Points

1. Jump with both feet.

2. Make sure to hold each jump for five counts.

Box-Drill Routine

When the athlete is able to complete the landing drills with balance and correct mechanics, we move to a series of more intense box drills.

DEPTH JUMPS

Purpose

To develop explosive vertical movements.

Procedure

1. Stand on top of a box with both feet.

2. Step off the box, land on both feet, and immediately jump as high as possible.

3. Swing both arms straight up as if making a block.

4. Do five jumps.

Key Points

1. Do not jump off the box; step off it.

2. Land on the balls of both feet.

3. When landing, the body should flex at the knees to absorb the weight.

4. Do not stay on the ground; jump up as quickly as possible.

5. Make sure that the landing surface is firm but has some resiliency (carpet, rubber flooring, etc.).

BOX SHUFFLE STEP

Purpose

To develop explosive lateral movements.

Procedure

1. Stand to one side of a box with the left foot on the box and the right foot on the ground.

2. Jump up and over the box with the left foot landing on the ground and the right foot landing on the box.

3. Do this continuously, shuffling back and forth for 20 seconds.

Key Point

1. Do the drill as quickly as possible under control.

DOUBLE-BOX SHUFFLE STEP

Purpose
To develop explosive lateral movements.

Procedure
1. Stand to one side of a box with both feet on the ground.

2. Shuffle onto the box, first with the left foot and then immediately with the right foot.

3. Shuffle off the box, first with the left foot and then immediately with the right foot.

4. Shuffle continuously back and forth for 20 seconds.

Key Point
1. Do the drill as quickly as possible under control.

LATERAL BOX JUMPS

Purpose
To develop explosive lateral movements.

Procedure
1. Stand to one side of a box with both feet on the ground.

2. Jump up onto the box with both feet.

3. Jump to other side of box with both feet.

4. Jump back and forth continuously for 20 seconds.

Key Point
1. Do the drill as quickly as possible under control.

Advanced Jumping and Landing Drills

Notice that we have included landing drills. Whenever we jump we work on landing too. Having our athletes jump onto boxes reduces pounding on the joints and forces players to lift their knees to get up and land in proper position. You will have to experiment with box size for your athletes. We use a couple of different heights and have mats for them to step onto after they have completed their jumps. I will list the drills that promote bilateral strength and increase vertical jumping ability through plyometrics. All of the jumps are volleyball specific. Learn the names of the drills and refer to the photos on the next page. Other drills not shown are:

- Approach jumps and land on box
- Counterstep and land on box

One-leg stick on the box

Block jumps to targets   Medicine-ball block jumps

Jump-Rope Routine

The ropes program promotes balance, good posture, extension, and coordination. You can do hundreds of exercises with your athletes. Below is a sample of what we incorporate in our program. The jump rope should be of a length that extends from the feet to the armpits. The athlete should hold the handles loosely in the hands and turn the rope using the wrists. Players should do the drills in place until they get the rhythm of the movement. Next, they work on smooth movements. As the movement becomes smooth, the players work on quickness. Use a surface that allows the athletes to jump freely and has a line 15 to 20 yards long.

DOUBLE BUNNY JUMP

Purpose
To develop timing, agility, and balance.

Procedure
1. Stand with both feet to one side of a line.

2. Jump back and forth over the line as you move forward.

3. Go 15 yards and come back the same way.

Key Points
1. Keep feet close together.

2. Stay as close to the line as possible.

3. Keep your eyes and head up.

4. Use quick feet.

SINGLE BUNNY HOP

Purpose
To develop timing, agility, balance, and leg strength.

Procedure
1. Stand with one foot to one side of a line.

2. Hop back and forth over the line with one foot as you move forward.

3. Go 15 yards on the right foot and come back on the left foot.

Key Points

1. Stay as close to the line as possible.

2. Keep your eyes and head up.

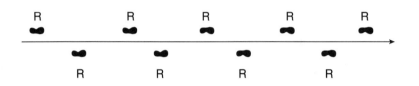

SHUFFLE STEP

Purpose

To develop timing, agility, balance, and lateral movement.

Procedure

1. Stand sideways with both feet on the line.

2. Shuffle step down the line.

3. Go 15 yards and come back facing the same direction.

Key Points

1. Stay on the line as you shuffle step.

2. Keep your eyes and head up.

3. Go to both the left and the right.

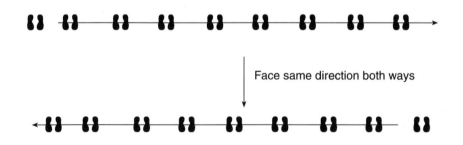

Face same direction both ways

ALI SHUFFLE

Purpose
To develop timing, agility, balance, and coordination.

Procedure
1. Stand sideways with both feet to one side of the line.

2. Do the Ali shuffle as you move laterally down the line (one foot goes forward of the line as one foot stays behind the line). Switch feet as you jump in the air to the front and back of the line.

3. Go 15 yards and come back facing the same direction.

Key Points
1. Go to the front and back of the line as you switch feet.

2. Keep your eyes and head up.

3. Go to both the left and the right.

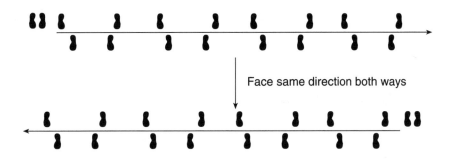

Face same direction both ways

SCISSORS STEP

Purpose
To develop timing, agility, balance, and coordination.

Procedure
1. Stand with your feet straddling the line.

2. Do a scissors step as you move forward down the line. (The feet cross over each other to the front and back. The feet should cross over on both sides of the line. Switch feet as you jump in the air.)

3. Go 15 yards and come back the same way.

Key Points

1. The feet go on both sides of the line as you switch.

2. Keep your eyes and head up.

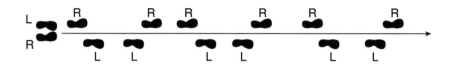

THREE TO NINE

Purpose

To develop timing, agility, balance, and hip flexibility.

Procedure

1. Stand facing forward with both feet to one side of the line in a six o'clock position.

2. Jump with both feet a quarter turn to a nine o'clock position (to the left) as you move forward.

3. Next, jump with both feet a half turn to a three o'clock position (to the right) as you move forward.

4. Repeat the half turns going from a nine o'clock position to a three o'clock position.

5. Go down and back 15 yards.

Key Points

1. As you turn the feet, they should be parallel to the line. The hips must rotate.

2. Lead the action with the feet, and the hips will follow.

3. Keep the shoulders square.

4. Keep your eyes and head up.

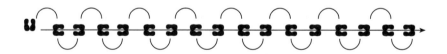

Core Strengthening Exercises

CORE ABS

Do all four sides of the body, starting at 15 seconds and working up to 60 seconds. The body stays straight. Athletes will shake on this one. Watch out for the athlete who compensates out of these positions.

BEAR CRAWLS

The hands and feet work together to move the body. Work on movement sideways and forward and back. Do not let arms or feet cross. The body part located in the direction of movement should lead. "It is better to lead than to push." Start with 10 yards per direction and work up to 50 yards. You will notice that all athletes will move better to one side than they do to the other. This tendency is a sign of dysfunction in the hips.

CRAB WALKS

Again, hands and feet work together. The athletes should move in all directions and keep the hips up when moving. Have the players start with 10 yards and ask them if they feel it in their hamstrings. This exercise is great for shoulder stabilization.

HAND-LEG OPPOSITES

Players can do this exercise lying flat on the ground, then on the hands and knees, and finally, in the advanced version, beginning on hands and feet. They keep the back flat and reach with the arms and feet to create a stretch. When the athletes get up on their hands and feet, you will see striking examples of bilateral deficiencies.

Lateral Movement and Conditioning

These drills promote lateral movement, defensive posture, and conditioning for long rallies.

MEDICINE-BALL PICKUP

Place three medicine balls (or cones) down a line about two or three yards apart. The athlete picks up a ball, shuffles five yards, lays the ball down, shuffles back five yards, picks up the next ball, and so on until all three balls are on the opposite line from where they started. The player must stay low throughout drill.

CONE-DRILL SHUFFLE

Place two cones about three yards apart. The player holds a medicine ball with the arms extended out in front of the body. In a defensive position the athlete shuffles from cone to cone, wrapping around the cone before changing direction. The player must stay low throughout drill.

Miscellaneous Drills and Concepts

The following drills incorporate extension, strength, and cool-down components. We do a couple of these on a daily basis.

1. The full or partial shoulder bridge promotes extension. We like the players to leave the gym in extension.

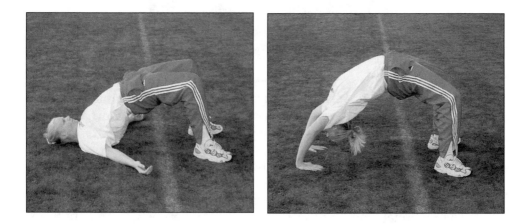

2. Lunges are a great way to develop hip extension, flexibility, and the ability to balance on one leg. Forward and backward lunges are both good exercises.

3. Pull-ups, or negatives for those who cannot do pull-ups, are effective for building strength. The negatives, done on a 5-10 count, are done on the way down.

4. For piggy backs, have a partner pull back.

5. We use striders or sprints because we feel it is important to run every day. Volleyball players move in a small area on the court, and running helps them stretch out their legs and hips.

I never fear a team that has dysfunctional athletes. I know that functional athletes will play to the level of their talent for a longer period than will dysfunctional athletes. We have a responsibility as coaches to train athletes in a functional way. Our lifestyle promotes poor posture, and our training methods develop imbalances in our athletes. Our goal at Nebraska is to develop functional athletes who play without pain and do not compensate on the court. If we can succeed with our program, the Huskers will always have an edge on the court.

PART IV

Individual Skills and Team Tactics

CHAPTER THIRTEEN

Serving

Mary Wise

Serving is often described as the first line of defense. In women's collegiate volleyball, effective serving has always been essential in preventing a team from siding out. With the rally score for both the men's and women's collegiate game, serving has become even more important. Whereas a weak serve once led to a side out, it now creates a point opportunity for the opponent. On the other hand, an overaggressive serve that leads to an error is a point, not just a side out. Coaches have to find a balance that results in effective, low-error serving. One must determine how effective is your team's side-out offense? How effectively can your team block or transition for points? These areas must all be analyzed to determine "serving risk."

According to NCAA serving statistics for the 2000 women's season, the team that led the nation in serving recorded 2.28 aces per game. The second best figure was 2.27 aces per game. Neither of those teams played in the NCAA tournament. As a statistic, aces are not good indicators of a team's success or an opponent's poor passing.

A comparison of the serving statistics in the 2000 women's national championship match reveals the following:

Team A recorded six aces and five errors.

Team B recorded four aces and nine errors.

If the ace-to-error ratio alone determined success, one would think that team A won. But those were the statistics of Wisconsin, which lost to Nebraska.

If the NCAA box scores had revealed the degree of difficulty a passer had with a serve, similar to the statistic that football uses to count "quarterback hurries," serving statistics could have been an indicator of the outcome. By themselves, aces are not the best indicators of poor passing.

How important, then, is serving? If you had seen the 2000 women's Division I NCAA finals, you would have noticed that good serving led to effective blocking. According to Nebraska head coach John Cook, "Our serving was a major factor in our winning the national championship. The pressure we put on our opponents with our serve helped us to become the best blocking team in the country."

At Florida we rate our serving by the opponent's efficiency in passing. We use the following scale:

- Zero-option pass: setter cannot set any hitter; server earns 3 points.

- One-option pass: setter can set only one hitter; server earns 2 points.

- Two-option pass: setter can set either of two hitters; server earns 1 point.

- Three-option pass: setter can set all options; server earns 0 points.

- Service error: server earns 0 points.

A poor pass can lead to a predictable set. As a result, even a team with average blocking ability can dominate with effective serving. It all starts with serving.

Basic Skills of Serving

The key to becoming an effective server, like the key to learning any other skill, is repetition. Golf instructors are quick to point out that perfect practice makes perfect skills. One must repeat correct technique for practice to make perfect.

Basic Floater Serve

- Keep it simple. Excess movement increases the chance for error. Teach players to use one step to the ball, not several. The hitting arm should come straight back, and the toss should be in front of the serving arm. Emphasize being in balance before and after the serve.

- The toss. Although it appears simple to execute the toss, a poor toss is often the single contributing factor to a poor serve. We ask players to toss a ball consistently with their nonhitting hand. Doing this is often a problem for young players with smaller hands.

The Draw

The player begins in a stride stance with the weight on the back foot. Place a mark on the floor to pinpoint where the toss should land if the server were to let the ball drop. This spot should be one step in front of the serving arm. Have players practice tossing the ball and letting it land on the mark.

- The draw. This refers to the movement pattern of the hitting arm. As the player tosses the ball with the opposite hand, he or she pulls the serving arm back with the elbow high (above ear level) and the open hand facing up (as in doing a high five). The arm follows a simple throwing motion by coming forward with the elbow leading the hand to contact the ball, where the hand is in front of the elbow.

Contact Point

Have players toss the ball, draw the arm back, and catch the ball at the top of their reach. A poor toss often negates a good arm draw. Players should work on the arm draw at the same time they practice the toss.

- Contact point. The contact point should be where the middle of the hand meets the middle of the ball. A strong, open hand at contact is best. The wrist should not be bent, but in line with the forearm. Contacting the ball anywhere other than the middle of the ball will often cause a spin that prevents the occurrence of the knuckle-ball effect. Players with large hands obviously have an advantage.

Follow-Through

By standing nine meters from a wall, players can work on their contact point with the ball. By picking a spot above what would be the top of the net, straight-ahead players can concentrate on the contact point of the ball. Only if they hit the ball solidly will it travel in a straight line to the wall.

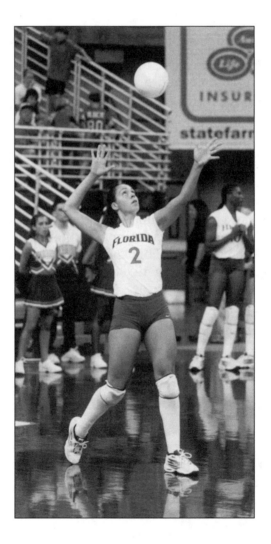

- Follow-through. To create the floating effect, the follow-through must be brief. Ideally, the hand comes off the ball immediately after striking it, as if a string attached to the back of the hand would pull the hand off just after contact. The word cue we use is to "pop" the ball. The theory is that a ball struck briefly will come off the hand and float.

Where to Stand

With the rule change that eliminated the right hash mark, servers gained an immediate advantage. By moving along the end line, players can develop different types of serves. With the right hash mark, the options were standing close to the end line or backing up deep. By being able to use the entire end line, players have many more options.

Some of the most effective collegiate servers are those with varied serving skills. They can stand close to the end line and serve a ball that gets to the passers quickly. By standing deep—10 feet or more from the end line—they can aggressively attack the ball and create a floater that changes direction several times before it reaches the passer. We encourage our players to have more than one standing position.

During a summer tour of Europe in 1997, every team we played had their servers stand at least 10 meters from the end line. We quickly learned that the serving skills of European high school and college-age women were significantly more advanced than what we see in NCAA competition. Standing deep off the court, these aggressive servers served a ball that I describe as a missile because of the way it changed direction and came so quickly to our passers.

By moving left or right, short or deep, the server can create different angles and thus force passers to make adjustments. Even a tough serve becomes easy to handle when it is made from the same spot, going in the same direction every time. Good passers will adapt quickly to a repetitive serve.

Keys to Becoming a Good Server

1. To be an effective server, you must serve. Why are coaches such good servers? Experience and repetition. Think about how many times they initiate a drill with their toss and contact. Like free-throw shooting for a basketball player, serving is a skill that players can do alone and outside regular team practice. Repetition is the key.

2. Players should develop a pre-serve routine. Just as free-throw shooters go through the same mechanics before shooting each foul shot, servers should develop a routine that centers their attention on serving.

3. Serving against passers is helpful. We judge the effectiveness of a serve on the quality of the resulting pass. We use passers with our serving drills so that the feedback to the server is the quality of the pass, not where the serve landed.

4. Players should serve under pressure. A good server in practice is not necessarily a good server in a match. Everything changes when the lights are on. As much as possible, serving drills should be done under some sort of created pressure. Standing behind the end line serving rapid fire is nothing like serving in a game.

Types of Serves

Beginners are better off having one effective serve rather than many different serves. The stronger the opponent's passing, the more important it is to have different types of serves. At the early stages, serving is often well ahead of passing. Just getting it in can make a young player his or her team's MVP.

Short Serves

The short serve that lands in front of the three-meter line can be extremely effective. It can clog up the middle by forcing players short to pass before they make their full approach. A short serve can often bring on a predictable set to the outside hitter. Also, by making a middle hitter pass the short serve, the server can disrupt the middle hitter's timing.

To serve short, the player must pop the ball with a short follow-through. This technique will get the ball to drop. A slow-spinning serve will not drop short but will tend to sail along. When contacting the middle of the ball with the palm of the hand, the player must quickly pull the hand off the ball after contact. The longer the follow-through, the farther the ball will travel. A high, lofty serve eliminates any advantage of a short serve by giving passers enough time to get under the ball.

Floater or Drive Serves

The server should toss the ball in front of the serving hand and slightly higher than maximum reach. As the arm comes through, the hand will pop off the ball, like a short serve but with a longer finish. By striking the ball harder with the hand, the server will create a knuckle-ball effect that causes the ball to change direction as it travels to the passer. The more the ball floats, the more difficult the serve is to pass.

To serve a floater, the player must use an open, firm hand. The wrist should be locked, not bent, and in line with the forearm. The serving arm should swing fast to the ball, and the hand should then pop off the ball. The speed of the arm will make the ball travel deep and then drop. Contact must be in the center of the ball to create the float. If the server does not contact the ball correctly (on the side, under the ball), an easy, predictable spin will result.

Jump Serves

The most difficult serve is the jump serve, a high-risk, high-reward technique. Rarely used at the high school level because of its difficulty, the jump serve dominates at the higher levels of competition.

During the 1998 women's NCAA volleyball season, we witnessed one of the best all-time jump servers in the women's game. Misty May, the setter for Long Beach State, dominated matches with her jump serve. Long Beach State went on to win the national championship, and May was named Player of the Year. The difference between May's serve and those of so many others was the height at which she contacted the ball. Misty's outstanding jumping ability allowed her to contact the ball at a point seldom seen with a serve in the women's game.

The jump serve starts with a toss in front high enough so that the player can make contact at the highest point of the jump. The length of a player's approach determines the distance from the end line. Ideally, the contact point is in front of the end line, with the player using a broad jump like that used in a back-row attack. Tall players and those with big jumps have the greatest advantage. Some players contact the ball so far above the floor that receiving the serve becomes less like passing and more like digging. The great jump servers are those who contact the ball well above the net.

• The toss. Most jump servers toss with their striking hand. The toss must be high and out in front so that the player can make contact at the peak of the jump. As when serving from a standing position, the toss is critical to the success of a jump serve.

• The approach. Having executed the toss, the player gathers the arms, swings them back, and takes a four-step approach, accelerating as the player would when making an attack approach. A right-handed player would step right, left, right-left into the jump. The final right-left is a quick plant with the weight going from heel to toe with the right foot and on the ball of the left foot. At the prejump position, the player should have the knees bent and the left foot slightly in front of the right foot. At this stage, the arms go straight back with the thumbs pointing down. At the jump, again like an attack, the player swings both arms in front, transfers weight from right foot to left, and generates power from the approach.

- The contact. The server contacts the ball out in front with the palm of the hand. By snapping the wrist at contact, the server puts topspin on the ball. The higher the contact and the faster the swing, the more topspin the server can place on the ball, forcing it to travel faster to the floor.

Variations

1. Topspin serve. Besides the jump serve, we have seen in the women's college game a serve in which the player stands on the floor and serves a topspin ball that drops quickly. The least effective serve is a slow spin serve in which the player does not contact the ball properly (under the ball, on the side, etc.). These serves cause little disruption to a good passing team. Jenny Manz, a two-time All-American at Florida, was an extremely effective topspin server. A lower-back injury prevented her from using the jump serve. To take advantage of her long arms, Jenny served a topspin ball while standing on the floor. The serve was effective because she made contact at a high point and the ball traveled quickly to the floor with a topspin rotation.

2. Sidespin. The server contacts the ball on the upper third, causing it to rotate down with a sidespin to it. Although this serve often happens simply by poor contact on the ball, the most effective sidespin serve results when the server slices the ball intentionally. The speed and spin of the ball cause it to be difficult to pass because the ball is usually moving away from the passer.

3. Jump floater. This serve results when the hand pops off the ball while the player is in the air. This action creates a serve that floats from a high contact point. Outside hitter Jessica Suddith used the jump floater with great effectiveness during her career at the University of Hawaii.

4. Let serve. New to collegiate volleyball in 2001 is the let serve, in which the ball hits the top of the tape and travels inbounds to the opponent's side. This rule allows servers to be aggressive and serve a lower, flatter ball. No longer is the serving team penalized if the ball hits the tape.

Serving Zones

An integral part of serving strategy is directing players to serve to predetermined areas of the court. We can divide the court into six zones of different sizes (figure 13.1).

The best servers are those who are able to serve all six zones with equal efficiency. In addition, the better servers do not give away their intentions. Where they stand and how they position themselves does not differ for the short serve, long serve, zone 1, or zone 5.

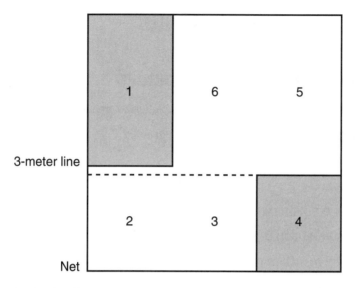

Figure 13.1   Serving zones.

One of our most effective servers at Florida was our All-American Jennifer Sanchez. She had the ability to serve each area of the court with the same degree of accuracy. At the same time, Jen never gave away the zone to which she was serving because she stood at the same spot for each of her different serves.

Common Zone Serving Strategies.

1. Serve zone 5. The server serves where the front-row hitter is passing. The player must pass first, then hit. By serving this player to the inside of the court or backing the player up, the serve disrupts the approach and timing of the hitter.

2. Serve short zone. By serving short, the serve can disrupt the timing of a first-tempo attack. The front-row player may be unable to be part of the attack because of the need to pass the serve first.

3. Serve behind the setter. This serve travels behind the setter's starting position as the setter moves to the target area at the net. The passers could lose sight of the ball by the setter's movement.

4. Serve line. By serving a ball down the line to zone 5 from the right side of the end line or to zone 1 from the left, the passer has less time to react to the ball.

5. A serve from the left side of the end line to zone 5 can drop in front of a left-back passer. With more distance to work with, the server can serve more aggressively and therefore create a serve that drops faster.

Florida Drills

30 PASSING POINTS BEFORE 15 SERVES

1. Servers work versus passers (using the team passing formation).

2. Servers alternate against passers for 15 total serves.

3. Each pass is rated on a 3-point scale:

> 0 points for an ace
>
> 1 point for a one-option pass
>
> 2 points for a two-option pass
>
> 3 points for a three-option pass
>
> 0 points for a service error

The drill ends after the 15th serve or when the passers reach 30 points.

This gamelike drill rates the serve by the pass it produces. Coaches can signal zones to the server or let the server decide. Passers can rotate or stay in the same position for each serve.

THREE IN A ROW

1. Servers work versus passers (using the team passing formation).

2. Passers are trying to get three consecutive "three-option" passes.

3. Servers are trying to get three consecutive passes that are not three-option passes.

4. A service error equals a three-option pass.

5. Serve rotates to each server.

6. Play the best three out of five games.

This drill requires the servers to execute a tough, gamelike serve three times in a row to win the game.

LET SERVES BEFORE 10 ERRORS

1. Servers try to serve 5 let balls (balls that hit the tape of the net and fall inbounds) before making 10 service errors.

This drill teaches the players to serve a hard, flat ball. A lofty serve caused by contact under the ball will not produce a tough let serve.

FIVE BEFORE TWO

1. Each server must serve five balls into each zone before making two service errors.

2. After the third error, the server must start over.

3. For more experienced servers, the game can require five successful serves before one service error.

The better servers are those who can serve to all zones in the court. This drill teaches that skill.

SERVING PROGRESSION

1. Servers serve 10 balls in. A service error requires them to start over.

2. They serve 5 balls in a row into the three deep zones. A service error requires them to start the deep serves over.

3. They serve 3 balls in a row into the three short zones. A service error requires them to start the short serves over.

This drill teaches players to serve a zone consistently. To master the drill, players must execute the serve to the same zone several times in succession.

SERVING POINT GAME

1. Mark the court for the six serving zones:

> Zone 6 = 1 point
>
> Zones 1 and 5 = 2 points
>
> Zone 3 = 3 points
>
> Zones 2 and 4 = 4 points

2. Service error = minus 1 point.

3. First player to score 15 points (exactly) wins.

This drill rewards serves to the more difficult zones and emphasizes that a serve into zone 6 is better than a service error.

SIX VERSUS SIX, SERVER VERSUS SERVE-RECEPTION OFFENSE

1. One server with five teammates in defensive starting positions serves against a serve-reception offense.

2. Each serve is rated based on the pass.

3. If the serving team wins the rally, subtract 1 point from the score of the passing team.

4. A service error is 3 passing points.

5. After five serves, the team receiving the serve rotates.

6. Low score wins for the server.

This drill emphasizes the importance of the serve as the first line of defense. If a server does not serve tough, then the defense must work that much harder to win the rally.

BALL AND PARTNER SERVING DRILL

1. Use one ball for every two people.

2. The server serves to a partner on the other side of the net.

3. Passers pass to themselves and catch it.

4. The first group to 10 catches wins.

5. A dropped pass does not count.

This excellent warm-up drill emphasizes ball handling control by the server. Serving tough produces no advantage. Partners who possess good ball handling and forearm passing control have the advantage.

BALL AND PARTNER, SERVE AND RUN

1. Players need a ball and a partner. The server starts behind the end line, and the passer starts directly across the net.

2. Player A serves to player B and runs under the net.

3. After running under the net, player A catches the pass from player B in the target position.

4. The first group to 10 catches wins.

5. A missed serve or dropped pass does not count.

This drill emphasizes ballhandling control. To be successful, the server must be able to control a serve to a partner on the other side of the net. After the serve, the server must sprint to the other side of the net to catch the pass.

SERVING HORSE

1. This drill is similar to the basketball game of the same name. Two people use one ball.

2. One person chooses a zone and then serves to that zone

3. If player A makes the zone, then player B must follow with a serve to the same zone to keep from scoring the letter H.

4. If player A misses, then player B chooses the zone and goes first.

5. The first one to spell "Horse" loses.

This competitive drill requires players to serve effectively to each of the different zones.

CHAPTER FOURTEEN

Receiving Serves

Steve Shondell

It was a lesson I will never forget. I was giving the pregame talk to my team before our biggest match of the season—Muncie Burris High School versus Muncie Central High School. A near-capacity crowd was on hand to witness the battle of the two most prestigious high school volleyball programs in Indiana. I had said to my team that the key to the match would be defense. "If we can outdig Central, we have a good chance of winning the match," was my specific statement. How wrong I was! My team outdug our opponent 37-16 but lost the match in two straight games, 15-12 and 15-7. Why did we lose? Deplorable serve reception. We overpassed 12 of our opponent's serves, which resulted in many immediate points, and Central aced us four times.

We virtually gave away 16 points through poor serve reception. I should have known better! How often had I heard that serving and serve reception decide the outcome of a match between evenly matched opponents? Our match with Muncie Central was no exception. The poor serve reception by our team was clearly the difference in the outcome. For years, I had believed that a team's ability to pass the serve accurately would largely determine the team's success in critical matches. My high school teams at Muncie Burris had won 95 percent of their matches since 1980, and the single most important reason for their success year after year was consistency in passing the serve.

Goal of the Serve Receiver

The goal of the serve receiver is to direct the ball accurately to the net in such a manner that the setter will have time to get under the ball and have the option of setting it to any of the attackers. This results in the team being "in system." An errant pass that results in the setter's having a limited number of options to set causes the team to be "out of system." An in-system pass is high enough for the setter to get under, one to two feet from the net, and 10 to 15 feet from the right sideline.

Height of the Pass

For an advanced team hoping to run a fast, precise offense, the serve receiver should pass the ball no higher than the top of the antennae. A ball consistently at this height will permit a team to develop an offensive rhythm that will allow the setter and hitters to develop a consistent, precise timing for their attack. A less-skilled team, such as middle school team or a less-skilled high school team, may find it advisable to pass the ball higher, perhaps three to five feet higher than the top of the antennae. A higher pass will allow the setter more time to get under the ball. On the negative side, the higher pass will slow the tempo of the offense, providing more time for the defense to prepare for the attack.

Passing Posture

In using the forearm pass in receiving the serve, the passer should assume the medium volleyball posture before the server makes contact with the ball. The medium position can be described as follows:

1. Feet spread slightly wider than shoulder-width, toes pointing straight ahead
2. Right foot slightly forward in a heel-toe relationship
3. Weight forward, transferred to the balls of the feet
4. Knees slightly bent so that they are forward of the toes
5. Slight forward lean so that shoulders are in front of the knees
6. Arms extended in front of the body and parallel to the upper leg
7. Palms up

The upper body must be relaxed when preparing to pass the serve. The footwork must be quick and aggressive to allow the passer to front the ball properly when making the pass.

Moving to the Ball

To be able to pass the serve consistently, the passer must be able to move efficiently to the ball. Getting the feet to the ball is critical to a passer's success.

When receiving the serve, the passer should usually be able to get to the ball by using no more than three steps. I like to refer to this movement pattern as the *step and plant.* The expression simply means taking a step toward the direction of the ball and then planting both feet to the ball in the spread position before making contact. The spread position is identical to the passer's starting position before the serve. As the passer moves to the ball, the passer's head must stay at the same level. I often tell my players that a barbed-wire fence runs an inch above their heads. They must work to remain under the barbed wire as they move to the ball. Once they get both feet to the ball, the passer's shoulders must be square, or perpendicular, to the oncoming ball.

Locking In

Simultaneous to the plant of both feet in preparation for making the pass, the hands "lock in." Although players can use several different hand positions with equal effectiveness, I prefer to teach the overlap grip, a grip that coaches have taught for years. The cues for this technique are as follows:

1. Fingers are across fingers.

2. Thumbs are side by side or parallel.

3. Heels of hands are together.

4. Push wrists down. Pushing the wrists down will help lock the elbows and assist in elevating the shoulders forward, which in turn will assist the passer in presenting an extended platform with the arms. I often tell my passers to form a "scared" cat back with the upper body. This is a great cue to help produce the extended platform.

Contact

The player contacts the ball by *lifting* the arms into it. I constantly remind my players to lift rather than swing the arms into the ball. There is a great difference between swinging and lifting, and the coach must understand the difference. By locking in, dropping the arms, and then lifting the arms in a swinging motion, the passer adds a great amount of impetus to the ball and constantly changes the angle of the rebound at contact. By simply lifting the arms into the ball with the shoulder shrug, the passer maintains a consistent rebound angle, thus producing a more accurate pass. The passer makes contact with the ball on the middle of the forearms. The key is to make certain that the platform of the forearms angles toward the intended target. The passer must work to front the incoming serve and direct it to the target by tilting the platform toward the intended target.

1. Midline. This is the simplest technique to execute. When the passer's body is directly behind the ball and the intended target is straight in front of the passer, the passer should pass the ball from the midline of the body with the feet in a parallel position.

2. Angle right. When a passer is directly behind the ball and the intended target is to the right, the passer must take the ball in front of the left hip, tilt or drop the right shoulder, and execute the pass with a lift-and-freeze motion (see figure 14.1). The feet should be in a spread heel-toe relationship, with the right foot being the lead foot. The angle-right pass is the most commonly used pass to receive serve.

3. Angle left. When a passer is directly behind the ball and the intended target is to the left, the passer

Figure 14.1 Angle right.

must take the ball in front of the right hip (see figure 14.2). The passer tilts or drops the left shoulder and completes the pass with the lift-and-freeze motion. The feet should be in a spread heel-toe relationship, with the left foot being the lead foot.

Emergency Technique

1. Clearing the shoulders. A ball served deep and above chest level is nearly impossible to play with the shoulders perpendicular, facing the ball. The passer will usually be shuffling backward and must clear the shoulders of the path of the ball. The passer must then tilt the shoulders and angle the platform of the forearms to the target (see figure 14.3). This technique allows the passer to maintain an extended platform and prevents the served ball from hitting the passer in the chest.

2. Shuffling through the ball. At times the passer will not be able to pass the ball from a stationary position. Under these circumstances, the passer must continue moving through the ball while completing the pass. This movement is typically a shuffle movement. Moving through the ball will impart a reverse spin on the volleyball, which, in turn will benefit the passer's ball control.

Tracking the Ball

To be successful, a passer must be able to track the ball from the time it leaves the server's hand to the time it reaches the passer's arms. The passer must never lose sight of the ball from the

Figure 14.2   Angle left.

Figure 14.3   Clearing the shoulders.

time the server tosses it up to initiate the serve. Passers should learn to track the ball with their eyes and should attempt to see the ball contact their arms. In practice, I sometimes do not permit my players to watch the ball after it comes off their arms, requiring them instead to keep their eyes on their arms until the ball is in the setter's hands.

Passers should also learn to keep the head still as they track the ball. The head should not move (bounce) as they move to the ball.

Keeping the Body Quiet

From the moment the server contacts the ball, the passer should be aggressive with the feet but keep the upper body as still as possible. The less the motion of the upper body, the better. I refer to this as keeping the body quiet. As the feet plant and the hands lock in to prepare to pass the ball, the body should be still, with the exception of the arms lifting into the ball.

Cushioning the Ball

One of the toughest skills for a passer to master is cushioning a hard-driven serve. The situation has come into play more frequently in recent years with the popularity of the jump serve. In men's volleyball at the college and international level, the jump serve has become the norm, and passers must master the skill of cushioning on serve reception. Passers should learn to relax the shoulders on contact when passing a high-velocity serve. Relaxing the shoulders allows the arms to give with the ball, making it possible for the player to pass a softer ball. The arms withdraw on contact rather than lift into the ball. A second technique that is popular in men's collegiate volleyball is for the passer to take small steps backward while passing the ball. Stanford used this technique in the championship match of the 1996 NCAA men's volleyball tournament to handle a UCLA team known for its powerful jump serving.

Communication

Communication between passers clarifying who will pass the serve is essential. A receiver who decides to pass the serve should call "mine" as early as possible. The passer's voice should be loud and clear! Teammates should then assist the passer by helping to determine whether the serve is out. The teammate closest to the line should make the call. If teammates close to the line feel that the ball is good, they should say nothing, and the passer should play the ball.

Passing the Seams

When the server places the ball into the seam between two passers, the passers must depend on decisions made in practice about who is responsible for passing the ball. We break down the seam into two parts: the short seam and the deep seam. In our system, the passer closer to the server is responsible for passing the short seam, and the passer farther away from the server passes the deep seam.

Serve–Reception Patterns

Teams use many serve-reception formations in today's game. The coach must decide which formation will be most effective for the team.

Two–Player Serve Receive

The two-player serve-receive pattern was made popular by the USA men's team during its Olympic gold medal years (1984 and 1988). Many collegiate men's teams used it with some success, but the growing popularity of the jump serve virtually eliminated it from the men's game in the mid-1990s. A coach may choose to use this formation when the team has two primary passers who are athletic and can cover a large area of the court. For this formation to be successful, both passers must have great range from side to side and up and back. The two-player pattern can be effective against the float serve but may be ineffective against the high-velocity serve. The two passers involved in the two-player pattern are usually outside attackers known as swing hitters.

Three–Player Serve Receive

The three-player reception pattern is popular when a team wishes to use three players as primary passers. One or two of the passers can be front-row players not involved in first-tempo offense. Teams commonly involve the two left-side hitters. When in a front-row rotation, they can run a swing type of offense moving to either side of the court, or a second-tempo offense in conjunction with a middle attacker who does not have passing responsibilities and is free to run a fast first-tempo attack. The court on serve reception is divided three ways, with the secondary passers at the net watching for the let serve or the short serve that can be passed using the overhand passing technique. The three-passer pattern is effective against both the jump serve and the floater. Area of coverage responsibility in the three-player pattern depends on the quickness and passing ability of each of the passers. The more mobile and precise passer will cover a larger area, and the poorer passer will defend a smaller area near a sideline when possible. Many teams, when the libero is permitted, incorporate an outstanding passer into this position, making this player an integral part of the three-player pattern.

Four–Player Serve Receive

The four-player pattern is useful for teams that are not particularly mobile and want to free up their first-tempo player for a quick attack. The pattern usually consists of two deep passers and two short passers. The two short players start outside the deep passers in what is called a U pattern. Its weakness is either corner or the 3 zone near the net. A modification of the U against the 3-zone serve is to move the two passers into a power-left or power-right shift. In a power right, the right-front short passer slides several steps to the left into the 3-zone passing position, changing the open zone from the 3 to the 2. In a power-left shift, the left-front attacker shifts from the 4 zone into the 3 zone, changing the open zone from the 3 to the 4. Employing the shift just as the server initiates the toss enhances the deception.

Five-Player Receive

The five-player pattern was at one time the most popular serve-reception pattern. As specialization became more prevalent in the 1980s and 1990s, the five-player pattern became less popular. The teams that now use the five-player pattern are primarily at the high school and middle school level. Its advantage is that each person has less area to cover. The five-player pattern is therefore perfect for smaller children just learning the game. The disadvantage is the confusion caused by having so many players in the passing pattern, several of whom are probably less accurate passers than others in the pattern. Having the middle attackers drop back off the net into the passing pattern can disrupt the timing of a first- or second-tempo attack, which is one of the major reasons that advanced teams do not use it.

Overhand-Passing Serve Reception

Another change in the international rules that allows a double hit on the first contact has brought the overhand pass back into serve reception. The overhand pass was the standard technique in serve reception from 1895 to the 1960s. Changes in rules interpretation virtually outlawed its use in receiving the serve, and coaches discouraged its use in the 1970s, 1980s, and 1990s. But the better teams are now counting on overhand-passing skill to help their teams pass more accurately. The overhand pass has become an efficient tool in passing float serves, especially the increasingly popular short serve.

Overhand Pass

When using the overhand technique to pass the deep, hard, flat serve, the player should keep the hands firm and hold them a little closer together than when setting or passing a free ball. These adjustments are necessary to counter the force of the rapidly moving ball. The passer needs to have a firm base with the feet in the spread position and the knees, hips, and shoulders square to the intended target rather than facing the serve, as would be the case when using the forearm pass. The passer makes contact with the ball over the forehead. The fingers and the hands should push straight through the ball toward the intended target. The recommended firm hand position will quickly push out the ball, minimizing the danger that the official will call a lifting violation. The advantage of the overhand pass on serve reception is control. A poorly handled ball will come down close to the intended target, a result that rarely occurs on a misdirected forearm pass. Players using this technique can extend their area of coverage by starting near midcourt and taking the deep serve by moving one step backward and cushioning the impact on the hands as they move away from the ball.

Conclusion

Serve reception is a critical aspect of a team's training program. In all levels of competition, serving and passing are highly correlated with team success or failure. These two skills should be an integral part of almost every daily practice plan. I prefer to incorporate serving and serve receiving in the early part of practice when concentration and focus are at a peak. The primary passers should receive as many repetitions as possible. The nonpassers can focus on other aspects of the drill, such as serving, attacking, blocking, or just being a target for the passes of the primary passers.

In practice, primary passers should receive serves as tough as, or even tougher than, those they will see in upcoming matches. This idea is commonly referred to as the overload principle. Passers should receive in practice all types of serves that upcoming opponents use. Competitive games in practice, with the servers taking on the passers, can provide valuable training experience. The competition will elevate intensity and concentration. These games can also indicate which players are mentally tough.

Consistency in passing the serve should be a goal for every team seeking to be successful. A breakdown in the passing game can take a team out of a match very quickly. A coach must never underestimate the importance of the passing game. A team that can consistently pass the serve to the setter in the target area has an excellent chance of reaching its goals and dreams.

CHAPTER FIFTEEN

Setting

Teri Clemens

Ahhhh! Witnessing the passion, competitiveness, and skill of a strong setter is seeing winning in the making! It is not the division or size of the school that defines success; rather, it is the *class* of the school that explains success. The same idea applies in the selection, style, and presentation of the setter. The division or size of the setter does not define success; the *class* of the setter defines success!

Train a winner, not a whiner! The coach makes the choice. I insisted that my setter be a winner. Make it clear from the start that whining is unacceptable. You should expect and reward a positive attitude in a setter. I like to reward good setting with more sets. This approach teaches a setter that setting is the end reward. Likewise, good blocking deserves more opportunities to block, strong serving earns more serves, and so on. I guarantee effectiveness of this theory in coaching. This is how you develop passion in your players.

I was able to witness several all-America setters. In fact, every starting setter in my tenure at Washington University was named to an NCAA all-America team. Why? Was that an accident? What did the setters have in common? What did they offer the teams they played for? Why did we win seven national championships with those particular setters running our offense?

These NCAA championship setters varied immensely in height, body build, personality, technique, training, academic focus, and experience. In some key areas, however, they did not vary. We often see teams in which it is obvious that the setter was selected by height—the shortest player in the group is the setter. Height is not the differentiating factor for success in the position, nor is technique or any other one factor. What makes an effective setter is a well-balanced combination of characteristics. Competitiveness ranks at the top of that list on my court. Each setter was an extension of me on the court—good and bad, I'm sure—but each uniquely copied my style in varied areas.

Lori Nishikawa

Lori Nishikawa, at 5-foot-2, was the NCAA III National Player of the Year in 1988 and 1989. She was painfully shy. If she spoke during her recruiting visit to WU as a senior in high school, I'm not sure I was present. The fans loved Lori—large crowds came to see her acrobatic, crowd-pleasing sets. Attendance averaged 26 in the pre-Nish days, and her final match drew 3,400.

Kelly Meier was 5-foot-10, lean, with hands that were so soft and sweet to watch set that she should have insured them. She lacked experience through her high school years and learned as much from studying Lori for two years as she did from our coaching staff. Kelly made hitters look better.

Leslie Catlin, 5-foot-7, loved learning and competing. She craved playing from her first day and valued coaching and responsibility for winning. We often referred to her "rocket fingers" as she chased shanked balls across the gym and, from her fingers, shot them great distances to hitters.

Those first three setters were Midwesterners—comfortable in this part of the country and with this Midwestern coach. The next setter, Stephanie Habif, from New Jersey, introduced the coaching staff and

Leslie Catlin

players to a new, different style on the court. Incredibly confident in her first year, 5-foot-9-inch Steph had the style of a coach on the court, always urging and pulling talent out of her hitters. Physically big and strong, she found early respect from her teammates. Steph was not quick, but she learned to make her movement on the court so efficient that by her senior year she was chasing down most balls. Coaches always commented on the speed she had gained, but what she really gained was power and smarts. I worked on cheating in movement—doing everything possible within the rules to get to a ball faster. This specific training was perfect for Steph. She had a background in volleyball with strong technical training. Steph saw early action in college.

Stephanie Habif

My last setter at Washington University was Meg Vitter, from New Orleans (and proud of it). I learned a great deal from Meg when she responded to my lack of interest in her as a prospective student-athlete. I thought I was going with another setter. After sharing this decision with Meg, I received a masterfully written letter from her. She was sure that she was our setter of the future. Her letter nearly exploded in my hands with her exuberant spirit, confidence, intelligence, and desire. She changed my mind. She was right. She was exceptionally good. It was great to be proved wrong.

Sharing the brief history of our setters sets straight the notion that a winning setter has a particular height, style, and spirit. The mutual characteristics that brought NCAA III national championships and all-America fame to these setters included maturity, unmatched desire to learn and win, leadership in creating team cohesiveness, respect for our coaching staff with lots of one-on-one conversations and extra training time, and finally massive competitiveness. They came to our program with varying degrees of this gift. Each was passionate about this program, their teammates, Washington University, and winning.

I believe each left with the highest level of competitiveness they could reach in those short years. I know each left with great satisfaction of accomplishment, higher expectation of self, and huge passion to transfer to an area of choice. Each was one of an elite few who gave what it took to be the best.

Training the Setter

The setter should be simple, efficient, and not dramatic in presentation of the movement of the feet or the ball to the hitter. The successful setter moves in a direct line to the ball and then takes a position to deliver it efficiently to the hitter, yet presents deception to the defense across the net. The set is a delivery of the ball, usually from the fingers above the head with a release by pushing the ball upward. The set appears to float to a hitter—not spin—from the forehead toward the ceiling. Arms would then fully extend upward. The setter can set the ball with her feet on the floor or jump set by jumping before setting the ball. Jumping provides greater delay for the blockers across the net, ideally providing the offense with greater chances of scoring. When the setter brings the hands up, thumbs should be high at the top of the forehead or above. Try this early in training—hands up high, thumbs at the forehead. The coach should toss the ball lightly into the setter's hands repeatedly. The setter, to return to correct starting position each time, touches the thumbs back to the top of the forehead before setting each ball. This drill trains the setter to keep the hands high—a difficult task to learn when one is neither strong nor experienced. Of course, as the setter improves the skill, she will not touch the forehead with the thumbs. Rather she will master the positioning.

Footwork includes an explosion to the ball, arriving early and in medium position with hands up. I yelled "run" to setters as much as I did any other word. It was often that simple—run to the ball. I was specific with footwork but tried not to overcoach. Left-right-left is ideal for footwork from the ready position at the net. Because every rule has an exception, setters who possess athletic prowess in addition to technique often perform better than the trained technical setter without born gifts. When arriving at the net to set, the setter should be approximately one yard from the net.

Many setters run in too tight to the net, causing a greater chance of fouling by touching the net. The weight at the net should be on the right foot, ready to take the first step with the left foot to chase down the ball. Ideally, the pass from teammates is right in the setter's hands. The reality is that the setter spends more time running to set the ball than setting the ball. I trained this movement with great repetitiveness and demanded intense explosion of the left foot to run. Even the slowest setter learned to get to balls faster because she became efficient at footwork.

Before movement toward the ball, the ready position for a setter includes the body in medium position. Again, I emphasize that the chase comes before the set. Because the setter must run before setting, it is not necessary to give the passer a hand-up-high target although I do like hands up early and fast to set. Finally, the extension and follow-through of the hands, arms, and body upward are critical to powerful setting.

I certainly love many variations in fast-paced drills, but one of the best and most efficient drills for training technique in setters and delivering thousands of repetitions is the triangle drill (figure 15.1). Infinite repetitions in sets are necessary for success.

Triangle Setting Drill

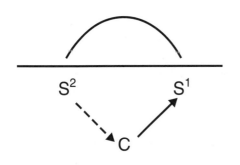

Figure 15.1 Triangle drill.

Requires 2-3 setters, 2 balls. Call the specific set(s) to be used in each series.

Coach or player tosses to the setter. Setter sets specifically assigned set to setter B who is standing in assigned hitting zone. Ball is caught by setter 2 (S2). S2 bounces a second ball to tosser who repeats toss to same setter. This allows one setter to do a series of repetitions on the assigned set and then the setters to rotate.

Note: This drill should move quickly and efficiently. An errant set is not retrieved until a series of 10 is complete. Many repetitions in a short time creates a better learning environment than a few sets over the same or longer period. S2 should give a brief constructive word to setter 1 (S1) after each set such as, "awesome," "tight" (too close to the net), "off" (too far from the net), "low," "high," or "flat." This is critiquing, not criticizing, and this communication creates accurate setters who treasure feedback.

Example: Coach assigns setter to do three series (alternating after each series of 10). Series 1: Set high outside to zone 1. Series 2: Set three foot high sets to zone 3. Series 3: Set high sets to zone 7. Repeat for a time period or until a predetermined number of series is accomplished.

Setter Presentation

In our program at Washington University in St. Louis we had certain behaviors and expectations that defined us as exceptional. I had enormously high expectations of setters. They had the same expectations for me as coach. I did not take their respect lightly. They had high regard for the tradition and history of our program. These setters were different. Each expected to be one of the best—a champion, a winner.

The following list includes the attributes and learned behaviors that differentiated championship setters (and often, great volleyball programs) from other setters.

- Is contagiously passionate for the game
- Expects to win a rally
- Competes in a way that defines winning as a work ethic that outshines the opponent
- Thinks intelligently and has good study practices in and out of the classroom

- Is efficient, prompt, and neat
- Digests information
- Communicates in a way that people understand, appreciate, and respect
- Respects and believes in the coach
- Craves infinite repetitions and sees the need for advanced training
- Doesn't play fair to hitters (by sharing sets with all) but instead plays to win
- Maintains an emotional level that is neither too high nor too low and stays off the roller coaster
- Boosts team rather than wears team out
- Transitions well
- Values varied offensive plays and understands the need for variation
- Likes the bluff and is deceptive and sneaky
- Welcomes physical training
- Focuses on strengths yet is aware of weaknesses
- Accepts role of playing defense as well as running the offense
- Plays within self
- Can step it up when necessary
- Wants to develop and believes there is another level

If the coach is comparable to an orchestra director, the setter must be the featured soloist. Many eyes are on the setter. Fans have high expectations. People watch setters because the setter touches the ball a lot. What the setter does strongly affects the team. There is both pressure and support. The encouragement never stops—"Get it," "Tight," "Set me," "High-out here," "Quick," "Go, go, go," "Cover." We taught our setters to walk into the arena expecting to win, to walk the walk of a winner, to wear the uniform more proudly than did the opponent.

Posture, eye contact, belief, and encouragement of teammates are qualities that coaches must cultivate in their setters. Opponents can easily read the confidence level of the setter. Presentation of the setter on the court often translates to points on the scoreboard. Even if the setter is not officially the captain of the team, opponents consider the setter to be the leader. They study the setter in warm-ups and early in a match, measuring skill, confidence, and general presentation. It all matters. Coaches are responsible for teaching their setters how to win. We cannot assume that setters, or anyone else, knows how to compete. Coaches should demand it rather than command it. Players respect high expectations, but none of us tolerate rough commands for long. I could laugh with my setters as easily as I could teach.

A championship setter knows that she or he is the captain of the court. That sort of setter presentation exemplifies a winner.

Tactics

The emphasis here is on the setter's individual tactics rather than the tactics of the team. We must emphasize this area even as we train beginning setters. They must learn where to look, when to look, what to look for, how to move and release the ball, where to set, who to set, why to set that player, how high or low to set, and where to go after setting. Wow! We, as coaches, may provide too little information, or we may overload a setter with too much information. A lot of pressure falls on a developing young person.

A knowledgeable, successful coach will give the setter simple and comforting information during a match. Overloading a setter with tactical information is usually detrimental. Err on the side of not enough information, Coach.

Tactics begin when we start adding combinations to drills. For example, we ask setters to start at the sideline, to explode to the ready position, and then, after we toss a ball, to set it to an outside hitter. Tactics involve the thought process as well as the technical skill.

The type and complexity of the offense depends on the ability of the setter, the knowledge of the coach and players, and the type of defense the team faces. I believe it is important to challenge players. I personally know many high school student-athletes who set challenging offenses in junior high programs and then, in their high school programs, have to run a simple game plan. It happens in the reverse too. The coach must study and be ahead of the talent in the program.

Coaches should think about several ideas in developing the thought process for a thinking setter.

1. Set to win! Most young setters share the sets among friends. Coach setters to set more sets to the top-scoring hitters. Discuss this idea frequently. I remember telling Meg several times early in her collegiate career during competitive drills, "Meg, was that your best choice of a set and who to set it to?" Let other players hear this at times to help them separate friendship from striving to win. Otherwise, they may assume that it is the setter's decision about which hitter is set rather than the coach's instruction.

2. Transition. This idea involves developing the setter's time management of the transition, the time spent between skills. For example, the setter sets the ball and then runs over to cover the outside hitter. The time between setting and covering (a defensive stance near the hit in case it is blocked back over the net) is a transition. Successful teams move efficiently in transition, using quick, efficient movement, with few steps and no wasted

motion. Improvement requires repetition. Winning teams are well rehearsed in transition. It takes planning to run these drills.

3. Choosing who to set, how high or low to set, and where to set. Before release of the ball and during transition time running to the ball, the setter must determine who to set, how high or low to set, and where to set. Developing this skill requires practice opportunities. Numerous offensive options are not necessary.

Some skilled and successful teams use few options but train at them well. A team can win with a high outside left attack, a quick middle attack, and a high right attack. When the setter has this series of simple options, the opposing middle blocker must wait in the middle for a time to guard against the quick attack there before she or he can advance to block the outside hitter.

Now the setter starts studying the position of blockers before the set to read whether the blockers are staying or going outside. It becomes a mysterious battle of the minds even at a young age. Choosing which player to set is fairly simple. The best-scoring hitter should normally get more swings than a lesser hitter. A strong setter chooses to win, not to make friends by sharing the ball equally.

Set Options

International teams, professional teams, many collegiate teams, and other high-level teams run many offensive options on sets and locations to hit those sets along the net. It is not important to hit in nine zones or to run a particular offense designed by a high-profile coach. This is the coach's opportunity to create. Build a simple offense with three zones or more advanced with more zones. It is important to run enough offense to challenge a team and to have a fair chance of defeating the opponents on the schedule.

I have colleagues at the collegiate level who run simple offenses successfully, and I know others whose players are bored and uninspired because the offense they run offers no physical or mental challenge. Give the team room to grow. A perfect balance of difficulty and repetition of success is hard to achieve, but finding that balance is one of the reasons we coach. Try to design your own brand of offensive game. Create sets that you see as successful within the program you are coaching.

Figure 15.2 shows all set options used in our 7-zone offense. The setter is positioned in zone 5. Note that zone 3 offers three different options, affording us the opportunity to run two attackers into this zone at the same time. The left side might hit a 33 while the middle hit a 31 on the inside of the zone.

Figure 15.2 Seven-zone offense set options.

Many repetitions of this specific positioning made our middle attack very difficult to read and stop.

Note that the setter goes to zone 5 to set. Zone 1 is typically high outside to the left zone. The setter can also shoot a quicker ball to the outside for the left hitter. This zone is the strong hitting zone for a typical right-handed hitter, so a high outside set to zone 1 is the most common and the first one that a setter should master. Use the net and antennae as guidelines about where to put the ball. In a high outside set, imagine a square 12 inches on a side that sits 12 inches off the antenna and 12 inches off the net. Hold a box or a ball basket there and show the setter where this imaginary box will be during the setting. I like this visual for setters. During drills, a setter can visualize the box. A good key phrase to use is "see the ball." On a high outside set, a hitter would wait to *see* where the set goes before taking the approach.

The setter might then develop a set in the 3 zone. Try a 3-zone set and a 3-foot-high ball lofted over zone 4. This is a 33. A left-side hitter, a middle hitter moving to the left, or even a right-side hitter coming from behind the setter and moving around the middle hitter could hit the ball. A high set behind the antenna that falls into a box in the 7 zone is a 75—zone 7 and a 5-foot set.

Developing an offense offers the imaginative and daring coach endless opportunity to be creative. Options abound for the advanced offense. The key to all offense is constant communication from the coach to the setter and from the setter to the team. The setter must master individual sets before adding these combinations. Prior to receiving service, it is most common for players to look to their setter for a verbal call and/or visual signal so hitters know the planned sets. During general transition play, hitters typically call out their desired sets. Since play can be fast paced, repetition is necessary for mastery.

Setting Drills

OFFENSE VERSUS DEFENSE

Three hitters and a setter on each side of the net. Drill should also be run with two hitters and setter in the front row when a 5-1 offense is used. Offers competition, scoring system, transition work, and many repetitions of sets.

One tosser on each side of the net. Side A tosses to setter. Hitters call their own attacks to setter. Team B hitters block while setter plays back row defense. (Coach may add other back row players as drill progresses.) Rally scoring to 5. Play until the ball is dead. The team winning the point gets the following toss, thus remaining on offense.

When one team reaches 5, coach makes necessary subs and play resumes. Improves setter transition and offers numerous set repetitions. Coach can instruct to work on specific attacks.

6 ON 6 VARIATIONS

Offer wash drills (rally scoring but team must score two in a row to get one point) but make it double points if the setter scores with a dump or a block. This puts additional pressure on the setter to play the full game with individual offense and defense. Coach can vary how double points are scored. The key is to work on only one double point skill at a time. Don't overload.

Final Thoughts on Setting

The personality and style of setters vary greatly, creating exciting and different offenses everywhere. We cannot change a boisterous, outgoing setter or a shy, introverted one. It took me a while to learn that good setters come with unique characteristics. The key is that they are competitive. They can learn to communicate. They must be able to run the offense, call the plays, and direct traffic on the court. These skills are absolute requirements. Success may come easier to a rah-rah setter, but a quiet, thinking setter can be successful too. Yes, the mild, thoughtful setter must call the plays. I've told more than a few setters over the years that it's OK to be quiet, but if she doesn't give the necessary information to the right people, her butt is on the bench. That's the given. She *will* run the offense.

This is a chapter on setting—not a book. What this short section should indicate to a coach is that the mind and emotions are as important as technique and tactics. Train the person, and a winning setter will evolve.

CHAPTER SIXTEEN

Attacking

Paula Weishoff

The attack, or spike, is the primary offensive weapon in volleyball. Teams use the attack to score points off serve receive and transition. At all levels the spike is considered the most fun and dynamic skill. Every player, coach, and spectator will tell you that the spike is what makes the game of volleyball so exciting. It is well known in volleyball that attack success correlates to winning games, especially with the new 25-point rally scoring system (international) or 30-point rally scoring system (women's college).

The attack breaks down into six basic movements: the approach (number of steps to the ball), plant or step close (positioning of the feet for the jump), jump (positioning of the body in the air), arm swing (bow and arrow, straight arm, circular swing, and roundhouse swing), contact and follow-through (hand position on the ball), and landing.

Approach

A good approach is essential for attaining the highest possible vertical jump and attacking the ball effectively at the highest possible point. The most common mistake for the hitter to make is running under the ball and thus not lining the ball up on their hitting arm. A good approach allows the hitter to hit in all directions and see the opponent's blockers and defensive players.

Individual preference or the distance the spiker needs to travel determines the number of steps to take in the approach. Remember that a quick-tempo attacker may use only a one-step approach, whereas a slow-tempo attacker will usually use a two- or three-step approach.

The three-step approach that I refer to is probably known as the four-step approach by many in the volleyball community. I like to call it a three-step approach because it comprises two steps and a hop, which is a quick, almost simultaneous step close with the last two steps. Ideally, the spiker performs the step close in one tempo, not two. Thus I consider it one step. Whatever you call it, the three-step approach for a right-hander is right-left-right-left (figure 16.1) and for a left-hander is left-right-left-right (figure 16.2).

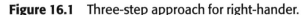

Figure 16.1 Three-step approach for right-hander.

Figure 16.2 Three-step approach for left-hander.

c

d

The first step shifts the body weight forward and allows the spiker to be in a balanced, ready position to go into the second step. The attacker uses the quicker, longer second step to adjust to the speed, height, and trajectory of the set. The third step of the approach (step close), the most critical one, should place the spiker about one foot from the ball with the hitting arm lined up behind the ball.

Plant or Step Close (Hop)

The third step in the approach, commonly referred to as the plant, hop, or step close, is where the attacker transfers forward velocity and momentum into vertical velocity. This step should be longer and quicker than the second step and should be an almost simultaneous touch with the right and left foot. For right-handers, the right foot explodes forward and touches at about a 45-degree angle to the net, first with the heel and then rolling forward onto the toe. The left foot swings quickly around to catch up with the right foot and pushes off on the toe close to perpendicular to the net (figure 16.3). For left-handers, the footwork is reversed so the left foot explodes forward and touches at about a 45-degree angle to the net, first with the heel and then rolling forward onto the toe. The right foot swings quickly around to catch up with the left foot and touches on the toe close to perpendicular to the net (figure 16.4).

- The tempo of the heel-toe-toe or sequence of step-close should be close to one count.
- The position of the hitter's feet in the step close should be slightly wider than shoulder-width.
- The lead leg plants at a 45-degree angle to the net, allowing the spiker to open the hips or body position in relationship to the setter. This positioning gives the spiker the ability to keep an eye on the ball being set, hit more angles of the court, and see the blockers and defenders.
- In the step close the front leg plants close to parallel to the net to stop the spiker from broad jumping into the net and to transfer momentum vertically.

For both right- and left-handers, when the lead leg explodes forward, the arms should extend backward (the arms will be straighter for an outside hitter than for a middle attacker). As the back leg swings around and makes contact with the floor, the arms swing and drive forward, continuing up over the spiker's head as the player leaves the ground.

Approach patterns vary depending on whether the hitter is right- or left-handed, the hitter's quickness and speed, the location of the pass, and the tempo of the offense. Spikers hitting a second-tempo or third-tempo attack

Figure 16.3 Step close for right-hander.

Figure 16.4 Step close for left-hander.

will see the ball set and then make their approach pattern, whereas a first-tempo attacker will be in the air before the ball is set or just as the setter is contacting the ball. Figure 16.5 illustrates the timing for the quick attacker.

a

b

Figure 16.5 Quick attack two step.

c

d

Normally, a right-handed spiker will make a wider approach when attacking a high outside ball from position 4 and a more straight-in approach when attacking a high back set from position 2. Normally, a left-handed spiker will make a more straight-in approach when attacking a high outside ball from position 4 and a wider approach when attacking a high back set from position 2. Figure 16.6 shows the court numbering system, and figures 16.7–16.10 show some of the possibilities for approach patterns.

4	3	2
5	6	1

Figure 16.6   Court numbering system.

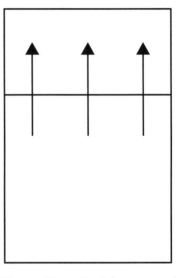

Figure 16.7   Straight approach.

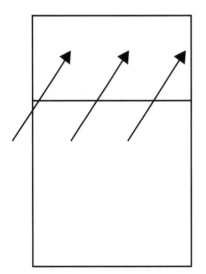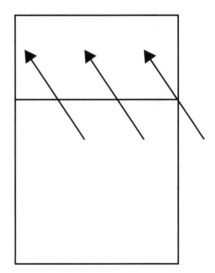

Figure 16.8a and b   Angle approach.

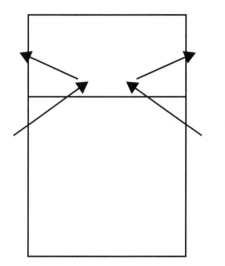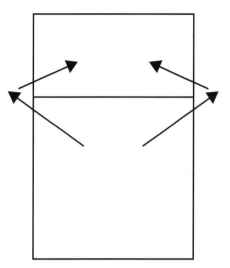

Figure 16.9a and b Fake approach.

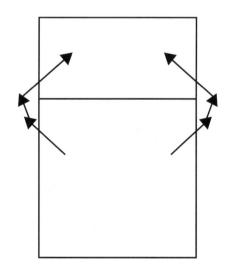

Figure 16.10 Loop approach.

Jump

The jump should start as soon as the back leg swings around, touches the floor, and the arms start their forward movement. The spiker should be in a coiled sitting position with the weight to the rear (the more bend in the legs, the higher the jump). From this position the attacker starts to uncoil the body by pushing up, starting with the ankles and legs and then thrusting the hips forward and extending the trunk upward. At this point a right-handed player will have the left shoulder closer to the net, and a left-handed player will have the right shoulder closer to the net. After takeoff the arms should come up over the head and quickly move into spiking position. Where spikers should jump depends on how far they broad jump. Ideally, front-row spikers will jump more vertically, whereas back-row attackers will jump more horizontally.

Arm Swing

The arm swing should allow the spiker to contact the ball at the highest possible point and generate maximum power. In my career as a volleyball player and coach, I have seen a variety of arm swings. Although some are not biomechanically perfect, all have been successful for elite athletes. What may work for one athlete may not work for another, and what causes pain in some athletes may not cause pain in others. I will give a few examples; the rest is up to you.

- Bow and arrow. As the spiker swings both arms up and starts to elevate, the nonhitting arm continues up while the elbow of the hitting arm bends and draws back. This motion simulates shooting an arrow. The elbow comes to about ear height, and the hand elevates slightly above the head, horizontal to the floor (at about a 90-degree angle). The hand of the spiker continues back farther, the elbow comes through, and the arm extends upward to contact the ball. This motion is similar to the motion of throwing a baseball. To initiate the arm swing the spiker rotates the trunk of the body forward, followed by the shoulder and forearm. As the spiker starts to swing up to the ball, the nonhitting arm swings down to counterbalance the movement of the hitting arm. The bow-and-arrow arm swing is fundamentally sound but can cause shoulder pain because the arm must come to a short stop before the spiker swings up to attack the ball (this action can jar the shoulder a bit).

- Circular arm swing. The circular arm swing is similar to the bow-and-arrow arm swing, but the elbow of the hitting arm, instead of drawing back to the ear, drives down beside the body, continuing in a circular motion until the elbow reaches the ear and the spiker extends upward to contact the ball. The circular arm swing seems to place less stress on the spiker than the bow-and-arrow arm swing because the arm does not have to come to a short stop before swinging up to the ball. The swing is a continuous movement from start to finish. The circular arm swing could cause problems if the spiker does not get the arm up high enough to contact the ball at the highest point possible.

• Straight arm swing. The spiker swings both arms up and, instead of bending the hitting arm back as in the bow-and-arrow technique, swings and contacts the ball with a straight arm. This type of arm swing puts a lot of stress on the shoulder, considerably reduces the range of attack, and is easier to block (blockers need only to line up on the hitter's arm).

• Roundhouse swing. The roundhouse is an interesting type of arm swing. I do not recommend that players use this arm swing regularly, but I do recommend teaching it to your players for use in emergencies and for occasional use to throw off the timing of the blocking and the defense. (Of course, a good tip or roll shot would have the same effect). The hitting arm swings straight down toward the floor. As the hand swings past the body, the palm turns out and up toward the ceiling, continuing in a circular motion until the ball is contacted. In an emergency the spiker usually contacts the ball behind the head, but the spiker can contact the ball at any point to throw off the timing of the block or defense.

Contact and Follow-Through

The spiker makes contact in front of the body over the hitting shoulder at maximum extension. Before contact the spiker rotates the trunk forward. The shoulder and forearm follow. The heel of the hand makes first contact (usually toward the top of the ball to direct it downward). While the wrist snaps forward, the fingers wrap around the ball for control and direction (the hand can be slightly cupped). The spiker's arm continues forward, following through in the direction of the spike and finally stopping near the side of the body. Spikers need to learn where to contact the ball to hit in the intended direction. Volleyball is about angles, angles, and angles. Spikers should be able to hit any set to any part of the court. To learn where the hand needs to contact the ball to hit a particular target, spikers can work on hitting different spots on the opposing court. Towels can serve as targets.

Landing

It is critical for the spiker to make the landing as softly as possible. The greater the bend of the knees on landing, the more shock they will absorb.

The spiker should land with their weight distributed evenly on both feet and flex the knees to absorb impact. Landing on both feet is important. Occasionally, spikers will find themselves in awkward or off-balance positions, so they should know the proper technique for landing in those types of situations. In a controlled environment, tossing balls behind the hitter's head, over the nonhitting arm, and outside the body will help players kinesthetically feel what they need to do with their bodies to land properly.

Back-Row Attack

The back-row attack has become popular in both the men's and women's game. Instead of having only two or three attackers, the back-row attack allows teams to have three to four attackers at all times. The approach for the back-row attack is similar to the approach for a front-court attack. The only difference is that the back-row attacker will usually broad jump more than the attacker will on a front-court attack. Although the back-row spiker must take off behind the 10-foot line, he or she can land inside the 10-foot line and therefore contact the ball closer to the net than 10 feet. The farther the set is in front of the 10-foot line, the greater the pressure on the opponent's blockers. The back-row spiker can hit the ball quicker and has more shots available to hit.

Setter Attack and Dump

When the setter is in the front court, he or she is a viable attack option. Coaches occasionally yell out in the middle of the game that the setter is live or front row. By passing the ball close to the net where the setter is, front-row setters can be a threat every time he or she touches the ball. This puts more pressure on the other teams and increases attack possibilities, especially if a back-court attack is part of the mix. A left-handed setter can be effective by spiking the ball, but most right-handed setters learn to dump the ball with the left hand, which can be just as effective as a spike. The setter should approach the ball with the intent of setting the ball. After seeing that the blocker has released or committed with an attacker, the setter knows that the attack or dump is available.

One-Leg Takeoff or Slide

The one-leg takeoff, or slide, is different from a two-legged approach because the spiker does not get the feet to the ball but instead floats sideways to attack it. The one-leg takeoff is effective because the spiker takes off and broad jumps to the ball (parallel to the net) with the ability to attack the ball at any point along the path of the set. The advantage of the one-leg takeoff is that the attacker can use it to hit at different speeds and heights, thus confusing the opponent's blockers and defenders. Quicker middles can hit a fast-tempo set, and slower middles can hit a slow-tempo set. Both types of spikers can hit with high efficiency. Right-side spikers can be back in a three-person serve-receive formation and still hit from the one-leg takeoff as a second-tempo option. A right-handed spiker makes the motion from left to right, and the footwork is left-right-left. As the spiker plants the left foot the right leg and hip along with both arms drive up, allowing the spiker to broad jump along the net (figure 16.11). A left-handed spiker makes the motion from right to left, and the footwork is right-left-right. As the spiker plants the right foot, the left leg, hip, and both arms drive up (figure 16.12). For both right-handers and left-handers the movement is similar to that of a high jumper or a basketball player shooting a layup. The tempo of whether the spiker is past the setter, even with the setter on contact, or chasing the set after setter contact depends on the speed and height of the set. The most important thing to learn about hitting the slide is that no matter where takeoff occurs or how far the attacker broad jumps, contact with the ball must occur when it is aligned with the hitting arm so that the attacker can hit both line and angle. Attackers too often jump past the ball and thus limit their shot selection to angle. Or they do not broad jump far enough, which means they never quite catch up to the ball and are thus obligated to hit line. By being creative with the one-leg takeoff, the attacker can hit anywhere along the net and incorporate it into attack combinations or use it on its own.

Other Attack Options

Another attack option is a pump. The objective of the pump is to get the blocker to jump so that the hitter can hit the ball when the blocker is coming down. The spiker approaches for a first-tempo attack, makes the movements for a normal approach, but does not jump. The attacker must sell the body language of a normal approach, especially the arm movement used in takeoff. Instead of jumping, the attacker pauses, counts to one and then pumps the arms to take off and attack the ball. The pump should throw off the vertical timing of the block and keep the defense off balance. The pump is effective when the opposing team is committing on the quick hitters or during transition when the blockers may not have time to notice the approach patterns of the attackers. Fakes, fades, or trick plays are other options. The objective of these options is to get the blocker to think that the attacker is hitting or jumping in one place when the hit and jump is occurring in another zone along the net. Teams use these trick options to beat the blocker laterally along the net. Quick hitters use trick plays and fades. Fakes are used for second-tempo attack combinations.

Figure 16.11 One-leg attack for right-hander.

c

d

e

Figure 16.12 One-leg attack for left-hander.

d

e

The trick play is run like a pump. The first-tempo attacker makes the movements for a normal approach but does not jump. The attacker then steps to the right or left to attack the ball. The footwork for a right-hander is the same as that used for a normal approach except that immediately after the back foot (left) comes around to plant, the attacker pushes off with that same foot (left), does another right-left step close, and jumps off both feet (figure 16.13). The footwork for a left-hander is just the opposite. Immediately after the back foot (right) comes around to plant, the attacker pushes off with that same foot (right), does another left-right step close, and jumps off both feet. Another option would be to hit the trick play off one leg instead of both legs. To do this, the attacker makes the same approach and finishes with the last two steps of a one-leg takeoff (figure 16.14).

The trick play has many variations. A popular trick play is for the quick attacker to make an approach to hit a quick 3 about 3 feet from tge setter and then step out to hit a 1 set (quick front of setter). Other trick plays include making an approach for a 1 with the attacker stepping out to hit a quick right behind the setter (this can be hit off both legs or one leg) or attacking a quick right and then stepping out to hit a one leg slide. Teams can use the trick play anywhere along the net, run it from left to right or from right to left, use it

a

b

c

Figure 16.13 Trick play with two-foot takeoff.

Figure 16.14 Trick play with one-leg takeoff.

with both right-handed and left-handed attackers, and use it to attack from locations other than in front of the setter. Trick plays can be deceptive and useful attacking tools in keeping the opponent's blocking and defense off balance.

The object of the fade, like the trick play, is to beat the blocker laterally along the net. The fade is a little different from the trick play in that the quick attacker broad jumps from one attack zone to another without juking or pumping, flying past the opposing blocker. A good time to use the fade is when the quick hitter or middle blocker in serve receive in area 2 and comes around to hit a 1 in front of the setter. Instead of hitting a 1 close to the setter, the quick attacker broad jumps from where the 1 would be set and hits the ball about two feet from the setter, hopefully hitting past the opposing middle blocker.

The outside and right-side attacker use fakes to beat the opposing blockers by changing their approach patterns in the last two steps of the approach. Fakes are usually used in second-tempo attack combinations. If the attackers are running a left-side combination and the quick attacker is hitting a quick 3, the combination attacker would come in behind the quick attacker. As the pass is in its downward flight to the setter, the attacker would change direction to hit a second-tempo set one zone to the left or right of the quick hitter. (The combination attacker waits for the downward flight of the ball to the setter to change the direction of the approach pattern because at that time the opposing blockers should be taking their eyes off the attackers to focus on the setter, momentarily losing sight of the attackers' approach patterns.) If the attackers are running a middle combination and the middle is hitting a front 1 or a back 1, the combination attacker would come in behind the quick attacker and hit a second tempo set two feet in front or behind the setter.

Shots

To be effective, an attacker needs not only be able to hit the ball hard but also to have a variety of shots available. The more shots an attacker has, the harder it will be for the opponent to predict where the attacker will hit the ball, and the more success the attacker will have.

• Sharp angle hit. The attacker hits the sharp angle by dipping the shoulder nearer to the net. The left-side attacker contacts the left side of the ball using the wrist and forearm to cut the ball inside the block, following through with the thumb pointing downward (reverse for right). The ball should land between the two front-court and back-court defenders or in front of the 10-foot line.

• Line hit. The attacker should make the normal approach and turn in the air to attack down the line. Attackers should always make the same approach so that the opponents cannot anticipate the shot. On seeing that the line is open, the attacker should rotate the hips toward the line and contact the ball before it crosses the midline of the body, aiming about two feet from the corner of the court.

- Deep corners hit. Attacking the deep corners of the court instead of hitting straight down keeps the defense guessing. The defense cannot be everywhere, and most defensive systems leave the corners open. The logic is that the block should take away this part of the court and if an attacker hits over the block into the corner, the defense should have enough time to run the ball down. But it is amazing how often the attack to the deep corner scores.

- Roll, or off-speed shot. To hit the roll, or off-speed, shot the attacker should contact the ball toward the bottom of the ball with the heel of the open hand. At contact, the attacker rolls the fingers over the top of the ball and finishes by snapping the wrist, which creates backspin on the ball. The most common mistake attackers make when they hit an off-speed shot is decelerating into the approach, giving the defense an indication that they are not attacking the ball.

- Tip, dump, dink. The tip is executed by opening the hand and contacting the ball with the pads of the fingers. The attacker makes contact toward the bottom of the ball and follows through with the hand in the direction of the tip, softly lobbing the ball over the block into an open space in the opponent's defense. Another option on the tip is to contact the ball at a higher point and quickly shove the ball down into the opponent's court. This option is especially effective if the block is late or there is a hole in the block and the ball is set tight to the net.

- Tool, or wipe off. Tooling, or wiping off, the block is frustrating for the block, and every attacker should know how to perform this attack. Attackers are often afraid of the block and try to avoid it altogether. Instead, attackers should feel comfortable going after the block. The attacker makes contact on the side of the ball opposite where he or she wants to hit the ball. The attacker hits partially into the block and then follows through out of bounds. A left-side attacker hitting from position 4 would contact the right side of the ball and follow through to the left of the body. The same would apply for an attacker hitting from position 2. The attacker would contact the left side of the ball and follow through to the right of the body.

- High and flat. The high, flat hit is a good option when the set is not in the perfect spot (off the net, inside, or wide), or when the attacker wants to push the defense back. Contact should be in the center of the ball, and the attacker should swing hard, high, and flat (aiming for the back wall), sending the ball off the block and past the defensive players.

- Seam, or hole, in the block. The seam shot is always a smart shot for attackers, especially if they are not sure what to do with the ball. Hitting the seam in the block can cause a lot of stress for the opponent, especially if the block is not well formed. Deflections can rebound off the blockers and catch the defense off guard. By attacking the seam the attacker may take advantage of a hole in the block or occasionally get a tool off the block.

- Rebound, or replay, off the block. When the attacker is trapped and cannot hit around, over, off, or through the block, the replay off the block is a smart option. The attacker should tap the ball into the opposing blockers and play the ball as it rebounds off the blockers' hands.

Set Nomenclature

The set nomenclature, the numbering system that you to use to name your set options, is based on individual preference. All coaches have a system based on what they have learned and what works for them. Diagramed in figure 16.15 are two popular systems. The first system is numbered in the circles with the sets in front of the setter using numbers and the sets behind the setter using letters (1–5 and A–D system). The second system is numbered in the boxes and uses numbers from 1 through 9 (1–9 system). The back-row attack is labeled with colors. For both systems the numbering system for first-, second-, and third-tempos sets is simple.

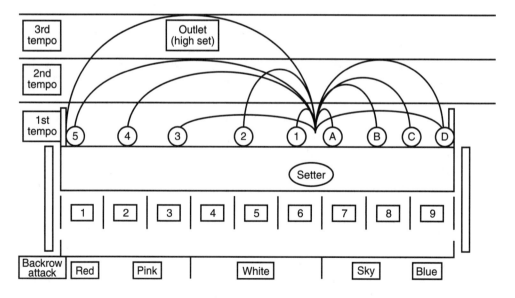

Figure 16.15 Set nomenclature.

Using the 1–5 and A–D system, the first-tempo sets would be labeled by adding a 1 to the number or letter. For example, a first-tempo quick in zone 1 would be an 11, and a first tempo in zone A would be an A1. The second-tempo sets would be labeled by adding a 2 to the number or letter. For example, a second tempo in zone 2 would be a 22, and a second tempo in zone B would be a B2. The third-tempo sets would be labeled by adding a 3 to the number or letter. For example, a third-tempo set in zone 5 would be a 53, and a third tempo set in zone D would be a D3. This pattern would apply to all zones across the length of the net.

Attack Patterns

Running attack patterns and combinations is an enjoyable and complex part of building an offensive system. Remember that the more complex the attack patterns, the more important it is to pass consistently to target. Work on patterns for all six rotations and have between three and five options or plays in each rotation. Here are some ideas to play around with (figures 16.16-16.20). Be creative and keep in mind the abilities and limitations of your players when developing your offensive system.

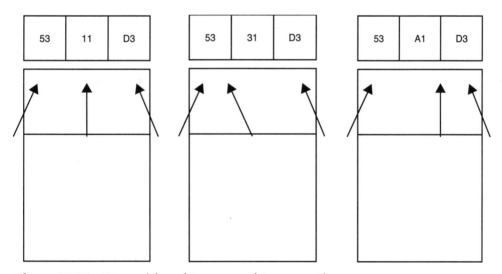

Figure 16.16   One quick and two second-tempo options.

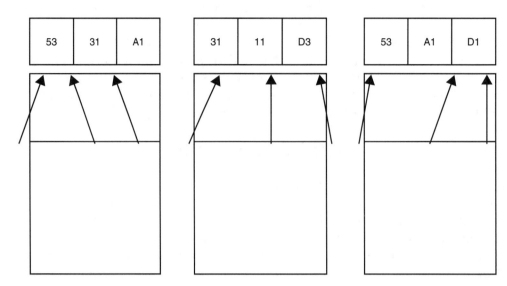

Figure 16.17 Quick and one outlet.

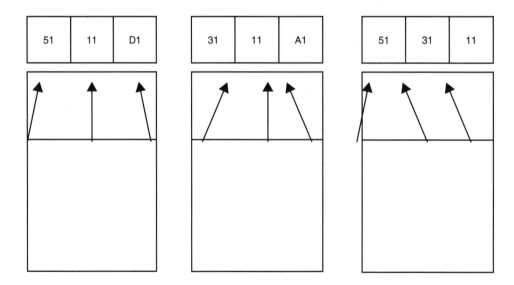

Figure 16.18 Triple quick options.

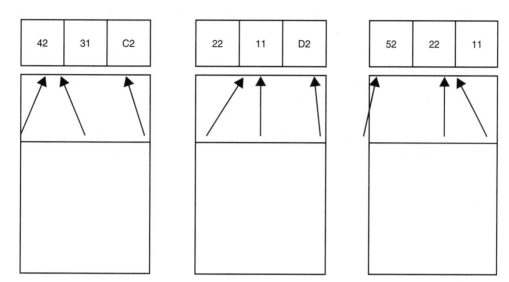

Figure 16.19   Combinations–tandem plays.

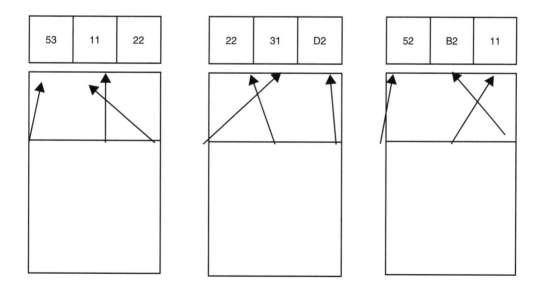

Figure 16.20   Crossing patterns.

Conclusion

For spectators, coaches, and players alike, the attack is the most exciting and dynamic skill in volleyball. When an elite athlete performs the approaches, attack patterns, and various shots mentioned in this chapter, the skills appear easy to perform. All players, regardless of age or level of experience, can learn these skills. The more that players practice and play, the easier it becomes for them to perform the approaches, attack patterns, and various shots. By playing hard, being disciplined in practice, being open minded and creative, and remembering to have fun, the player can achieve whatever goals and aspirations he or she has in volleyball.

CHAPTER SEVENTEEN

Digging and Ball Control

Jim Stone

The primary purpose of floor defense is to play the attack of the opponent in the backcourt, redirect the ball to a setter, and counterattack with a spike. The first line of defense is the block. The second line of defense involves the defenders behind the block. For the purpose of this book, the second line of defense will be referred to as floor defense. These two lines of defense are deeply interrelated. For younger ages, floor defense is a primary factor in team success. Because blockers are smaller and less physical and attackers hit the ball at slower speed, defenders can successfully pursue and play the ball in the backcourt. In higher levels of play, however, attackers hit the ball extremely hard, and the ability of the blockers largely determines the success of the backcourt defenders. To defend a hard attack, the blockers must take away a portion of the court from the attacker, forcing the attacker to place the ball toward the backcourt defenders.

At all levels of play, when playing rally score, most points are determined in the following ways:

- Service aces
- Attack from serve reception
- Stuff blocking
- Transition (defending an opponent's attack and scoring with a counterattack)

The potential of a team to score large numbers of points with transition play is significant. Coaches must therefore spend many hours developing this aspect of team play. The performance of a team on defense reflects its fighting spirit, pride, and desire to win. A good defensive team will always be difficult to beat because its characteristics—competitiveness, good talent, good skills, mental and physical toughness, and focus on winning every point—are the same as those of teams that are generally successful. A great defensive play may inspire a team more than a great attack does. Opposing attackers often find it difficult to cope mentally with repeated failure to put the ball away.

Developing individual defensive skills and ball control is a time-consuming part of the practice routine. Repetition of these defensive skills is the only way that players learn to play defense and develop the ball control necessary for a successful counterattack. Don't underestimate the importance of the counterattack. Successful teams not only defend the attack in the backcourt but also successfully set the dig to an attacker who scores on the counterattack. There are no shortcuts in developing ball control. Teams must spend many hours to develop this aspect of the game.

This section will focus on two parts of defense. First, we focus on the concepts of individual defensive skills and techniques. Then we focus on controlling the ball and being able to dig the attack into an area that will lead to a successful set and counterattack. These parts are certainly interrelated, and we present them in that manner.

Basic Concepts of Floor Defense

One half of a volleyball court contains approximately 870 square feet. With six defenders, every player must successfully defend about 145 square feet. This calculation points out the importance of the following:

- Six defenders must operate within a team system to cover the court.
- Individual defenders must be able to move quickly to play the ball that is not hit directly toward them.
- Individual defenders must be able to play the ball from a variety of postures and court positions.
- Defenders must be able to play hard-driven or softly attacked balls.
- Blockers and defenders must work together to cover the court.

Coaches and players should not consider defense a passive event in which defenders wait for the ball to come to them. Good defenders develop the ability to "attack" the ball. They aggressively pursue any ball that the spiker attacks. For the purposes of this section, I will focus on the perimeter defensive system. Within this system, the defenders assume positions toward the perimeter of the court, facing the attacker, with most of the court in front of them (see figure 17.1). This system places little emphasis on playing balls hit behind a player. Instead, it emphasizes forward and lateral movement.

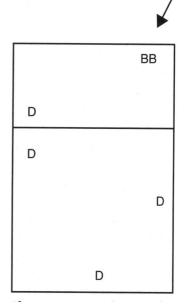

Figure 17.1   Perimeter defense system.

Ingredients of Successful Defenders

To excel at the refined aspects of defense, defenders should possess several attributes:

- Leg strength. To defend attacks successfully, the defensive player must be able to play attacks that are sometimes falling low to the floor or outside the defender's feet. In both cases, the defender must be able to bend the

knees and drop the hips lower than the ball. In addition, the defender must have the ability to lunge to an attacked ball, driving the hips behind the attack to facilitate ball control. See figure 17.2.

• Excellent hand-eye coordination. The defender must place the forearms behind and under the fast-moving ball with consistency.

• Flexibility. The defender must be able to play the ball from a variety of postures.

• Fighting spirit. The defender must never give up on the attacked ball and must be willing to sacrifice his or her body to keep the ball off the floor. The defender approaches this skill as a one-on-one game versus the attacker by thinking, "Nothing the attacker hits will beat me."

Figure 17.2 Using leg strength to attack the ball.

• Ability to manipulate the passing platform. The defender must be able to angle the passing surface to rebound the ball to the desired target area.

Training the Defensive Player

Retrieving the hard-hit ball is a reflex action. Little conscious thought takes place in the defensive action. To achieve this reflex action, the coach must train the motor skills of the player to respond successfully to attacks that are hit hard or soft, high or low, directly at the player or a distance away from the player. In drills the coach controls the pace of the attack and the distance from the player. At the beginning the coach attacks the ball at a medium pace and places the ball fairly close to the player. As players develop their skills, the coach can attack the ball harder and place it at increased distances.

Many teams limit the defensive training of their players to playing pepper. Although this drill is a good warm-up, it will not produce the variety of shots that defenders will face. Another problem with playing pepper is that the ball always comes from the same point and players always direct it back to the same point. In a game the ball comes from a variety of angles, and players must direct it back to the target areas. The coach must develop the ability of the defender to play attacks from the variety of angles and speeds that will occur in competition. In collegiate women's competition, the ball goes from the hand of the attacker to the defender in 0.3 seconds or less. Defensive training must prepare players for attacks of that speed.

When training defensive skills, the coach must provide a balance by offering players successful contacts while pushing them to their maximum ability and challenging them to play balls hit away from them.

Defense Before Ball Is Attacked

The defensive player has limited time to react to attacks after the ball is struck. Good defensive players prepare themselves before the ball is attacked. They accomplish this by establishing a good initial court position, or base position, and by establishing a positive body posture or defensive stance as the attacker contacts the ball.

Base Position

Base position is the position defenders take before the opposing setter contacts the ball. Many factors influence base position. Is a front row setter capable of attacking? Will the opponent set a quick set (1 or 31)? Do the opposing hitters have specific attack tendencies? Does the opposing setter use a pattern of set distribution? With all these variables, base position is not a specific point on the court but a general area of the court. The defender should guard first against the quick attack and then respond to the higher set.

Adjusted Defensive Position

Defenders place themselves around the block when the opponent is attacking the ball. They assume that the block will direct the attack to areas of the court where they place themselves, outside the block and on the perimeter. Defenders take positions based on the offensive patterns of the opponent and the speed and location of the set.

Body Posture and Foot Movement

Volleyball players use multiple postures. For example, players use a high posture for serving and blocking, a medium posture for setting and serve receive, and a low posture for performing defense (figure 17.3). But the defender must be aware it is physically impossible to play a long match with long rallies in a constant low posture. This posture will fatigue the legs and inhibit court movement. The defender must establish base position and

Figure 17.3   Low defensive posture.

defensive court position in a medium posture. Only as the attacker contacts the ball does the defender assume a lower defensive posture.

In training defensive skills, the coach must emphasize efficiency in moving the feet to the attacked ball. Two points are important in this area. First, it is always easier for defenders to move their feet if they are in constant motion. Defensive players should avoid having their feet stationary. The preferred method of moving on the volleyball court is to shuffle step to the ball, a movement that keeps the shoulders and hips facing the middle of the court, the target area.

Defense is a forward-moving skill. Defenders must attack the ball, regardless of the speed of the attack. They must avoid waiting for the ball to come to them. Reaching sideways or behind the feet is ill advised. They should make every attempt to play the attack with both arms and with the body and shoulders behind the ball, although this is not always possible, especially on hard-driven balls landing outside the feet. Defenders must be comfortable playing the ball while moving their feet. They must also be proficient at extending their platform laterally and turning the ball back to the target.

Areas of Court Coverage

The defender is responsible for three areas of court coverage. Balls that land at close distance, medium distance, and long distance from the defender present different challenges and require different techniques by the defender (see figure 17.4).

Initial training of the defensive player should focus on balls hit close to the player. This preparation will allow the player to gain confidence and develop ball-control skills. If the block is successful in channeling attacks to the defensive players, balls hit close to the defenders should account for most of the attacks. Balls hit a medium distance from the defender will require a step and reach. Defenders should learn to step out or perform a shuffle step to the ball and avoid turning the hips or shoulders away from the target.

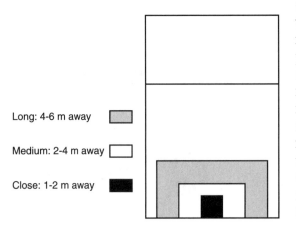

Long: 4-6 m away

Medium: 2-4 m away

Close: 1-2 m away

Figure 17.4 Areas of court coverage.

Types of Digs

Players should master a variety of digs to deal with the various attacks that are hit toward them.

Two-Hand Overhead Dig

• Hard-hit ball (figure 17.5). Recent rule changes allow players to play hard-hit attacks with open hands without double contact being called by the referee. This rule has dramatically changed the way defense is played, in both how defenders contact the ball and where they position themselves on the court when defending. Players must become comfortable with overhand passing a ball that comes to them above the height of the shoulders. They acquire this skill by first becoming comfortable with playing soft attacks with the hands similar to the technique they use to defend against the free ball. As players gain skill and confidence, the

Figure 17.5   Attacking a hard-hit ball.

speed of the attack should increase. Players must understand that overhand passing an attack is different from setting a ball to the hitter. Although the skills are similar, overhand passing requires the use of firmer fingers and wrists, allowing players to play a hard-hit attack without risking injury to the fingers. Players should focus on making the play with their shoulders behind the ball, using firm hand and wrist action to perform the pass (figure 17.6).

• Free ball. For balls passed or set over the net, players must learn to play these attacks with an overhand pass to the setter. The setter will release early to the setting position, and the remaining five defenders will cover the court equally to defend against this soft attack. Defenders should be able to direct these balls with great accuracy to the setting position to initiate the counterattack. Players must become skilled at playing these attacks, which may come over the net with a variety of spins or from different heights.

Figure 17.6 Making a play with shoulders behind the ball.

Figure 17.7 Keeping hips lower than the ball with forearms angled.

Two-Arm Dig

• High, above knee. This pass, used to retrieve balls coming at high or medium velocity from different angles, is similar to the technique used to receive a serve. The hips should be lower than the ball, and the forearms should be angled so that the ball will rebound toward the target area (figure 17.7). When the ball comes to the defender outside the bodyline, the defender must shuffle quickly to get the hips and shoulders behind the ball. Sometimes, the ball comes at a speed that makes this impossible. In this case, the player should reach forward and sideways and drop the shoulder that is nearer the target area to deflect the ball to target. Players must avoid reaching sideways or behind them to play the ball, a practice that will inhibit the accuracy of the dig.

• Low, below knee. To defend against the low attack, the player must focus on driving the hips and passing platform lower than the ball. At times, it will be necessary to drop to one or both knees to get below the trajectory of the ball. The player may also need to bend the elbow or wrist slightly to keep the passing platform parallel to the floor. This method will ensure that the ball comes up and stays on the defenders' half of the court. Much time and repetition are necessary for the player to become comfortable enough to execute this skill successfully. The coach must be able to run defensive drills that place the attacked ball below the knees of the defender, thereby forcing the defender into the low posture.

Sprawls

• Forward sprawl (figure 17.8 a and b). Players use the forward sprawl to play a ball hit in front of them and very close to the floor. The defender must observe fundamentals and still attempt to get the hips and passing platform lower than the ball. To accomplish this, the defender extends the platform under the ball and drives the body forward to the floor. When the ball comes to the defender below the knee, the defender must change the passing platform to keep the forearm passing surface parallel to the floor.

a

b

Figure 17.8   Forward sprawl.

To accomplish this, as the body extends forward to the ball, the defender bends the elbows and curls the wrists under the ball. If possible, the defender takes a step forward before contacting the ball. Should the defender not have time to take a step, he or she thrusts the arms forward and under the ball, extending the body to the floor. To prevent the hips from banging into the floor and causing injury, the defender should rotate the knee toward the body midline as the body goes to the floor.

- Side sprawl (figure 17.9). A technique used to play balls hit hard and low outside the feet is the side sprawl. This technique is similar to the forward sprawl. The primary goal of the defender is to drive the hips and passing platform underneath the ball. The player makes every effort to manipulate the passing platform and shoulders in the direction of the intended target. The player must become skilled at dropping the shoulder that is closer to the target area, thereby angling the passing platform so that the ball will rebound to the target area. The player must perform many repetitions with this type of platform manipulation to become accurate with the dig.

Figure 17.9 Side sprawl.

Extension Roll

- Close range (figure 17.10 a-c). The defender uses the extension roll to expand the area of coverage. Defenders should focus on playing the balls within one step and a reach. If court positioning is correct, most attacks will be in that range. Occasionally, however, defenders must expand their area of coverage to play balls tipped by the attacker or balls that deflect off the block. Defenders must pursue these balls with the same intensity they use in going after hard-hit balls. They must extend their arms to the ball and let their bodies go to the floor without fear of injury. Coaches should slowly expand the area of coverage for the defender. The principles of keeping the passing platform and hips lower than the ball still apply.

Figure 17.10 Close range extension roll.

Close-range balls are those that land at medium or slow speed three to four meters from the defender. Players should move their feet quickly to the ball and stay on their feet. In an effort to place the passing platform below the ball, however, the player must occasionally drop to the floor. The difference between the extension roll and the sprawl is minimal. The player extends the arms to the ball, lunges forward, drops the hips below the ball, turns the knee in to the midline, and rolls over the shoulder. With repetition, the player will become comfortable with the skill.

- Medium to far range. Attacks that land from four to six meters from the player require emergency plays. The defender runs quickly to the ball, extends the passing platform, drops the hips lower than the ball, plays the ball, and rolls. The coach should emphasize that the roll is a means of recovering balance after pursuing the ball, not a means of transportation. The player runs to the ball, makes the play, and then follows through with a roll.

Developing Ball Control

The first level of skill development is for players to improve their defensive technique so that they can prevent the ball from hitting the floor. As players become comfortable with defensive techniques, they should begin to focus on controlling the ball to ensure a quality counterattack. The coach must consistently emphasize the importance of playing the ball to the appropriate target area. This target area changes with the type of attack being defended. For a free ball or a down-ball attack, defenders should play the ball back to the net to allow the setter to set any of the attack options. When defending a hard-hit ball, players focus on a target area in the center of the court at the three-meter line. When the player is playing a ball off the court, or making a stab to play the ball, the target area is any place where a teammate can make the next contact. Only through consistent repetition will players react to the attack and determine the appropriate target area.

Several principles apply to acquiring the ball-control skills that lead to quality counterattacks.

- All defensive drills should be done with a target for the dig.
- With three-person pepper, players can work on digging balls to their left or to their right to a setter.
- Coaches can hit balls to a defender who works on digging the ball to the target area.
- Players should be comfortable playing the ball while moving their feet.
- The preferred method of movement when defending is to shuffle step to the ball. Defenders should avoid turning the hips away from the

center of the court or the target area. If a ball lands far from a defender, he or she should shuffle and then turn and run to the ball.

- Defenders should attempt to play the ball at the body midline. To accomplish this, players must move the hips and shoulders behind the ball when making the play.

- When playing a ball outside the body midline, players must become skilled at manipulating the forearm passing platform to angle the ball to the intended target. Players accomplish this by dropping the shoulder that is closer to the setter to angle the passing platform toward the target area. Players must attempt to keep their arms straight while reaching to the side.

- When making the defensive play, players should attempt to have their hips lower than the ball.

- Players must become adept at playing the ball with either the hands or the forearms.

In summary, the importance of repetition in acquiring ball-control skills for defensive play cannot be overemphasized. Coaches must be able to hit and toss balls to their players so that they can attain proficiency in the skills. Many coaches work only on team defense, not individual defensive skills. Although players practice team defense during competitive scrimmages or formal competition, they may not perform sufficient repetitions to acquire comfort and proficiency in the various defensive postures and angles that will confront them. Besides providing adequate repetition of individual defensive skills, the coach should establish an atmosphere in the team that takes pride in defensive effort. In every sport, defense wins championships. Players and teams become skilled at what they do the most. If a team is to become proficient in defensive skills, the coach must plan activities that focus on defense in the daily practice routine.

Blocking

Rudy Suwara

Blocking is the attempt by one, two, or three players to stop an attacked ball at the net and deflect it down into the attacker's court. Although the block can score points quickly, it is the most difficult volleyball skill to learn and master. All blocks are timed to the attack of the opponent. Touch blocks or controlled deflections into the player's own court can be converted to good passes and lead to an effective attack to score points. The block is the first line of defense in volleyball.

The player should stiffen the hands and arms just before contact to stop hard-hit balls. The thumbs should be about six inches apart so that the ball will not go through the hands. Blockers must keep their eyes open to see the hitters when they contact the ball. As blockers reach forward to block, they should see the backs of their hands as they penetrate across the net.

Balance

An important aspect of blocking is balance. The player should be about one-half arm's length from the net, with weight equally distributed on the balls of the feet. The feet should be pointed straight at the net or slightly to the outside. The blocker should stay balanced just before making the move to get in position in front of the attacking opponent. By maintaining balance while reading the setter, the blocker can react to the set and move quickly along the net. The blocker reading the setter must not lean one way

Figure 18.1 Maintain balance in the air while piking.

or the other or guess which direction the setter will set. The blocker should keep equal pressure on the balls of both feet until he or she sees the set and then starts the move to get in position to block the attack.

Maintaining balance in the air is an important skill that players can develop by practicing blocking and reaching over the net as far as possible while not touching it (figure 18.1). Players who have poor balance often touch the net while jumping to block. Players can improve their balance by learning some trampoline skills. Jumping on a trampoline and doing simple drops, rolls, and flips can help players become more skilled at body control in the air. The players can then practice piking in the air to simulate blocking over the net by moving the feet forward slightly while simultaneously extending the hands and arms forward.

Eyes

1. The blocker's eyes should watch the pass coming to the net in case an overpass can be attacked.

2. The blocker then looks at the ball in the setter's hands to see the direction where the ball is set and to judge the flight of the ball as soon as the setter releases it.

3. To time the block, the player watches the hitter's approach and jump.

4. The blocker then decides on the timing and gets over the net or seals it so that the ball will not go between the player and the net (figure 18.2). The best blockers make their decisions quickly, just before the hitter swings, about the best way to block the ball. The blocker must make the blocking move before a hitter with a fast arm attacks.

5. The blocker should strain to keep the eyes wide open as the ball is attacked. Keeping the eyes open will allow the blocker to achieve more blocks and follow the ball for the next possible contact.

Figure 18.2 Blocking with eyes open.

Preparing to Block

• The jump. The blocker must time the jump for the block to the attacker's approach and jump. The general rule is to jump to block a split second after the attacker takes off to spike. The blocker keeps the back straight and the head looking through the net at the attacker. The knees bend to 60 to 90 degrees, depending on the height of the blocker and the strength of the legs. The hands and arms shoot up close to the net as the blocker jumps off both legs. The player should shoot the hands and arms over the top of the net after clearing the top of the net. The longer the player can keep the hands and arms over the net, the better the chances of blocking the spiked ball. As the player reaches the top of the jump, the arms should be straight and stiff to stop hard-hit spikes. As the player descends to the floor, he or she should pull the arms and hands back across the net and land on both legs to be ready for the next contact.

• Landing. When landing, the blocker should be turning to follow the flight of the ball. He or she will then be able to react to a ball that is hit past the block and dug up in the air by another player. Drills can help the player learn to land and step away from the net with balance and speed. The player must have good body control to avoid netting and making foot faults across the centerline. Players should avoid making the common error of stepping over the centerline after landing as they turn to start their move away from the net. Some players practice landing on one leg so that they can turn more quickly to follow the flight of the ball. Although this can be an effective technique, it may contribute to knee and ankle injuries.

• Footwork skills. Practicing footwork drills along the net and centerline will help improve speed and balance in blocking. The easiest blocks to execute are those that do not require the blocker to move along the net. The blocker simply crouches and jumps right in front of the attacker.

All players should learn and practice the following skills, which use different steps to move quickly and efficiently along the net to block. Players can practice footwork drills along a wall with an outline of a net taped on it.

• Slide two steps. The slide step to the right is a step to the right with the right foot and then a closing step with the left foot. The player starts in a slight crouch with the hands above the head and the elbows at or slightly above the shoulders. The player moves quickly to the right and jumps to block. The same drill is done to the left from the starting position.

The slide-two-steps block jump is the easiest to learn. Blockers use it when they need to move only a few feet to get in front of the attacker. Outside blockers use this skill to move short distances to block sets to the outside attackers.

Crossovers

Blockers use crossover steps to move longer distances along the net to get in position to block. Crossover steps are faster than slide steps.

• Crossover two steps. Starting in a balanced position near the net, the player turns the hips in the direction of movement to make the block. Moving to the right, the player pivots on the right foot while crossing the left foot over in front of the body to take a large hop step to the right. The player lands on the left foot first, pivots on the left foot while turning the body back toward the net, and lands on the right foot.

The player then pushes off both feet to jump up and reach over the net. This technique allows the blocker to jump higher and move more quickly along the net. The crossover-two-steps move allows the blocker to travel long distances quickly. This technique is the best way for two blockers to move along the net together because they will avoid stepping on each other's feet.

• Approach jump two steps. This technique allows shorter blockers to get higher on blocks, but it takes skill to avoid netting. The player starts one or two steps away from the net. Timing the set is difficult, and the player approaching the net must have excellent timing with the center blocker coming to the outside to close and make a two-person block.

• Crossover three steps. Taller players usually need only three steps to get to the sideline from the middle of the court. Top players use two footwork patterns.

Technique One—Moving to the Right

The player starts in a balanced position with the weight equally distributed on both feet (figure 18.3). The player turns the hips to the right and steps with the right foot first. Next,

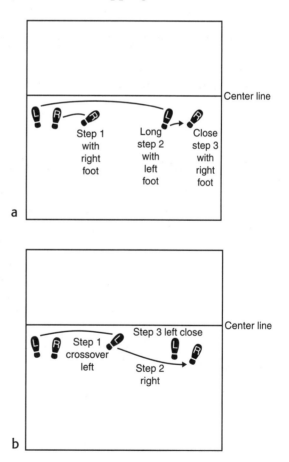

Figure 18.3   Crossover three steps.

the left foot crosses over in front of the player and makes a long step toward the sideline. The right foot closes next to the left foot as the player lands in a crouched position, turning the hips back to the net to jump. The right foot must be planted hard to stop the movement toward the sideline and to transfer the force of the approach into the vertical jump. This technique, which is similar to a spiking jump, allows the player to move quickly and jump high.

Technique Two—Moving to the Right

The player starts in a balanced position with the weight equally distributed on both feet.

The player begins the movement with the crossover step. The player turns the hips to the right and crosses the left foot over in front of the right. He or she plants the left foot and steps out with a long step with the right foot, quickly followed by the left foot. The left foot closes to the right foot with the player landing in a crouched position ready to jump. The player turns the hips back to the net while jumping and reaches over to block.

Technique Three—Moving to the Left

Blockers should practice the crossover steps to the left also, so they become able to move in both directions quickly and balanced.

• **Crossover four steps.** Shorter middle blockers may need this technique to get all the way out to the sideline on wide sets.

Technique Four—Moving to the Right

The player starts in a balanced position with the weight equally distributed on both feet (figure 18.4). The player turns the hips to the right and steps with the right foot first. Next, the left foot crosses over in front of the player and makes a long step toward the sideline. The right foot steps past the left and lands toward the sideline. The left foot closes to the right foot as the player lands in a crouched position and turns the hips back to the net to jump. The right foot must be planted hard to stop the movement toward the sideline and transfer the force of the approach into the vertical jump. This technique, which is similar to a spiking jump, allows the player to move quickly and jump high.

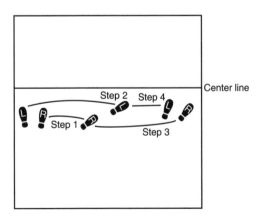

Figure 18.4 Crossover four steps.

Blocks

- Two-person blocks. In two-person blocks, the players should time their jumps so that they reach forward over the net together to make a solid wall of hands and arms. The outside hands should be turned in slightly to direct the spiked ball back into the opponent's court. The outside blocker must be good at turning the ball in so that the attacker cannot hit off the blocker's hands. The phrase "setting the block" refers to lining up the block to allow the defense to get in position behind the block. The outside blocker usually sets the blocks at the sideline, and the middle blocker closes to the outside blocker. The two basic ways of setting the block are taking the line and giving the line. When blocking the line, the blocker must be sure to line up his or her nose on the ball to take the line completely and remember to turn the outside hand in to face into the attacker's court. The middle blocker should set the block on sets to the center of the court. The outside blockers should move to the center to close the block.

Figure 18.5   Two-person block.

- Three-person blocks. Men use the three-person block more often than women do. With three players blocking, each of the outside blockers tries to turn the outside hand in to avoid deflections off the outside edges of the block. Timing the block is difficult. Verbal cues can be helpful in timing triple blocks. For example, the blockers can say "1-2-3" or "Ready-set-jump." With triple blocks, the blockers usually take away most of the court so the defensive players must be good at fielding touches and tips.

Blocking Skills for Women

1. Arms-together block. Women are more flexible than men and find it easier to use this technique of pressing the arms closer together, about three to four inches apart.

To perform this technique, the blocker rotates her wrists and points her fingers to the outside. The thumbs point up. This technique brings the arms and wrists close together to form a tight block with smaller seams or spaces for the ball to go through.

2. Stopping the one-foot takeoff attack. The one-foot takeoff is difficult to block because the hitter is flying along the net. The blocker must be able to move along the net and reach over the net very quickly. Usually the middle blocker should receive help from the left-front blocker. The blockers must talk and call out the attacker's approach. One way of doing this is for both blockers to call "Slide, slide" as the hitter starts the approach. The left-front blocker must read the setter to be ready to block the quick back sets to the quick hitter in his or her zone.

I believe that a one-foot takeoff blocker can block a one-foot takeoff attacker. I use a player-on-player blocking plan that allows a skilled blocker to front a slide hitter and simply run along the net parallel to the attacker, fronting her. The player blocking must be an excellent athlete with good balance. The other left-outside blocker must give her middle blocker the net to move along and take an approach jump to get back to the net on crossing plays.

Attack Blocks to Go for the Stuff

To stuff the ball, the blocker reaches over the net as far as possible to block the ball down on the attacker's side of the net. Players using this technique must be tall or have good jumping ability. They must be able to jump high enough to press their hands and forearms over the net. The player who can also get the elbows over will score more blocking stuffs.

Soft Blocks

Shorter players can often block effectively by using the soft-blocking technique. If an opposing spiker is consistently hitting the ball over a player, that player should use the soft block. This block will make it more difficult for the attacker to hit over a shorter blocker's hands. The player tilts the hands slightly back at the wrists to deflect the ball up in the air into the player's own court. The technique is like an overhand dig. The blocker uses the palms and fingers to slow the ball down and make it easier for teammates to pass for a counterattack. Coaches should give statistical credit to players who use this skill to help their team score points.

The soft-blocking skill is useful when a blocker is late getting up in front of the attacker. The blocker who is faked out and jumps on a quick set can make a soft-block attempt of the next hitter by keeping the hands up and soft blocking the combination set.

Read Blocking

In read blocking, blockers at the net start in a balanced position and then read the ball as it leaves the setter's hands. The blockers react to the set and move to block the attacker. All the blockers should use the following sequence of reading the setter:

Figure 18.6   The soft block.

1. Ball. The blockers watch the flight of the ball as it is passed up to the setter.

2. Setter's hands. The blockers focus on the ball as the setter releases it.

3. Ball. The blockers watch the flight of the ball and move quickly to get in front of the attacker and jump to block.

4. Hitter. The blockers switch their focus to the hitter as they move to block. The sooner they see the hitter, the better. A common error that blockers make is watching the ball as it goes up high in the air instead of looking at the hitter. Blockers who do this will be unable to time the hitter and consequently will not block effectively. The hitter's percentage will be much higher against a blocker who does not see the hitter's approach, shoulder turn, and arm motion in attacking the net.

Read blocking is standard among the best collegiate teams in the United States and the USA teams. This system can be extremely effective for a team that has tall middle blockers who can keep their hands high and get touches on quick sets.

A good scouting report will help blockers prepare for the tendencies of the attackers and the setter in running the offense.

One-On-One Blocking

The best blockers know how to get stuff blocks and touches when they are one-on-one against an attacker. The best way to start to block one-on-one is to be out far enough to the sideline to block the attacker's line shot. The player then takes a quick step to the center and reaches in to block the crosscourt power hit. Great blockers have the mental skill of being able to keep track of the attacker's tendencies in certain situations. For example, if an attacker has been turning back to hit the line often, the blocker should stay wide and take that hit away.

Figure 18.7 One-on-one blocking.

Commit Blocking

A tough game situation for blockers at the college level occurs when the other team is passing well and the setter is scoring by setting quick attacks most of the time. Read blocking may be ineffective against a hot quick hitter.

In the men's international game the quick attack is the highest percentage play on a good pass. The team must commit a blocker to stop it or get a touch.

Commit blocks offer a way to stop the opponent's quick hitter. The blocker starts as if he or she is going to read block. Instead of reading, the blocker takes the quick hitter as his or her only hitter. The blocker gets in front of the quick hitter's approach and takes a big, early jump, trying to get over the net before the hitter attacks. The blocker reaches over and takes away the attacker's best hit. The best result is a stuff block. The commit block should cause the setter to start setting some of the other players to the sidelines, attacks that are not as effective as the quick hitter.

When I was an assistant coach with the USA men's team from 1992 to 1996, we noted that Japan would run a quick set almost every time we served the quick hitter a short serve. The hitter would pass overhand and receive the set most of the time. We used commit blocking in this situation and were good at scoring points that way against Japan.

Blocking Situations

Coaches can use many adjustments and drills to work on special problems in blocking. I will outline a few of these situations and some drills that will help solve these problems.

Split Blocks

In some situations hitters will aim around the blocker or blockers at very sharp angles. When great spikers are having a blast hitting past the blockers, the coach must adjust the blocking plans. One option is to split two blockers, leaving the middle open and taking the line and the sharp angle (figure 18.8). This adjustment works well against hitters who do not see the block and just hit their shots. Putting an excellent digger in the middle back to dig the straight-on hit also helps in this situation.

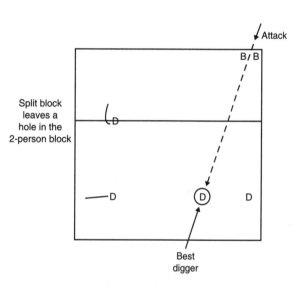

Figure 18.8 Split blocks.

Man to Man

In this plan, each of the front-row blockers follows and blocks a specific player. Against three hitters in the front row, each blocker takes one of the hitters. To front a hitter, a blocker gets in front of the approach path of the hitter.

The USA men's team used the man-to-man, or "man," system of blocking when the opponents used a lot of double-quick sets, which made read blocking very difficult. Cuba and Brazil were best at doing this.

We came up with a successful plan against Cuba. In the rotations that had a double quick, we used the man system to place one blocker in front of each quick hitter. Cuba often responded to this by running right crossing combinations. As soon as we saw a combo, the blockers called out "Combo" and switched to the read system of blocking, which was effective at blocking combo or crossing plays. The USA men's team used these tactics to beat Cuba twice at the 1994 world championships.

Short Blockers

Shorter blockers should try to develop the approach-jump technique. Players who still cannot get their hands above the net cannot be effective blockers. These players should learn to cover tips and dig angles rather than attempt to block. The remaining two blockers should be skillful at reading the setter and moving quickly.

Short blockers must have soft-blocking skills to be effective in game situations. A good touch that deflects the ball to the blocker's team can be passed and set up to score a point. This sequence can score points just as a stuff block does.

Switching Blocking Positions

Teams can switch the front-row blockers to different positions to make it difficult for the opponent's setter to keep track of where the short blocker is. The short blocker should become skillful at faking the direction of movement to confuse the opponent's setter.

Players are usually specialized at higher levels and switch to block in one position at the net. This system has the advantage of allowing the player to practice more often in one area. Outstanding blockers are able to block in the area from which the opponent's best hitter is attacking. The coach must know the ability of the players and assign them to block where they have success.

Key Words and Phrases

See the backs of your hands when you reach forward to block.
Face your hands to the middle of the court to block the ball into the center of the court.
Press over the net before the hitter swings.
Keep your hands strong to block the ball back at the hitter's court.
See the hitter attack by keeping your head level and eyes open.
Follow the ball with your eyes after it passes you and goes into your court.
Balance is the key to read blocking effectively.
Balance is important while you are jumping in the air to block over the net.
Read the setter while staying balanced and ready to move to follow the ball.
Move like a big cat, agile, mobile, and hostile to the attack.
Land like a cat and you will save your knees and avoid errors.

Drills

KEEPING THE EYES OPEN

Many players have the habit of closing their eyes when they are blocking. But to make the best possible adjustments with the hand and arms to block the ball, players should keep the eyes open to see the hitter's arm swing. If the ball passes the block, players should make the landing by turning toward the flight of the ball to react as a teammate passes it back up to the net.

The coach can have one player hit balls at the hands of a blocker standing on the floor. The standing player practices keeping the hands stiff and firm at the time of contact. A third player watches the eyes of the blocker to make sure that the blocker is straining to keep them open. This simple drill can help players warm up for blocking drills, saving their legs while they work on timing the pressing of their hands and facing correctly to block the ball with their eyes open.

The next drill is to have players block live hitters. Players should see the hitters spiking the ball and block over the net before the contact. When blocking one on one, hitters should turn as they land to face the side on which the ball passed. An easy place to do this drill is in the center of the net with sets four to six feet above the net. The next drill is to block quicks, or low fast, sets.

STACK BLOCKING VERSUS COMBINATIONS

The first time we used blocking stacks, in which one blocker stands behind another at the net, was in 1972 when we played Poland just before the Munich Olympics. Poland was running right crosses using oral calls. Jon Stanley and I decided to try stacking, having the blocker off the net simply follow the hitter's path and move in front of him. This method required the front blocker to stay in position to block the 1 set. This blocker did not move laterally, so the blocker stacked behind him could move forward quickly to block the second hitter on the combo with no interference. The stacked blocker had to be good at reading the approach of the crossing or fake-crossing hitter to get to the net in front of him.

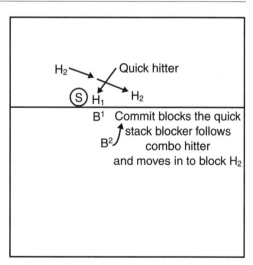

Figure 18.9 Stack blocking.

I had my men's teams at the UCSB practice these skills in the early 1970s. I found that only a very athletic player could make the movements away from and back to the net.

The San Diego Breakers professional team used these blocking tactics in 1975 to defeat the Santa Barbara Spikers with Poland's Stan Gosciniak, one of the best setters ever to set combinations.

BLOCKING LOWER ON SETS OFF THE NET

On sets more than two meters away from the net and on high sets that have allowed three blockers to form a solid block, it is important to form the block lower and over the net to prevent the spikers from using the blockers as a target for balls hit far out of bounds. The blockers should use oral timing cues such as "Wait" or counting "1, 2, 3."

The cues should help the blockers coordinate their jumps and press over the net to form a solid wall of arms and hands. These solid blocks can be intimidating to the hitters and cause them to tip or make hitting errors. Giving the hard hitters less to aim at often causes them to change their spikes.

PADDLES OVER THE NET

One of my favorite coaching cues is "Paddles over the net," which simply means that the player should have the hands and forearms over the net. This position gives the blocker a greater chance of scoring or making a stuff block. Players who time their blocks well are over the net just before the attacker hits the ball. This timing of the spike is one of the most difficult skills to teach in volleyball.

One way to get good reps is to set up a video camera just above the net to film the blockers from the side, at the same angle that the up official sees them. To start, a coach can hit off a box. Then live hitting can begin with medium-height sets. Gamelike situations and lower faster sets can follow. The video can provide the blockers with feedback that will help them improve their ability to spend more time over the net.

ONE-HAND BLOCKS

An important skill in blocking is independent hand and arm movements. To help players develop this skill, I have them practice blocking with one hand and arm. Practicing one-hand blocks takes good concentration and balance.

First, have the players block tosses with each hand on a lower net. Then hit the ball off a box directly at the blocker. The blocker uses one hand to block the ball. Finally, hit the balls at the one hand and arm blocker from a box. The player should get the feel of facing the hand into the court and reaching over the net. Usually each

Figure 18.10   Paddles over the net.

blocker will be better with one of the single hand and arm blocks. The coach should give extra repetitions blocking with the weaker hand and arm.

This simple work with each arm really helps blockers become better at controlling the way their hands and arms deflect spiked balls.

SPLIT BLOCK

The split block is a natural progression after learning to block one-handed. To block using the spread, the blocker must be high above the net with both arms. The arms are spread wide keeping the hands above the net.

This is a good technique to use against a quick hitter hitting repeatedly around a blocker. The split block should get at least a touch. A danger is that a hitter seeing the blocker do the split may hit straight ahead at the face of the blocker.

SHOW AND TAKE

One of my favorite techniques for blocking one on one was to "show" angle or line as the hitter took a look and then "take" it by blocking it late. For example, I would start as if I were going to block the line giving the angle crosscourt. Then I would take away the crosscourt by jumping into the angle and blocking crosscourt. By blocking it late after showing the shot, a blocker can take some of the initiative away from the hitter.

This can also be done with two blockers coordination to give cross-court early as they block the line. Later in the match, it is good to change the block to taking away the cross court and giving the line. These strategies should be coordinated with the back row defense.

THE BATTLE BETWEEN HITTERS AND BLOCKERS

Hitters have the advantage against blockers when there is a good pass and set. Often there is only one blocker up and that gives the hitter a lot of open court to aim at. Great blockers still score in these situations by using strategy and knowing the hitter's best shots. The blocker that blocks a hitter in a one-on-one blocking situation wins a big point and puts a lot of pressure on the hitter. I have seen hitters mentally break down after being stuffed one on one. The blocker also can break down by making nets, foot faults, or blocking the ball out of bounds often. The blocker that nets when the hitter makes an error or is dug up by a teammate feels just awful.

Figure 18.11   Blocking over the net for a stuff block.

COMMON BLOCKING PROBLEMS AND SOLUTIONS

1. Net violations are the most common error. The blocker who is out of balance on the jump to block will net and lose points. The blocker must learn to block without touching the net. Net touches should be avoided, especially on sets where the spiker has a poor set far away from the net. Swinging the arms back and then forward over the net will frequently cause net violations. Blockers should practice footwork and block jumps as part of warm-ups and as a finishing drill at the end of practice when they are fatigued. Playing balls that come out of the net develops the players' ability to retrieve balls from the net without netting.

2. Poor footwork technique often causes foot faults. The most common error occurs after the blocker lands and turns to move away from the net. Drills in which blockers practice blocking jumps and landing skills can be the starting point for hitting and digging drills.

3. Sieve blocks result from holes between blockers or a blocker's wildly swinging arms. Blockers should practice making a solid blocking wall by hitting balls across a low net as they stand on the floor. The blockers press their arms forward and form solid blocks.

4. Balls going in front of the blocker are tough to play and lose points. Blockers should seal their hands and arms to the top of the net to keep balls from getting through their hands. The distance between the hands and arms and the net should be less than three inches.

5. Blocking balls out of bounds can be avoided by facing the hands into the center of the attacker's court. When blocking the line, players should take the ball completely or give a clear shot at the line. If they line up to block half the ball, the hitter can easily wipe off the blocker.

6. Players should avoid guess blocking and then being caught out of position to make the proper block. The blocker should simply stand in front of the setter, staying balanced to read the ball coming out of the setter's hands. The blocker simply reads front or back sets to the sidelines to start this drill and then moves to the outside to block. The blocker must follow the ball and not guess. Next use a 2 set in the middle. Now the blocker has to deal with three hitters. Then lower the outside sets and make the middle set a quick to create a gamelike situation. The coach should watch the eyes of the blocker to make sure that the blocker is following the read sequence of passed ball, the ball in the setter's hands, the flight of the set ball, and then a focus on the hitter.

CHAPTER NINETEEN

Components of a Successful Offense

Fred Sturm

In the sport of volleyball a good offense is also a good defense and on of several performance elements required for top-level success. No longer can a team superior in only one dimension of play achieve championship status. However, if a team only has time to focus on one dimension that should be offense. Many of us are playing with the rules of rally scoring (one point per serve). The large majority of points are produced by the offense in the form of kills by attackers. The level of productivity of your team's offense from serve-receive or from its transition to offense from defense is very important to its success.

The task for coaches is to choose the offense system that will give your team the best opportunity for success (i.e., produce the highest hitting efficiency for your team). This is an important decision which requires some thought. One must take inventory by assessing the talents of your players and abilities of your setters. Training time and the length of your season are important considerations. Statistical information about your team's offensive performance is a great tool for determining the best way for your team to plan on offensive. Other important elements are your choice of training drills and their role in your team's improvement process.

What follows is a more complete explanation of the above and their relationship to the development of a successful offense.

About Concepts and Definitions

Outstanding offensive systems are composed of several elements. The following are some of the things to consider when evaluating your team's offense.

You should know the sequence of sets made by your setter. Study your setter's decision-making process. In what situations is the *sequence* predictable, and in what situations is it unpredictable? I like my setter's decisions to be aggressive, smart, and, whenever possible, unpredictable.

Repeatability occurs when your setter sets either the same hitter or the same type of set twice in a row. In what situations does your setter repeat in a predictable way? In what situations does your setter repeat in an unpredictable way? In what situations does your setter not repeat in a predictable way? Both you and your setter should know these habits. Most setters have unconscious habits that they need to become aware of. For example, your setter may never repeat a hitter after that hitter has made a mistake.

Streaking occurs when a setter delivers the ball to the same hitter or sets the same type of set five or more times in a row. An example of this occurs when the setter streaks sets to the quick attackers.

In today's game many teams want to play quickly on offense. A fast-tempo offense doesn't give the opponent enough time to set up its defense, creating a good opportunity for an attacker to score. How fast can the offense be? The answer depends on several things. First is your team's level of serve-receive. The more frequently they make a good reception, the more often they can use the fast offense. Second is the ability of your setter. Does your setter have the skill and knowledge to run a fast offense? Third are the physical abilities of your hitters. When determining speed, look for hitting control and hitting range. Hitting control is the ability to hit without making too many unforced errors. Is the speed of the set too fast, causing your hitter to make too many unforced errors? Hitting range is the ability to spike the ball to many different places on the court. The speed of the set should not limit the hitter's range of shots.

A *gap* is the space between two blockers or the space between an outside blocker and the sideline. Attacking into a gap is an excellent offensive tactic.

Either the setter or the hitter can generate *motion*. One popular tactic is for the setter to move in one direction and set the ball in the opposite direction. Hitter motion has to do with the direction of the approach angle relative to the point of attack along the net. A hitter's movement to the left or right of the defenders is more effective than movement that occurs straight in front of the defenders. The tendency is for blockers and defenders to lean (shift their weight) in the direction of the motion. For example, hitter motion to the right causes the blockers and defenders to lean in that direction. Because the defenders are leaning to the right, they will move much more slowly when they have to move to the left. The two most common types of motion are *flooding* and *isolating*. Flooding is the tactic of having two hitters run routes into the zone of one blocker. When the attackers move quickly, one blocker will find it extremely difficult to cover both hitters. The setter should keep this blocker guessing by mixing the distribution of sets to these hitters. Isolating is a tactic that matches one hitter against one blocker. The most common way to create isolation is to run a pattern that has two hitters flood the zone of one outside blocker, leaving the third hitter isolated against the other outside blocker. The ideal matchup is to place your best hitter against the opponent's worst blocker. To isolate your hitter with one blocker, your setter must hold the opponent's middle blocker by periodically mixing the distribution of sets to the other hitters in the pattern.

The slide behind the setter is popular in the women's game. A hitter running an approach parallel to the net creates a difficult blocking situation. Often the blocker must guess where to position the block because it seems that the hitter can attack from more than one place along the net. The hitter can make the floating action along the net with either a one-footed jump or a two-footed jump. Offenses with attackers who use both vertical and horizontal (floating) actions create a difficult situation for the defense.

The setter dump is used much more often in the women's game than it is in the men's game. The reason for this is that few women's teams use the back-row attack in the same way that men's teams do. Typical men's teams use the back-row attack approximately 25 or 30 percent of the time. Typical women's teams use the back-row attack less than 10 percent of the time. In the women's game, the setter is an important part of the attack when she is in the front row. By jumping hard to set the ball in the same way that she jumps hard to attack, the setter creates a big distraction to the opponent's blockers and defenders. The setter who creates this double-threat effect (to make a strong attack or set one of the hitters) adds an invaluable dimension to the team's offense.

About Styles of Systems

You can use two general ways of choosing the right system for your team. The first is to focus on core sets and core patterns. Each hitter learns how to hit two or three different types of sets. The setter learns how to set the hitters. This offense typically has only a few patterns in each rotation. The goal is to execute this offense at a high level of efficiency as measured by hitting efficiency and side out percentage. By focusing your work on offense to a small number of tasks, you can rapidly improve efficiency. In other words, your team can become a master of core tasks instead of a jack of all tasks. This is a good system of play for inexperienced, modestly skilled players because it allows for the possibility of keeping your setting and hitting errors to a low percentage. The error percentage often decreases over time as the setter and hitters improve their skills and become more familiar with each other during the season. This style of offense is good for teams with limited training time. At the beginning of the season identify and develop the core sets and patterns of your offense. Later in the season you can add new sets and new patterns to give your offense some new wrinkles. Remember that your goal is to execute your offense at a high level of efficiency. Over time you can gradually increase the number of different sets and patterns while continuing to execute your offense proficiently and efficiently.

On the other end of the spectrum is a wide-open style of offense. Unlike the offense with core sets and core patterns, this offense gives the opposing defense many different looks. The wide-open offense includes many types of sets leading to many kinds of patterns (offensive looks). This is a good system for a team composed of highly skillful, knowledgeable, and experienced players. If your team has an experienced setter and versatile hitters, this is a great offense. If your goal is to confuse your opponent's defense and to prevent them from getting into a groove, this is the offense for you. If you like the idea of matching up any one of your hitters with any one of the opponent's blockers, this system will allow it. The wide-open offense has several downsides. You will need more training time and the majority of your players will need to have some experience playing together. Your players will need more time and repetition work to learn more tasks. This system has a higher risk for errors. In the beginning stage, miscommunication between your setter and hitters may cause errors. In addition, your setter and hitters will need time to find the right rhythm for each of the attack options and to learn to execute the attacks efficiently. Over time, the frequency for errors will decrease as your setter and hitters learn how to communicate and as they develop the right rhythm.

In the beginning of the season, have your players experiment with many offensive options. This is a time of discovery and creativity for your players, and a time for you to take inventory. After a while, you can identify the elements of your team's offense that you wish to continue and those that you want to discontinue.

About Your Setter

A team with a great setter and a group of good hitters has a better possibility for achieving greatness than a team with a good setter and a group of great hitters.

Your setter can affect the level of play more than any other player on the court. Therefore, you should do everything possible to aid the rapid development of the setter.

Each setter has a unique blend of talents and skills. Take inventory and identify those physical, mental, and emotional gifts. Then customize the role of the setter to maximize those strengths.

Your setter's two most important jobs are to set a hittable ball and a smart ball. Setters need years and many repetitions to acquire the skill and confidence to make sets with good location and rhythm. Becoming a smart setter requires countless hours of experience on the court along with a lot of study time off the court.

The setter is the center of your team's offense. Mentor and tutor your setter. You can make no better investment in your team's offense than by spending time with your setter.

About Training Time

You should know the total volume of training time you will have during the season, specifically, the number of hours per practice session, the number of hours per week, and the number of weeks in your season. Generally, the less training time you have, the fewer things your team can develop and master.

Practice is the best time to build your skills and improve your team's offense. By carefully planning your practices, you can make the best use of precious training time.

How Much Do You Want to Know?

You can use several methods to study your team's offensive performance. During the competitive phase of our season I use statistical information from our matches to measure our performance. From this information I learn what our strengths and weaknesses are. After identifying our problem areas, I begin the process of finding solutions.

Four matches provides the minimum amount of statistical information you will need to identify your team's norms. If you wish, you can separate this information into groups according to the quality of your opponents or other characteristics. One set of data might cover matches against teams whose record is below .500, another set could include matches against teams ranked in the top 25, and a third set might include matches against conference opponents. I keep an ongoing summary of all matches throughout the season. In addition, I keep a continuous summary for each specific group. The information I glean from these statistics has a significant influence on my coaching decisions about how we will play. Much of what we work on in practice comes from what I have learned from our statistical analysis.

The two most important offense statistics are side out percentage and hitting efficiency. I like to know three kinds of information about my team's offense: information from the scoresheet, information from a side out chart, and the Coleman statistic.

From the match scoresheet you can learn about your team's side out percentages. The side out percentage can be calculated by dividing the total number of side outs into the total number of serves. For example, when your team scores 6 side outs in 10 serves, the side out percentage is 60. I want to know the side out percentage breakdown for each of the six rotations as well as the sum of all rotations. In addition, I like this information for each match and a continuous summary of all matches. This statistic clearly identifies the strongest and weakest side out rotations. During the season, the goal is to improve our weak rotations and, if possible, our strong rotations.

Another excellent statistical tool is the side out chart. This chart gives valuable information about your team's performance in each of its six rotations. I like the chart to include information about passing and hitting, offensive patterns, and set distributions. I like to know the hitting efficiency for the rotation as well as for each individual hitter. In addition, I like to know what types of sets each player was given to attack. From this information I can learn many things. The most important thing I learn is the smartest and most efficient way to play each rotation. I can also learn the best use of the time we spend in practice on rotation work. My college coach at UCLA, Al Scates, is a master of maximizing team performance during practice and matches through study of the side out chart. Like the score-sheet statistic, I like the side out chart information for each match as well as an ongoing summary of all matches during the season.

The late Jim Coleman, former USA men's national team head coach and the nation's foremost authority on volleyball statistics, invented the Coleman statistic. One of its sections has information organized by skill. There are two readouts—one for each player and the other for the team as a group. This statistic contains good offensive information about passing and hitting. The hitting-efficiency information falls into three categories—serve-receive attack (first attack only following serve receive), all other attacks for side outs, and attacking for points. The information from the statistic is an excellent tool for measuring the performance of your team.

All of these statistics and charts can be kept during matches (that is, if you are lucky enough to have people who can take these charts). Another option is to develop the information from videotape after the match.

A crucial factor for success for your team during the season is the rate and amount of improvement. Study your team's performance through statistical analysis. This information will help you identify ways to maximize your team's offensive performance.

How Do You Play on Offense?

Time and good statistical information will allow you to identify the best way for your team to execute its offense. Efficiency is everything. For each of your rotations you should know the side out percentage, the hitting efficiency, and the passing level. Next, look at individual player statistics. What is the hitting efficiency for each player? What percentage of total sets does each receive? Generally, the players with the highest hitting efficiencies receive the most sets. What is the passing level of each player? I also like to know the offensive patterns and corresponding set distributions. I recommend that you know the hitting efficiencies by offensive pattern and by the individual players in the pattern.

Having this information, you are now able to find the best way for your team to execute its offense. Examine each of your rotations. Begin with the ones with the lowest side out percentages. Examine your team's serve receive. If there is a problem, what is your idea for a solution? Look at your team's hitting efficiencies. Is your setter running the best patterns? Are your attackers hitting their best kinds of sets? Are the sets being distributed to your hitters in the smartest and most efficient way?

About Training Drills

Many drills are available to improve the offense of your team. I am going to tell you about two training drills I use during the season. One focuses on the team's side out percentage and the other on the team's offense.

The first one, which I call "Do or Redo," focuses on your serve-receive attack. It is a great drill for rotation work. Here is how it works. Use two teams of six players—one team on offense and the other on defense. Each team works on two rotations at a time (1-4, 2-5, 3-6). The team on offense receives 20 serves from the defense team. Each team stays in the same rotation for 10 balls and then changes to the other rotation for 10 more balls (for example, 10 serves in rotation 1 followed by 10 serves in rotation 4). Identify a goal for the offense. For example, the offense must win 12 of 20 serves. Each serve is worth 1 point. Service errors are worth 1 point for the offense. To win, the defense must win 9 or more points. For this drill I have our starting six on the offense team. The goal is to win 12 of 20 serves in three different ways (rotation 1 and 4, then rotation 2 and 5, then rotation 3 and 6). The offense team remains in the same rotations until it reaches the goal. If it fails to reach its goal, we "redo" that part of the drill.

Here are some variations. Instead of having the defense team stay in the same rotation for 10 balls, have them change after every 3 serves. I use this variation when I want the offense to receive a variety of serves. At the same time the offense practices against a variety of blocking groups. Another alternative is to create competition between the two teams. For example, the winner is the first team to win three times on offense and in all six of the rotations (1-4, 2-5, and 3-6). The defense team must prevent the offense team from winning 12 balls before it can play on offense. In other words, when the offense team wins (12 or more serves of 20), it remains on offense and changes to the next rotation. When the offense team loses (fewer than 12 serves of 20), it becomes the defense team, and the defense team switches to offense.

I like to initiate the action with a serve. Or you can use balls less difficult to handle, such as balls put into play by a coach. Use these or other variations to meet the specific needs of your team. This is an excellent drill for rotation work and, in this example, for focusing on your team's side out percentage. When the offense wins 12 out of 20 serves, its side out percentage is 60. My Boise State team goal is 13 out of 20 serves for a side out percentage of 65.

Another drill I use is designed to develop all hitters in each of the rotations. Using all your hitters in your offense is important. The more ways your team can play on offense, the more ways it can attack the opponent's defense. When your setter is in the back row, you have a left-side, middle, and right-side hitter in the front row. When the setter is in the front row, you have a left-side, middle, and possibly one back-row hitter. A team has a great offensive situation when it can use each of these hitters successfully at any time and in any situation. Your setter will need time and practice to learn how to use all the hitters in a pattern and how to sequence the sets. The drill promotes awareness and creativity in your setter. Moreover, this drill teaches your hitters an extremely important habit—to expect the set every time.

This is how the drill works. One team is on offense, and one team is on defense. When the setter for the offense team is in the back row, the offense must make five side outs in a row, using each of the three hitters at least once. When the setter is in the front row, the offense must make four side outs in a row, using each of the two hitters at least once. This rule applies only to the first attack after the serve receive. No rules apply to the offense for any transition that follows. The offense team has five opportunities to meet its goal (i.e., before the defense wins five balls). You can adjust this number according to your situation. When the offense meets its goal, it changes to a new rotation and repeats the drill. When the offense fails to meets its goal (i.e., the defense has won five balls), the teams switch roles and start again. The winner is always on offense, and the loser is always on defense. Only the offense team can score a point. The winner is the team that first scores a point in each of its six rotations. You must have rules for serving because your players will be tempted to use low-percentage serves. This circumstance could create bad habits. To prevent this problem, I allow the defense team one service mistake per competition. For each additional service error, 1 point is deducted from its offense total. You can adjust the number of permissible service errors to meet your level.

During the early part of the season, I have a coach put an easy ball into play from across the net. I want players to run the offense off perfect passes to build skill, rhythm, and confidence. Later we initiate the drill with a serve.

About Improvement

Among the most important factors for success are the rate and degree of improvement your team makes during its season. Improvements in your team side out percentage and hitting efficiency come gradually. I do not know any quick-fix solutions. Keep yourself well informed about the performance level of your team. Know your strengths and weaknesses. Obviously, it is advantageous to find solutions to your team's problems quickly. But the amount of time you will need to find the right answers is difficult to predict. The process is often an experiment with trial and error. Finding solutions through the process of elimination can take a long time.

Before your season you should identify your team's goals for side out percentage and hitting efficiency. Let's say 65 percent is your side out goal for November 1. On September 15 your percentage is 61. Your team has six weeks to reach its side out target. If your team can improve by 1 percent every 10 days, it will meet its goal by November 1. This is one example how you can make the process both progressive and gradual. You can use a similar strategy for hitting and passing efficiency. You can establish targets for the team as well as for individual players.

Keep a record of year-end team statistics and use it to set appropriate performance standards for your team.

Conclusion

Volleyball is a game of many elements. In my opinion the most important element is offense. You may select from many styles, concepts, and tactics. How much you want to know about each of them is a personal choice. Regardless, from your base of knowledge you choose the offensive system most suitable for your team based on its physical ability, skill level, knowledge, and experience. You can put it to the test during competition. You can measure its effectiveness with statistics to identify the smartest and most efficient way to play an offense. Statistics can also give you direction about how to use your training time to effect crucial improvements in your team's offense. This evaluation and development process requires you to invest time and work, but the payoff of seeing your team's offense execute at high level of efficiency can make it all worthwhile.

CHAPTER TWENTY

Devising a Talent-Based Offense

Peter Hanson

Although I have coached volleyball for 17 years, I am still learning new things about offense and offensive systems within the game. Every new team we play, every coach I speak with, and every player I have ever coached has given me insights into the complicated game of volleyball. Each year a new team with a unique blend of personalities, talents, athletic abilities, and skills steps into our practice gym to prepare for the season. When I try to jump ahead and turn to a page in chapter 2, I learn each time that I must start with chapter 1. Developing a team is far more complex than issuing practice gear and hitting the court. You as a coach must develop a plan to help your team prepare, practice, and succeed on the court. I have learned a few strategies that may help you begin the development and analysis of an offensive team system and strategy.

Understanding Talent on Your Team

A coach must be aware that no two teams are alike and that the offensive system that he or she implements must fit the talents of the team. A team is to some degree malleable and may be able to adapt to a particular offensive style and system, but ultimately the coaching staff must structure an offense around the players to develop a team that is productive at their level of play. Will you be able to run a 5-1, or will a 4-2 offense better fit your personnel? Perhaps you have two capable setters who are strong attackers and a 6-2 offense would maximize their strengths. Once you as a coach have made this decision, you can begin to plan the offensive structure.

To arrive at a strategy for your team's offensive system, you should evaluate the key components of your team's talents and weaknesses early in the preseason. You can generally count on the skill level of returning players, but even their strengths will change with physical and emotional maturation. I have seen a young player leave for summer break at 160 pounds and return in the fall two inches taller at 180. I have also seen a shy, unsure athlete return the next season as a developing leader. Never assume or count on the talents of your returning players. They will change, so your offensive strategy must change as well. The final measure will be how well your system uses the physical and technical capabilities of your players.

Maximizing Strengths

What are your team's strengths? Are they passing, attacking, setting, athletic ability, or the setter's tactical abilities? Will your strength be individual skills, or will it be team tactical superiority? Can your team win by having individuals overpower opponents using a basic offensive plan and their physical prowess, or do you need a carefully orchestrated attack to mask individual weaknesses and highlight the team's collective strength? Once you have answers to these questions, devising your offense plan will become easier.

A good example of this comes to mind with the first team I coached at Ohio State. I came onto the court with the philosophy that the best way to win was to implement a high-level tactical offense with many offensive plays to keep the opponent guessing. We spent a lot of time showing diagrams to players to impart knowledge through bookwork. In practice after practice and drill after drill, it became obvious that my choices involved three major problems. Number one, we did not have the individual skills (serve receive and spiking) to carry out the proposed offense. Number two, we were running out of time before our conference competition began. Number three, the players were becoming frustrated with themselves and their teammates, and they started to believe that they were not good enough to execute the offensive system and win. I was trying to create an effective team with my sheer will power and little high-level volleyball talent. After both the players and I had become extremely frustrated, it suddenly became obvious what we should do—scale back. Find the things that each individual could do well on the court and fine-tune them. Make the team revolve around those strengths. Make the strengths a factor for other teams to contend with. We pulled back, returned to basics, and started to play as a team. We simplified our offensive tactics, continued to spend practice time improving the parts of the players' game that were already strong, and minimized the time spent on developing new or higher-level tactics. Only after we mastered a skill did we implement a new strategy or tactic.

From this early lesson I learned that an offensive system could function well only if the players have mastered the individual skills associated with the offensive philosophy and then are placed into an offensive structure that maximizes those skills. As a coach, you must outline a plan that will accomplish both of these tasks within the context of your team's abilities.

Introduction of Your Offense System

To develop your team's offense, you must train and develop both individual skills and tactics within the context of the offense. We must teach players to receive, serve, and spike, but we must also teach them to do this within the context of the offense. To delay the introduction and implementation of your offensive system until player have acquired the necessary skills serves only to postpone your team's offensive development. Although you may not have identified all your offensive options at the beginning of training, introducing concepts and offenses to the players early will allow you to evaluate and structure your training routine accordingly. Start with the basics, as noted earlier, and let the players become comfortable within the structure. Although we introduce higher-level offensive tactics early in the development of the players and team, basic skill acquisition is still the highest priority. We will not implement higher-level tactics and fail because of poor skill. Instead, we will pursue higher-level skills and succeed with simplified tactics and high levels of execution.

Our goal at Ohio State, although it sounds oversimplified, has been to have each of our attackers hit the best type of set for them as often as possible in the position that will produce the most kills. Our passing and setting abilities dictate how far we can take our offensive scheme. We never want to try to do more than what our players are technically able to achieve. Ohio State was fortunate to have an excellent setter from 1997 to 2000. The young man's name was Angel Aja (pronounced "anhal aha"). This young athlete was able to rocket our offense from a keep-it-simple mentality to a complicated, successful system that took our team to a 25-4 season and into the final match against UCLA in the 2000 NCAA championship. We were able to be successful with an intricate offensive system that kept all our hitters succeeding at a high level. Angel's skill as a setter gave our hitters confidence and allowed our offense to have a diverse, potent attack from virtually any position along the net.

During Angel's years at Ohio State we had a collection of athletes who had developed first-rate individual skills early in their careers at their respective positions. We could therefore spend more practice time on team tactics. Our primary passers (Jose Rivera and Pieter Olree) were consistent with their passing to Aja. We had two capable and athletic middle hitters, 7-foot Colin McMillan and 6-foot-6-inch René Esteves, who over time developed a chemistry with Aja to become extremely effective at hitting a variety of quick sets from the middle. Having a consistent force in the middle allowed our outside hitters to succeed at a high level as well. Our outside hitters, as well as a very effective opposite (Chris Fash), allowed Aja the option of using many offensive combinations and tactics. With the superior individual skills of these players, the offense of the game and its tactics suddenly seemed easy. Not having to spend a great deal of time on rudimentary skill acquisition in practice allowed us time to fine-tune the tactical capabilities of our offense. Some of these players arrived at Ohio State with the necessary skills to perform the way we had hoped. Others developed their skills in our gym while learning our offensive system.

We have now completed our 2001–2002 year at Ohio State. With this team we returned to a more basic offensive structure and spent more time in practice to develop basic skills before we tried to increase our tactical capability. We had a young team and a freshman setter. This team showed great promise, but we had to focus on the basics.

Each season brings a new set of challenges and processes. This year, men's collegiate volleyball has adopted the rally scoring system, which is being used at the international level and junior levels. The side-out offense and strong, consistent serving are now the highest priorities for a team. A missed serve means 1 point for your opponent. The game moves quickly. A deficit of even 5 points can be difficult to overcome. This year we also have the let serve rule that keeps the ball in play when it hits the net but goes over and into the opponent's court, and the libero player, who adds defensive ability as well as more consistent passes to improve the effectiveness of the offenses. Whether these changes will improve the game from the viewpoint of the players or fans is yet undetermined. One thing is clear—the game has changed and we must change as well.

Time Constraints

Another major consideration in developing an offensive philosophy is the time limitation that you always have in coaching. How much time will you have, as a coach, to polish your developing offensive system before you need to use it in competition? Will you have enough time to get all your players to a comparable level of effectiveness and execution within your offense?

Men's collegiate volleyball has a 22-week period in which to train players and compete during a regular season that allows for 28 dates of competition, culminating in the national championship. Typically, each university spends 5 to 7 weeks in the fall in a preseason-training phase, allowing them a 15- to 17-week regular-season training and competition phase. This is an ideal format for individual and team development. During the preseason phase a coach is able to implement, experiment, and evaluate the offensive tactics and philosophy that the team will use during the regular season.

Collegiate women's volleyball and most girls high school volleyball teams do not have this luxury because their preseason usually consists of a two- or three-week period before regular-season play begins. Therefore, the coach must consider distinctly different plans and goals. Under this schedule you may have to limit the high-level tactical aspects of your offensive system until you have had enough training time to achieve your desired level of success. Identifying and implementing a well thought-out practice plan will be one of your most important tasks before the start of your season. Realize that time constraints will define your offensive strategies as much as the talents of your players do.

A team must make the best use of its practice time. From the beginning, many teams must compete for court time when scheduling practices. This circumstance makes it even more important to plan every practice to maximize gym time. I always have an outline of our practice before the team hits the court, from warm-up to finish, with time estimates for each drill. Never allow your athletes to be idle. Maximizing quality repetitions is the key to acquiring and developing high-level skill. A coach with a good practice plan keeps the volleyballs and players in constant motion.

Practice Setting

Early in our training phase as we work with small groups of hitters, we work on all the various sets of our offense. We occasionally combine multiple groups of hitters and hit different sets to begin to identify combinations of sets and personnel that will work with each one. As we see combinations begin to have success, we continue to add additional elements to the general offensive scheme. We are always looking for that point when we have attempted to do more than what our hitters or setter can execute at an acceptable rate of success. Each stage of competitive volleyball requires you as a coach to determine what level of offense effectiveness you must achieve to succeed. You must find that standard and then put into place the practice plans and offensive tactics that will help your team achieve those numbers.

We train our offense in separate parts and then in multiple combinations. Our first goal is to teach our hitters the location and tempo of each set. We spend a large amount of time in each practice throughout both the preseason and during the season using fundamental pass-set-hit drills in which we work on a specific type of set with a specific group of hitters. A progression of drills will help you through this process, beginning with the most basic warm-up hitting drill and leading up to a combination skill drill versus blockers and defenders. We spend only a limited time in warm-up hitting lines because that exercise is not typical of game conditions. Once our hitters have warmed up we use drills that usually have a small group of hitters working with the setter on developing their spiking ability and gaining a feel for the tempo of the setter's offense. We have the hitters working on specific shots and target areas as well as developing a rhythm with the setter. These types of drills are combination skill drills in which the hitters hit after passing a ball to the setter or reacting to someone else who has passed the ball. The hitters work on their specific approach patterns to different zones along the net and continue to work on specific shots. Although rudimentary, these drills serve a useful purpose by allowing the coach to evaluate the capabilities of each player. Perhaps you have a hitter who cannot hit a fast-tempo set after passing the ball but is quite good at spiking a fast-tempo set when not passing. This is the kind of information that you must extract from your drills and practices to devise your offense.

The next progression requires your hitters not only to react to themselves or another passer passing the ball but also to succeed against some form of defense, either blockers or diggers. You can have the hitters compete against the defense to achieve a certain number of kills from a certain zone with a certain tempo of set, either by themselves or in combination with other hitters. This progression will help you analyze the locations and tempos where each hitter will be successful.

As the hitters and setters begin to gain confidence in one another and themselves, the next level of challenge is to have the hitters compete against both a defense and the scoreboard. Hitters must learn the consequences of every swing they take. The more accountability you can manufacture in your practices, the greater the success your hitters will achieve during game and match situations. The accountability that you create in your drills and practices will provide you with additional information on how to develop your offense. Find out which hitters are more successful in serve-reception offense versus transition offense. Which hitters can be successful against two or more blockers? Which will need to be one on one to be successful? Perhaps you will find a hitter who is deceptive and explosive when hitting in combination with a middle attacker but ineffective hitting a high-tempo set against a well-formed block. As a coach you must evaluate every offensive swing that your hitters take to define your offensive strategy.

We work constantly with our setters to develop a good tempo in setting each set to the various hitters. The setters must learn what each hitter likes and how that relates to the success rate for that spiker. We find that each hitter requires a slightly different tempo for the set that is being delivered to a particular area along the net. Some hitters may be able to succeed with a faster tempo set because of their particular skills, whereas other hitters may need a higher and slower tempo set at the same zone to be successful. Having consistent tempo and location with sets is one of the fundamental building blocks of the offense. It is extremely important to identify what slight variations, if any, each of your hitters needs to be successful. Repetition is the best solution.

When you have identified the strengths of your hitters and setters, you need to look at combining different hitters and different types of sets that will lead to your multiple-attack offense.

Typically, you do not have all your offensive options available at the beginning of the season for competition. You are probably working on those combinations in practice. When you feel you have reached the desired level of performance and your players have gained an appropriate level of confidence in practice, you can give the green light to the setter and hitters to use offensive options in a game situation. As the season progresses we increase our tactical options as well as the offensive tempo of the sets. The ultimate goal is to develop each hitter and the setter to their maximum ability and creativity by the end of the season. Be aware, however, that you should never attempt to do more than your athletes are technically or tactically capable of executing at your desired level.

Offensive Basics

The main offensive strategy that we have developed at Ohio State has been to attack from the different zones along the net with single or multiple hitters at a tempo that will put pressure on the opposing blockers. We teach our setters to put a hitter in a one-on-one situation as often as possible, either through misdirection or by overloading a hitting zone. *Misdirection* is a term we use for setting against the flow. As your setter moves in one direction, he or she sets to a hitter in the opposite direction. Young blockers typically react to this movement by being out of position. The second tactic is to overload a specific zone along the net with more than one hitter. This tactic forces the blockers to guess which hitter will be set. The faster the tempo that your setter and hitters can attain, the more pressure they will place on the blockers. You can use the principle of overloading a zone with both front-row and back-row attackers in each rotation. If we can bring enough offensive pressure to bear on the defense, then we may be able to dictate to the opponents what they will defend and what they will have to give up. At both the collegiate and international level we are seeing four or five hitters available and capable of spiking on each side-out attempt. This type of offensive pressure makes it extremely difficult for three blockers to defend the whole net and establish a well-formed double block at each offensive option.

Components for Your Offense

Most men's collegiate offenses involve a basic repertoire of sets used in either a few or many combinations. Our middle attackers are usually training to hit four types of sets:

1. A front quick, which is a 1 set in front of the setter;

2. A back quick, which is a 1 set right behind the setter;

3. A 31 or wide 1, which is a 1 set about three feet from the setter toward the left-front antennae; and

4. A front slide, which is an approach in which the hitter drifts a little from right to left across the setter and tries to hit a 1 set that is slightly past the traditional 1 position.

We have two types of sets for our left-side hitters to attack from the left-side pin:

1. A high set called a "hut" and

2. A faster tempo set called a "go."

Our right-side hitter has three types of sets that allow him to attack from the right-side pin:

1. An x5, which is a high set;

2. A red, which is medium tempo; and

3. A green, which is a fast set to the right-side pin.

These basic sets allow us to spread the blockers from antennae to antennae. The next group of sets that we try to incorporate is the play set series, which we use in combination with the middle attackers. Either front-row outside hitter, depending on his or her abilities, can use each play set. We use three sets in combination with our middle attackers: an x1, an x2, and an x4. The x1 is a wide 2 ball set in the 2-3 zone. The x2 is a 2 ball set just to the left of the middle attacker in the 5 zone who has run a quick, and the x4 is a 2 ball set in the 8 zone behind the setter.

The addition of multiple back-row attacking options in conjunction with a front-row offense can overwhelm the opponent's blocking. We have attempted to create a minimum of two and sometimes three back-row attack options with our outside hitters. Our back-row attackers are using the traditional zones such as the D in right back, the pipe in center back, and either an A in left back or a blue in the zone between the pipe and A. Figures 20.1–20.11 show both the locations for the basic sets that I have described as well as a 5-1 offense with the basic approach patterns that have four or five hitters involved in each offensive play.

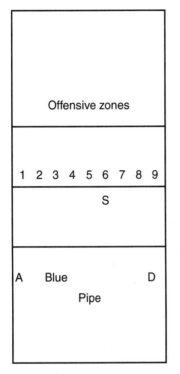

Figure 20.1

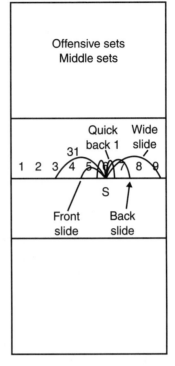

Figure 20.2

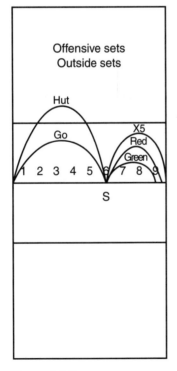

Figure 20.3

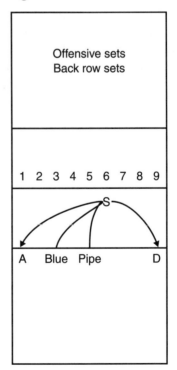

Figure 20.4

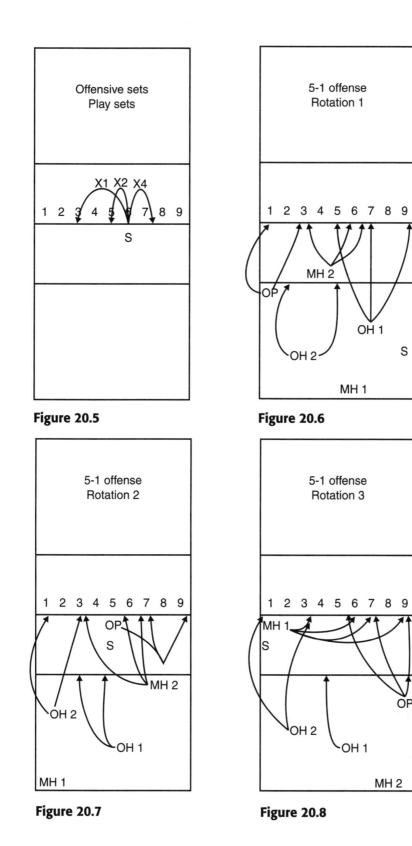

Figure 20.5

Figure 20.6

Figure 20.7

Figure 20.8

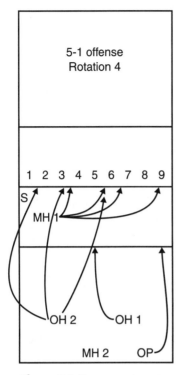

Figure 20.9

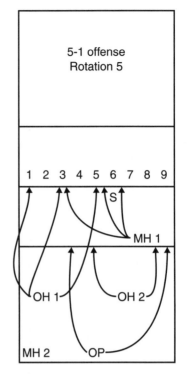

Figure 20.10

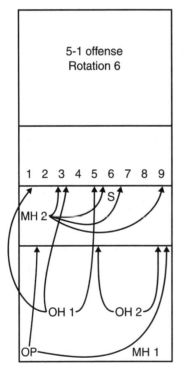

Figure 20.11

CHAPTER TWENTY–ONE

Dominating Defensive Systems

Taras Liskevych

In all my years of coaching I always felt that defense—individual defense and team defense—is the tactical area that determines which team will ultimately win. You have no doubt heard the coaching cliche "Defense wins championships." Good and great defense depend on the interplay and co-ordination of the block and the backcourt defense. My philosophy has always been that good defense begins with a good block.

With the advent of rally point scoring (scoring a point after every rally), serving, blocking, and floor defense will be even more critical to the out-come of a match. A key ingredient to the success of your team will be your ability to sell your team on the concept of great team defense—blocking and digging versus being satisfied to be just a good attacking team.

Occasionally, a coach has the luxury of watching his or her team put all the elements of great defense together. I vividly remember a match in Stock-ton, California, on April 7, 1991, when the USA women's team did just that against the USSR. We continually thwarted the Soviet attack with timely blocking, precise defensive positioning, and a never-quit attitude. I can easily picture similar matches with my Ohio State men's team (1974–76) and my University of Pacific women's team (1976–84). The calling card of all out-standing teams is an outstanding defense.

Definitions of Defense

1. Team defense is what a group of players does to keep the opponent from scoring or siding out.
2. Defense is the action that a team takes from the time its opponent contacts or controls the ball until the ball crosses the plane of the net to its side and is either stuff blocked back to the opponent or con-trolled for an offensive play.
3. A team is on defense once the ball crosses the plane of the net to the opponent's side of the net—after a serve, after an attack, after a down ball or a free ball.
4. Defense includes both blocking and backcourt digging or contacting the ball.
5. Defense is a reaction to offense.
6. Defense prevents the other team from siding out and from transition scoring.

Defense Philosophy and Concepts for the Player

Your objective as a player is to position yourself between the flight of the ball and your half court so that you can either block or dig the ball and then to convert your defense contact to an offensive play by your team. As a defender, you want to have the mentality that *nothing* will ever hit the floor. Your pursuit of the ball should be relentless.

When a ball is in play, always follow it with your eyes. Play with the philosophy that *every* ball is coming to you. Be in a position where you can make the play when it comes to your specific area. The most important aspect of defense is reading the development of the point of attack correctly. Put yourself in the correct defensive position *prior* to the attacker's contact with the ball.

You are responsible for a defensive area, not just one spot on the court. Players often ask, "Am I in the right spot?" I always answer, "If you can block, dig, or get to the ball, you are in the right spot." Figure 21.1 is a sample diagram of some backcourt responsibilities for a perimeter middle back defense.

Moving from the perimeter toward the center of the court is easier and more efficient than moving away from the center of the court. You and your teammates should avoid congregating in the center of the court. Use the sideline and end line as your guide. Wing players, the left back (LB) and right back (RB), use the sidelines. The deep player, the middle back (MB), uses the end line. Players digging in the backcourt should use parallel movement in opposite directions (figure 21.2).

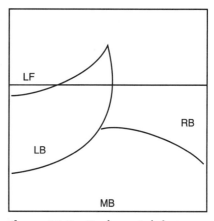

Figure 21.1 Backcourt defense.

Defensive position requires the backcourt player to be on the balls of the feet, in medium or low body position, with the body forward, and with the butt down (so that you can come up to contact the ball, not go down with the ball). Taking this position ensures that your arms will be between the ball and the floor. Do not fall to the floor unnecessarily. You should never touch the floor before your arms make contact with the ball. Lunge, sprawl, roll, or dive as a last resort. Be aggressive but under control.

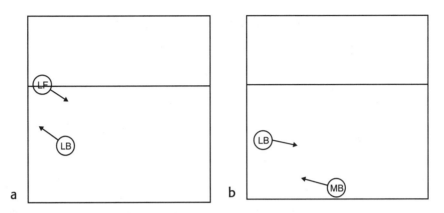

Figure 21.2 Parallel movements for defense.

Defense Philosophy and Concepts for the Coach

A defense is designed to prevent the ball from being hit off your block out of bounds and to prevent the ball from hitting the floor on your side of the net. Your side of the court comprises 900 square feet. You cannot cover every inch of it. Therefore, you must determine what zones of the net or areas of the court you are willing to give up and what zones of the net or areas of the court you will protect and defend.

You must consider not only the opponent's strengths and weaknesses but also the capability of your team. How good is your team's backcourt defense? How good is your block? What are the strengths of your opponent? From where (which zone of the net or which back-row position) do they most often attack the ball? What area on your court do they hit the ball to? After you answer these questions, design your defense with the following points in mind (in rank order):

1. Strengths of your players
2. Areas where your opponents are most likely to attack, along the net and in your backcourt
3. Weaknesses of your players and where you might hide a weak blocker or weak backcourt defender

You must teach your team where most attackers (hitters) attack (hit). Every attacker has a tendency. Most players hit the ball cross-court (on an angle). In addition, in using correct biomechanics, everyone hits the ball between their right and left shoulders.

Your six players on defense must respond as a unit, even though separate coordination is required among the players in the first line of defense, the blockers, and in the second line of defense, the back-row diggers.

The block is the foundation of your defensive alignment (formation). You make back-row adjustments based on the following blocking actions and principles:

1. Attack (stuff) versus area (zone) blocking
2. Numbers of players blocking—one, two, or three
3. Positioning of your blockers—cross-court angle, line, or straight-on blocking (blocking the ball)

Determine what blocking system you will be using. If you are area or zone blocking, you must emphasize the following concept to your players. They can let the opponents hit the ball anywhere they want, over and around the block, but your players will not allow the opponent to attack the ball through the block. Are you attack blocking? That is, have you designed your defensive scheme to have your blockers aggressively go after each attack to intercept it before it breaks the plane of the net? Are you emphasizing a combination of these two philosophies? Do you teach one-on-one blocking or a two- or three-person block scheme? Once you determine your blocking system, you must teach the on-court defense starting positions and sequencing. You will have to coordinate your backcourt positioning and movement sequences with your blocking system. Here are some concepts, definitions, and illustrations that you should establish and teach before you work on backcourt movement and sequencing:

1. Behind the block, inside the block, outside the block
2. Blocking straight on (the ball), blocking cross-court, blocking line (figure 21.3 a–c)

In all defensive schemes, you must identify the following: your main blocker, your main digger, and the player responsible for the tip. Have you covered the court area to which the attacker most often hits the ball (main tendency)?

Aldis Berzins, a former collegiate all-American, the defensive star on the great USA men's teams of 1983–86, and my first assistant coach with the USA women's team in 1993–96, often said, "The most important aspect of defense at the international level is attitude." Really, attitude is important at all levels. It is the most difficult part of the game to teach because it involves intangibles that we can't draw on a chalkboard. These attributes include hard work, discipline, focus (concentration), perseverance, and desire.

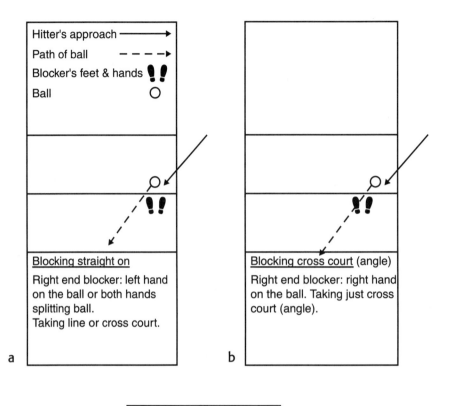

Hitter's approach ——→
Path of ball   – – – →
Blocker's feet & hands
Ball

Blocking straight on

Right end blocker: left hand on the ball or both hands splitting ball.
Taking line or cross court.

a

Blocking cross court (angle)

Right end blocker: right hand on the ball. Taking just cross court (angle).

b

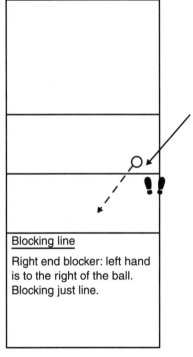

Blocking line

Right end blocker: left hand is to the right of the ball.
Blocking just line.

c

Figure 21.3 **(a)** Blocking straight on the ball; **(b)** Blocking cross-court; **(c)** Blocking line.

Preparation starts with the coach and carries over to the players. The worst thing that a coach can do is look at a diagram in a book and say, "Our players should be 12 feet from the net just as the diagram shows." Coaches need to determine their defenses based on all the points discussed earlier. Obviously, you must scout your opponent (live or on video) and chart their tendencies, play patterns, strengths, weaknesses, and so on. The most important chart you can produce shows where the attack came from and what the result was (kill, error, out of bounds, in net, stuffed by block, in play, etc.). This information will help you determine what area of your net or court you need to defend. You should do the same scouting analysis of your team in your scrimmages or matches so that you can really begin to know your strengths and weaknesses in both attacking and defending.

As mentioned earlier, the most important aspect of defense is *reading* the play correctly. Positioning on the court involves a series of adjustments that are both mental and physical. No matter what defense you are playing—middle back, middle (setter) up, rotation, and so on—you should begin by teaching your team the four positions of defense. When you and your team master these four team-defense sequences, you will have a better understanding of how to read the opponent's attack and how to counter it by deploying your preassigned defensive formations and patterns.

Four Positions

   1. Starting position. Defense begins from the moment the ball crosses the net to your opponent. At that instant, every player must get to his or her basic starting position.

The goal is for the defenders to be in this predefined (assigned) position before the opponent's first contact. The starting position is a defined spot for each of the six players for perimeter middle back defense (figure 21.4).

   2. Read position. This position determines the defender's area of responsibility. Make sure that the defender is in stationary position as the attacker contacts the ball. The defender must follow the ball from the moment it crosses the net to the opponent's side (starting position) to the first, second, and third contact by the opponent. The defender focuses on what is happening to the ball.

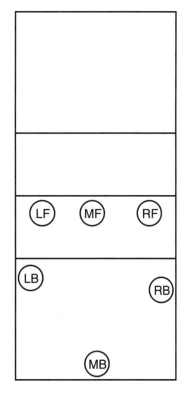

Figure 21.4   Starting positions.

The goal is for the defenders to be in the read position before the attacker's takeoff. These are some things a defender must pay attention to:

- *Overpass.* The opponent returns the ball right back to your court on the serve receive (pass) or dig.

- *Setter attack (tip or hit on the second contact).* Great setters can become an offensive weapon when they are in the front row rotationally. They can disguise their intent to set, tip, or hit on their second contact. The key for the defender is to watch the ball and the setter's body position. The player can read correctly by coupling careful observation with scouting knowledge of the setter's tendencies.

- *Set direction.* In a normal three-contact sequence, the set direction is essential to determining the defender's area of responsibility. Once the ball has left the setter's hands, the defender knows whether it's going to go forward or back, high or low, tight or deep. Great setters can set the ball from many different body positions, making set direction tougher to read. Again, knowing the setter's tendencies (in your scouting report) or reading the body-position cues (arching the back on back sets, jump setting on quick sets, etc.) will help the defender to pinpoint his or her area of responsibility.

- *Set placement and position (height, depth, and zone of the net).* The farther the ball is from the net, the closer it will be to the top of the net when it goes over and the longer it will take to get to the defender. The closer the ball is to the top of the net, the quicker the attack. A ball set right on the net is the blocker's responsibility to defend.

- *Attacker approach (angle or straight, early or late).* To have the option of hitting the ball in any direction, the attacker must be on time. The approach angle of the hitter will determine whether the attack will be an angle (cross-court) attack or a line attack. An approach near a 45-degree angle (to the net) is more likely to be an angle, or cross-court, attack. A more perpendicular, or straight in (90-degree angle), approach will more likely produce a line attack. An attacker who is late or early is probably just going to try to get the ball in. A blocker defending an early attack must jump early, of course, and must be patient and wait longer for a later attack.

- *Attacker tendencies (line, cross-court, deep, sharp, seam, off hands, straight down, off-speed, roll, tip, wipe, etc.).* Only world-class attackers have the ability to hit all shots effectively. Often, a hitter doesn't have good roll, wipe, or tip shot. For example, Mireya Luis, the outstanding Cuban player, hits as hard as anybody in the world. She also has an excellent tip shot and a good off-speed shot. But she doesn't hit the ball off the block (wipe) very often. With Luis, like most great hitters, the defenders must touch the ball on the block. If the block doesn't touch Mireya's hits, she is probably going to score on 80 percent of them. Hitter tendencies also come into play at the lower levels, where the best hitters are likely to have favorite shots. In high school or college volleyball, one thing you can be sure of is that players will not hit many line shots because it is much easier to hit angle (cross-court). Knowing the tendencies of the attacker will help the defender make the correct read.

- *Use of the antennae and court.* If the ball is set outside the sideline, the defender knows that the attacker will not be able to hit the line. The farther outside the ball is, the more angle (cross-court) attacks the attacker will hit.

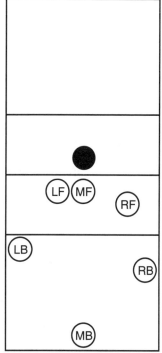

Figure 21.5 shows the shift that occurs from a starting position to a read position during a quick middle hit. Note the adjustments made by the left front and right front.

3. Adjust position. This position is the exact spot where the defender should be to intercept the ball. The defender moves to this position after the attacker contacts the ball, adjusting within a range of a few (one to three) feet. Remember that the ball is traveling at 40 to 80 miles per hour, depending on the level of play. The player has little time to react, let alone take a step or two. Thus, the defender must be in the right area (the correct read position) before adjusting a short distance to the exact spot.

Figure 21.5 Position shift from start to read.

Figure 21.6 is a standard perimeter defense for a left-side attack in the adjust position. Note the movement capabilities of the nonblockers.

4. Emergency position. The defender moves to the emergency position in the pursuit phase, moving more than three feet to intercept a ball that has changed direction after a block deflection, an errant dig, or a mis-hit by the attacker (figure 21.7).

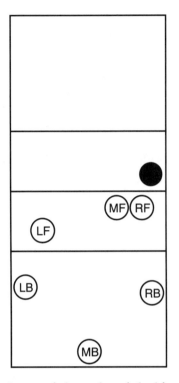

Figure 21.6 Standard perimeter defense for a left-side attack in the adjust position.

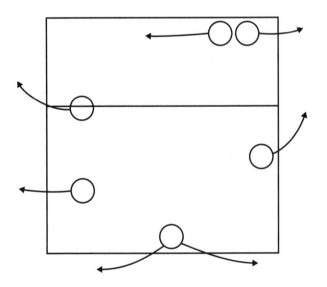

Figure 21.7 Emergency position.

Team Defense Systems and Patterns

During the last 60 years, indoor volleyball has evolved several different defense systems and patterns. These fall into four distinct categories:

The *perimeter* defense (figure 21.8) places at least three defenders on the court lines (sidelines and end line). This defense is commonly called *middle back, middle back-back, 6 back* (6 is the international designation of the middle back player in the rotation), or *white defense* (the latter name was first used by Val Keller in *Point, Game, Match,* Hollywood, California: Creative Sports Books, 1968).

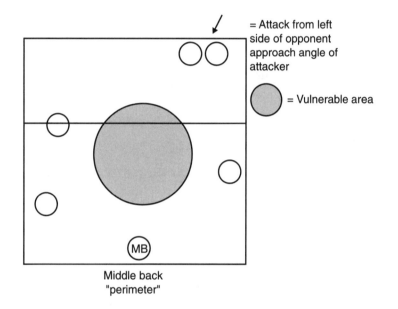

Middle back
"perimeter"

Figure 21.8   Perimeter defense.

In the *up* defense (figure 21.9), one defender, usually the middle back or the setter, goes to the 10-foot line (3-meter line) behind the block. This defense is commonly called *middle up, middle back-up, 6 up, setter up* (often the up person is the back-row setter), or *red* (Keller definition).

The *rotation* defense uses a predefined rotation (movement) of players during the read position based on set direction. The defense has many variations. Through the years, I have called some of the variations *strong rotation* (figure 21.10a) or *counter rotation* (figure 21.10b).

Miscellaneous defenses use one or two elements of the other three systems. Figure 21.11, a through c, depicts three of these systems. In the first, the left-front player on defense slides behind the block. By Keller's definition, this is the *blue* defense. The second, known as *black,* is one that we used with the USA women's team in 1995–96. It uses a three-player block

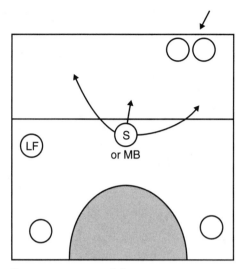

Figure 21.9 Up defense.

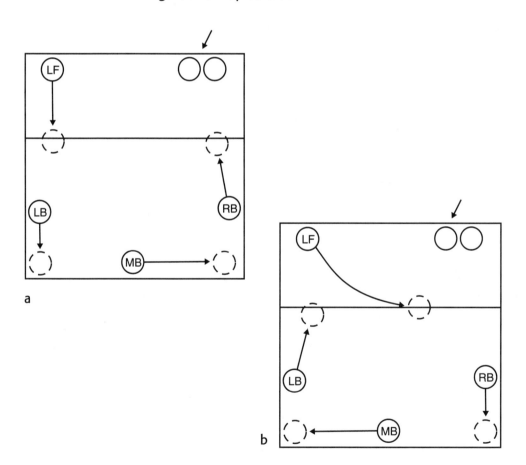

Figure 21.10 **(a)** Strong rotation; **(b)** Counter rotation.

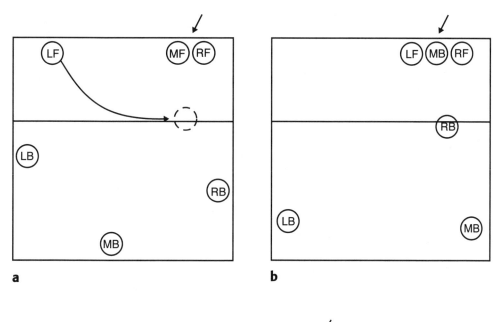

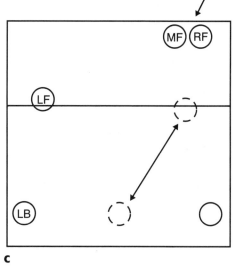

Figure 21.11 Three defense systems: **(a)** Blue defense; **(b)** Black defense; **(c)** Rover defense.

and a player up. The third is called *rover* (who plays like a free safety in football), in which a player can play up or back depending on her or his read of the situation.

In the next few pages are samples of defenses I used at University of the Pacific (UOP) with my women's teams from 1976 through 1984 and with the USA women's teams from 1985 through 1996.

Nonblockers and back-row players take these four steps in playing defense:

1. They begin in the basic defense position, assuming this position as soon as

   - the ball hit to the opponent has crossed the net (serve),
   - the ball has passed the block and crossed the net on a spike, or
   - the ball has been hit over the net in any other way.

   In all three cases, players should be in the basic position before the opponent touches the ball.

2. Players go to the read position, determining it by the pass to the setter, the set direction, and the approach by the spiker. The ideal is to be in the read position when the hitter slaps the foot at takeoff. Players should be in a stationary position as the spiker contacts the ball.

3. Players adjust position with a two- to three-foot movement (in the primary zone of effectiveness) after the spiker hits the ball. They make the movement with a step, hop, or sprawl and must be stationary when making the dig contact.

4. Players use the emergency position (secondary zone of effectiveness) for ball deflected off the block.

Knowing the basic steps for blocking and playing the back row, we are ready to describe the different defenses that we used at Pacific and by the USA National team. Each has particular strengths and weaknesses. The key to the success of each is coordinated movement among the front-row blockers, among the back-row diggers, and between the front row and the back row.

I. Middle Back (MB)

Figure 21.12 shows the basic starting position for the middle back defense. The left back is primarily responsible if the setter dinks the ball on the second contact. For a set to the opponent's left (our right), the block takes the cross-court shot, and the diggers adjust accordingly (figure 21.13).

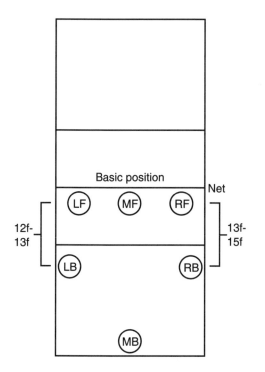

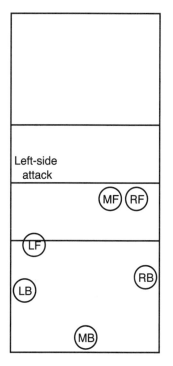

Figure 21.12   Basic starting position for the middle back defense.

Figure 21.13   Left side attack middle back defense.

The players have these responsibilities:

1. The middle back (MB) is responsible for any ball on the end line or any ball that others cannot get. In the rover defense, the MB tries to get everything.
2. The left back (LB) is the main cross-court digger.
3. The right back (RB) covers the dink or down the line. Although the RB prepares for one or the other, she or he must be ready for both.
4. The back-row players should use parallel movement.

For a high set in the middle, the team takes the positions shown in figure 21.14. The LB and RB have to adjust for dinks outside or over the block. Once the ball has passed the block, the blockers should also go after the ball.

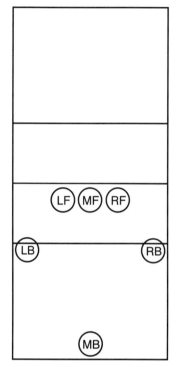

Figure 21.14 Positions for a high set in the middle in a MB-back defense.

II. Strong Rotation

The most effective defense that the University of the Pacific teams used in the past was the strong rotation defense. Its purpose is to defend against high outside sets. It is a read defense that reacts first to set direction.

III. Counter Rotation

This defense is similar to the strong rotation defense. The counter rotation has two variations.

1. Counter rotation. In this variation the nonblocker rotates behind the block, and the back row rotates away from the set direction.
   - For a set to the opponent's left front, the team rotates as shown in figure 21.15.
   - For a set to the opponent's right front, the team rotates as shown in figure 21.16.

An advantage to this rotation over strong rotation is that the setter can be protected from digging the ball. In addition, this defense may be more effective at defending quick outside sets.

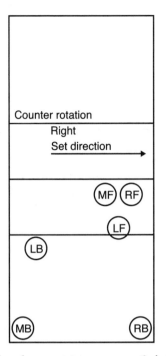

Figure 21.15 Counter rotation for a set to opponent's left front.

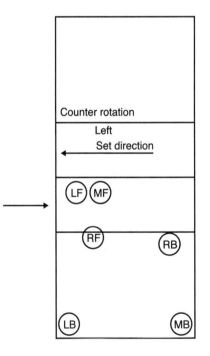

Figure 21.16 Counter rotation for a set to opponent's right front.

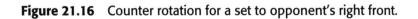

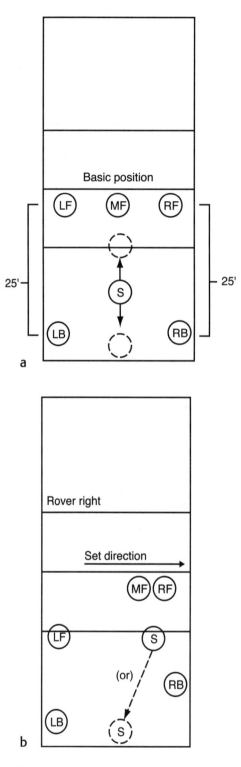

Figure 21.17 Rover defense.

IV. Rover

The read positions for this defense are shown in figure 21.17, a and b.

The rover defense is similar to the middle back defense, with these differences:

1. The middle back starts in the middle but can go wherever she or he thinks is best to dig the ball.

2. Back row players LB and RB start and stay at 25 feet back.

3. The back-row player behind the block digs only. Ideally, this player has no responsibility for the short dink.

4. If the setter moves to middle back, the nonblocker has full responsibility for the dink. This player straddles the 10-foot line and lines up slightly inside the block.

During the year we may use all of these defenses at one time or another. The key is to use a defense that takes away the opposition's prime hitting area and that we play well. The system that best meets these requirements will change from team to team. We may also modify the defenses as the situation demands. Our goal is to let the opposition hit the ball as hard as they can to areas that we are giving them. Our defense will be there waiting.

Final Thoughts

I believe that once you understand and are able to teach the process of defense—the definitions, the philosophy for the player and the coach, and the four positions—you are ready to design and implement a specific defense system for your team.

Above all else, remember the importance of *learning to read* the situation on the other side of the net. Teams must play defense before the opponent contacts the ball. Practicing the various situations that your opponent might put you in is the best way to improve your defense. Couple this concept with adequate individual defensive skills and the proper teaching of the points in this chapter, and you and your team will be on your way to becoming a great defensive team.

Regardless of how quick your players are and how skilled they are in individual defense techniques, if they do not put themselves in the right position *before* contacting the ball they will not become outstanding defenders. Your team defense is the summation of all of your players' abilities—innate physical talent, volleyball skills, and perhaps most important the cognitive understanding of the concepts and ways of playing the game.

PART V

Game-Winning and Tournament-Winning Strategies

CHAPTER TWENTY–TWO

Giving Players and Teams the Competitive Edge

Pete Waite

When volleyball coaches prepare their teams, they spend hours upon hours training physical techniques on the court. But the coaches who really understand the mental aspects of the game have teams that often seem to find ways to win. These coaches may not always have the most physically gifted teams, but in the end they put it all together to create champions. Within the best teams and players, the mental and physical parts of the game intertwine. Combine the two in the right way, and you have a team that is very difficult to beat.

Training the Brain

As I prepared to write on this topic, I thought of all the ways the mind is connected to the sport. To see it as a clear separation of the physical and the mental didn't seem quite right. To discuss the mental aspects of the game, we must also address the emotional and spiritual sides. To be a good coach, you need to recognize the effect you have in everything you do with your team, say to your team, or behave around your team. Once you understand the effects of your actions, you'll find it much easier to move with your team toward a common goal. Your job as a coach is to guide your players, to nudge them along through areas they don't always want to go. If you develop a good feel for what is happening within your team, you will be able to sidestep obstacles that could hold some teams back.

Some of the most obvious mental aspects of volleyball take place on the court, whether in practices or games. The first hurdle blocks the path of both novice and elite teams. Players must learn to trust the coaches so that they can begin to learn. You must show your players that what you're saying will work. Whether it's a hand position on a block or a defensive alignment against a certain hitter, the players need to see proof that what you say will get them closer to the win. The road to winning begins with that first small step. Once trust is in place, your players will become more confident every time they step on the court. As you know, a confident team is hard to beat.

Some of the best teams have an understanding between the coaches and the players that it is all right to take risks. The best coaches encourage and challenge their players to take risks and grow. To become better, players need to try things outside their comfort zone. They need to improve their weak areas and try new approaches. Have you ever had a camper or a new player tell you, "I wasn't taught it that way!" To improve, that player will have to take a risk and try a new technique. That's where trust comes in. If players are going to take a risk, they have to trust you. Most players feel their way is the right way (even when it's not working), and you need to persuade them to try another approach. To serve different zones or serve harder serves, they need to risk looking bad for a while until they perfect the technique. If you yell at them after every mistake, you will stifle their growth. They will become tentative when they need to be aggressive, and their minds will get in the way of their progress.

As you build the strength of the team through improving the players' techniques, you give them the ability to look beyond themselves. Inexperienced players are concerned only about their own game, so they find it difficult to focus on the opponent. Experienced players know not only what they are doing but also what the opposition is going to do. They don't learn that on their own; it's something you as a coach need to teach them. Your players should always know what defense the opposing team is using. Scout upcoming opponents and teach your players to watch defenses while the ball is in play. Teach them to communicate with each other about play as it happens. Where is the tip open? Is the setter front row or back? Who are the weak blockers? At any point in a practice scrimmage or a match, I ask my team what defense the other team is in. When I'm with a team for the first time I'm amazed at how many blank stares I get. Some players have never thought about looking across the net during play. Those same players will drive you nuts by tipping directly to a player who for the entire game has been rotating up behind the block. Can you afford to give up one easy play when you could have scored with a better shot? Teams win or lose championships because of plays like that. Take care of the simple things so that your team has a chance to win. Teach them to use their minds, to learn as they play, and to find satisfaction in outsmarting an opponent.

One way to know if your hitters are mentally strong is to watch them attacking. When they get a bad set, do they back off and become tentative? Teach them to become more aggressive when the set isn't right. By attacking the ball while it is still above the tape, they have a great shot at scoring. Do they tip only when they're in trouble? By allowing them to tip only when they have a great set, your attackers will catch the defense on their heels. When your hitter sees a double and triple block, does he or she hit the ball out? I call that an avoidance shot. That hitter would rather hit it out than challenge the block with the chance of being stuffed. Teach them to attack the block. They'll find that many blocks are breakable. The main thing is that you let them know that it's OK to be blocked occasionally. If they learn to attack with confidence, their hitting percentage will go up quickly. As hitters finds confidence, they become stronger mentally and seek that great feeling of scoring. When you have them fighting for a kill on every set, you have created a strong-minded attacker who wants the ball in crunch time. Then you can count on them when the game is on the line.

When you think of mentally strong teams, you might also think of the intimidation factor in games. Intimidation generally occurs between a strong team and a weak team. A team should learn to carry itself without showing signs of stress. Teach them to minimize negative body language and to avoid showing frustration. If you can level off the highs and lows, you might find that your team plays a more steady, consistent game. Players feed off the

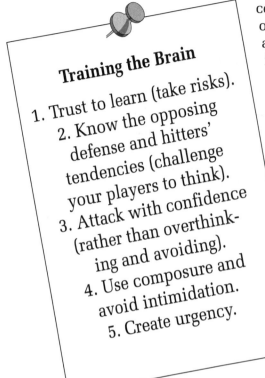

Training the Brain

1. Trust to learn (take risks).
2. Know the opposing defense and hitters' tendencies (challenge your players to think).
3. Attack with confidence (rather than overthinking and avoiding).
4. Use composure and avoid intimidation.
5. Create urgency.

coaches, so be sure you know what kind of signals you are giving off in practices and games. Some of the most intimidating teams I've seen are the ones who play steadily point after point. They are the teams that you can't seem to score on, the teams that enjoy the tough volleys. Teach your team to stay composed no matter what happens on the court.

The overriding philosophy of good coaching is to get your team to play with an urgency to win. If you can instill that mind-set in your players, then they will focus on figuring out an opponent, outworking them, and being the first to score the final point of each game. If you see them being satisfied with average play, then you need to emphasize the importance of each part of each play. Passers should get great satisfaction from giving a perfect pass to start the play. A small blocker who deflects a ball but doesn't stuff it should feel great if the team transitioned back to score. These sequences are the beauty of volleyball. Many skills intertwine to make the whole machine run smoothly. Work hard as a coach to create an atmosphere of focus and urgency to win. Your team should strive for perfection in every part of every play, fight for every point of every game for the entire match. When your team mentality becomes that focused, you have a chance to beat any opponent. No team can play a perfect game, but you will be amazed at the heights your players can reach when they learn about playing with an urgency to win.

Monitoring Mental and Emotional Needs

How many times have you heard people say that sport is 90 percent mental and 10 percent physical? As I think about all the aspects of volleyball, I tend to believe those percentages. If you as a coach are good at analyzing and adjusting the mental and emotional state of your team, then you will win many matches against coaches who don't understand it. If you understand that your players are not just physical beings executing techniques, you may see that they are all humans with many things going on inside them. Become skilled at guiding them through the rough times, and you'll find that your job becomes easier.

You will rarely have teams in which everyone gets along all the time. Athletes are competitive, and they bring their entire personal history to the court. They will act how their parents raised them, or how coaches allowed them to act. You'll be thrilled with some players, whereas others always seem to have problems. Keep an eye out for conflicts brewing in the group. Try to settle things before they get out of hand. You may have to straighten out a player who is disrespectful to teammates. You might need to bring two players together to talk things out. Talk to your players on the bus or during stretching. Try to feel the pulse of the team and find whether a positive feeling exists among the group. If you are oblivious to player conflicts or ignore them, you will probably pay for it later. Male players tend to go head to head with each other and settle things quickly. If they don't really settle it, at least they're able to step on the court with their teammates even if they're arguing about something. Women tend to brew, and conflicts can build without your knowing it. Some players may cause internal problems you can't see on the surface. Those players can create a sickness that silently eats away at the insides of your team until it affects everything on the court. Stop the cancer as soon as you can or cut it out entirely. No matter how talented the player, you'll be happy that you are free of the problem, and your team will probably be better in the end.

Coach-player issues can stem from things you might never imagine. Sometimes you may need to handle matters right on the court. At other times you may be able to sit down and talk in private. Coaches are always critiquing players, and that process can be hard on their egos. Some will always feel that you're picking on them, that you never say anything positive. Other issues may be about playing time, or a player may believe that you're favoring someone else. The bottom line is that you are the leader of the group. You want to be sympathetic to their thoughts, but in the end you need to guide them toward the ultimate goals of the team. No coach can treat all players exactly the same way. I think the best coaches treat all players fairly and in a similar fashion, but they know how to tweak their response to each member to have them playing their best. The coach is like a race-car mechanic who adjusts the engine until it sounds just right. If you're good at listening to the engine of your team, it will be ready to take on all comers. If your players have unresolved issues with the staff, they won't play hard for you and they'll always fall short of expectations.

Besides having issues with teammates and coaches, your players will have personal situations that they have trouble keeping off the court. Watch for the stress of a starter who is unable to handle his or her role. Maybe you have a kid who comes off the bench but can't handle the stress. Teach the player to mature into his or her role or change the role to one that fits the player's experience or personality. Academics can be stressful, especially for the college athlete. On the men's side of the game, players aren't as likely to take their concerns about classes onto the court. But as a women's coach, I see occasions when players reach their breaking point because of their classroom work. Whether the cause is a big project, midterms, or finals, late-night studying and worrying about grades can affect the players' mental state in practices. Occasional meetings with players can help them through some problems and may give you a more focused team in the gym. How often should you meet? Some people meet individually with players every week, but I think that's too much. I try to make contact with as many players as I can every day in practice and then meet in a relaxed situation about every three weeks. Chatting before practice, during stretching, or during a water break can alleviate minor issues before they become major.

At some point during the season, tension will probably develop. It can be a build up through issues I've already mentioned, but the pressure put on by the staff everyday often causes strain. Everyone wants to win, and coaches find it hard to watch mistakes happen repeatedly. Coaching tests your patience and requires you to be creative with your team as you continually ask for improvement. After too much of it, you can almost see the players' spirits fade and their desire to be in the gym diminish.

You can try to alleviate that pressure by planning something enjoyable as part of every practice. We often think that just playing volleyball is fun for the players, but day after day, week after week, it gets old. They start feeling as if volleyball is a job, and they play it with no emotion. Occasionally give them enjoyable things to do, things that will make them (and you) laugh. These activities could be part of a warm-up drill, maybe some short-court doubles. One of the activities I throw in is a game of tag for warm-ups. Suddenly, the players become kids again and start laughing and smiling. Think about how long this generation of players has been in organized sports. T-ball and soccer in kindergarten? Many started club volleyball at sixth or seventh grade. Coaches or parents have been pushing them ever since to work hard, to be better. How often do they play just to have fun? You can even add 10 or 15 minutes at the end of practice for them to play triples or doubles. If you let them do this, don't try to coach them. This is their time to have fun, and it's a way to remind them why they play volleyball.

One of the most useful methods I've learned is to let the team design the practice. The players really seem to enjoy this, but I suggest that you do it only occasionally. Tell them they can pick any drills they want, set them up, and tell the coaches how they want to use them. They'll pick their favorite drills and enjoy performing them because they made the choice. I promise that your team will leave the gym that day feeling good about themselves and appreciating what you did.

The most significant use of this technique came for me in the 2000 season. Our Badger team had just come off a weekend at Indiana and Penn

State. We were about two-thirds of the way into the season, and every match was critical. We beat Indiana in four but didn't play very well. Then we had bad weather on our flight to Penn State and lost. Everyone was feeling the stress, including the staff. Coming into practice on Monday morning, I had to put together the next practice. We could have worked on many things we hadn't done well. We could have pounded balls at the players to try to raise their level another notch. I sat at my desk thinking that none of that felt right. I thought we needed something else, so I wrote nothing down for practice. When I walked into the gym, I brought the team together and asked them to split up into classes. I asked each class to come up with a part of practice. I didn't tell them to come up with drills. I just said that they would decide what we were going to do. Now an open-ended request like that might set me up for trouble, but it was interesting to see what they chose. Each class came up with a game, ranging from tag to triples. I was particularly impressed with the sophomores, who came up with kickball. Their choice helped me realize what really makes them happy. We went through each game class by class. They kept kickball for the end, and that event turned out to be amazingly fun and amusing to watch. Picture our team in the Wisconsin Field House with the outfielders up high in the second-level seats! You should have seen Sherisa Livingston, the Big Ten Co-Player of the Year, run up to kick the ball! Was I worried that she might get hurt? Yes. Did she injure herself? No, thank God. Was this a risky thing to do at this point of the season? Yes. Did it end up paying off? Absolutely. The spirit of the team came back, and the team mentality was much healthier. That team ended up winning the Big Ten and went on to play in the national championship match. That practice was a turning point for our season, and it all revolved around what I felt the team needed at the time.

A similar solution to giving life to a tired team can be as easy as taking a day off. Sometimes, especially in the college game, the best thing to do is to give players time away from each other. You'll really make them happy because they'll have time to do their laundry, study a little more for a test, or just relax with their friends. It's not something I do often, but a day off can be good for the players and the staff. Although a great practice the next day is not guaranteed, the rest you have given their minds and bodies will pay off when you need it.

All the areas I've discussed in this section have a connection to your success or failure. If you can monitor the mental and emotional health of your team, then you have a great chance of finding that elusive characteristic known as team chemistry. I've always looked at coaching as a job like that of a shepherd. Your job is to move your flock from one place to another, together. If one member strays, then you need to bring that individual back with the group so that you can move on. If a several players are straying in different directions, you're going to have a hard time getting anything done on the court. You will not be moving forward toward your goals. I call it getting stuck in the muck. Coaches who let their players become stuck in the muck will also fall by the wayside. Those who can move their teams together as one will begin chalking up the wins and the championships.

Visualizing and Positive Self-Talk

Many books and much information about using visualization in sport and life are available. Although I haven't spent much time on visualization with my teams, I have seen the benefits and I believe that your program will be better if you use some of the skills.

The basic premise of visualization is to repeat positive images in your mind in the hope that the body will do what the mind has practiced. Those images can be of group or individual situations. Visualization goes hand in hand with positive self-talk, another important skill that athletes should learn. As a coach you have to be alert to negative talk or actions that can be part of the downward cycle of losing. Remarks or body language that conveys messages like "We're never going to beat them" or "I can't pass a ball" almost certainly bring about those outcomes. In the reverse, a player who thinks or says, "We're going to win no matter what" or "Serve me, this one's mine" will likely achieve positive outcomes because of how the player approaches every play.

To attain the right frame of mind, players can use visualization just before a practice or a match. Some people do it with their eyes closed in a favorite private spot, whereas others can do it with their eyes open walking to class. Either way, all you have to do is imagine yourself in the situation in which you want to be strong. You can even use visualization when you are preparing for something you've never done before, like a championship match or a making a speech in class. If you can repeatedly see yourself successfully executing the skill in your mind, then when you actually do it your body and emotions will react as if they've done it before. Coaches and players who are good leaders do this for their teams. Rather than just giving feedback after a play, they plant positive thoughts into the minds of players or teammates to help them execute the skill when the time comes. Some examples of talk that doesn't accomplish anything would be "Come on, pass the ball!" or "Don't hit it into the block!" Instead, if you say, "Move your feet and surround the ball," the player will visualize how to perform the skill. When the ball comes, the player will be in better position to make a good pass to the setter. The visualizing in this case takes place in an instant. In the blocking example you could say, "Just get up there and bang the line. It's wide open." You're giving the player a mental image of what you want him or her to do. You're also taking the burden off the player. The player is trusting you and may not take an error personally because the suggestion came from the coach.

Positive talk and visualization put a team into an attack mode. You are planting in their minds what you want them to do. Something I learned years ago as a water-safety instructor was to tell pupils what I wanted them to do, not what I didn't want them to do. The theory behind this is that the last thought in a person's mind before the person tries a skill will likely come true. Thus, saying, "We need this point, don't make an error!" has players thinking, "Don't make an error!" Coaches must work hard to tell players how to be successful in skills and situations. Give them the mental tools to find ways to win and soon you'll find them doing the things you suggest.

All teams want to win, and all players want to be successful. You and your players can also visualize your goals and dreams. First, I suggest that you write them down and put them where you'll see them everyday. Then spend time seeing them happen for you. If your team goal is to be the conference champion, then get them used to saying it in their heads and out loud: "I want to win the conference championship." Repeat it. Have your players picture what it would be like to celebrate the championship match and hold the trophy above their heads. Have them visualize it on a regular basis. If your goal is the state or national championship, do the same thing. You are causing them to talk themselves into it, to talk themselves into succeeding. If they can't picture it, it probably won't happen. If they believe it can happen, they will do the work necessary to make it happen. They will train harder, focus more, and make decisions that will lead them toward the mental image they have. I've seen many examples of this working in my life and in the seasons of the teams I've coached. I have no doubt that this saying is true: "What the mind believes, the body achieves!"

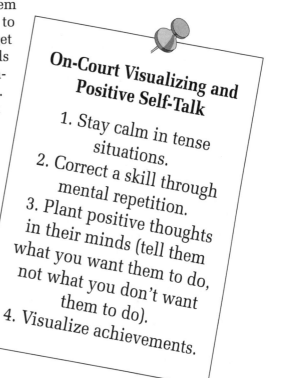

On-Court Visualizing and Positive Self-Talk

1. Stay calm in tense situations.
2. Correct a skill through mental repetition.
3. Plant positive thoughts in their minds (tell them what you want them to do, not what you don't want them to do).
4. Visualize achievements.

Players Roles and Personality Types

Part of deciding who goes where on the court must come from what you know about your players. Once you get to know them, you can work on expanding their roles or use who they are to maximize what they can do for the team. One of the biggest challenges for a coach is to get each player to accept a role and give total effort in that role.

Over the years I've seen enough classes come through my programs that I've narrowed the players into six common categories. These variations may not cover all players, but I've run into these a lot. Players of each type need slightly different coaching to get the most out of them, but all are vital to the success of the group. My best teams had a combination of these traits, and my average teams lacked one or more of these types of players.

First, the stud athlete. Every winning team needs one or more stud athletes—players who jump higher, move quicker, and hit harder than anyone else. These players may not be your hardest workers or deepest thinkers, but they can beat people with their raw talent. At times these players will have to put the team on their shoulders and carry it to the win.

Second, the hard shell. These players are resistant to change. They may question you and have a bit of rebel inside. You want to nurture the competitive nature of these players and take advantage of their toughness. The important part is to come to an understanding with them. They have to be willing to try what you're teaching them so that they can improve their game. Whether you consider their traits stubborn or competitive, you must stay patient and positive because they may be frustrating to coach. I describe these players as being tough nuts to crack. They may have hard shells on the outside, but you have to find a way to reach them and connect with them.

Third, the perfectionist. I've seen two kinds. One has a healthy level of perfectionism, and they get the most out of their bodies. They work harder than the others to be technically perfect, and they make corrections quickly after an error. This kid may not be a great athlete, but he or she can compete with the best because of an unbelievable work ethic. The second kind goes overboard with the pursuit of perfection. If they don't get it right every time, they become so negative that they distract the team or themselves from making the next play a good one. This distraction could come in the form of yelling, pouting, or crying. You have to try to change this habit because it will take energy and attention away from the pursuit of team goals.

Fourth, the reliever. This player is perfectly suited to come off the bench and give the team a lift. Players of this type may not be able to maintain their play at a high level for an extended period, but in short bursts they're invaluable. You can compare these players to the short relief pitcher in baseball who comes in to help close out the game. In volleyball they might give you a different pace of attack or variety in your serves. Sometimes if they don't understand how important it is to have someone strong coming off the bench, I'll ask them, "Which is it better to be, a starter or a finisher?" Even as seniors some players are better off the bench than they are starting. Find out what your players do best and use them in those roles.

Fifth, the clown. This player brings comic relief to the team and staff. In competitive sport a lot of tension can build up, and you need these players to lighten the mood. They often have a hearty laugh and can tell a good joke. You'll often see them as the center of attention on the bus or plane. The most valuable ones also know when to get serious on the court. The ones you need to straighten out pick the wrong times to get goofy in practice. I try hard to let these players be who they naturally are. If you have all serious players and no jokers, the team will probably be at each other's throats when you can least afford it. Loose teams will be calm in the thick of the battle. A word of warning, however; if you have too many clowns you won't be able to get anything accomplished in practice and the matches will be a mess. Some kids are born this way. Some emerge. Either way you'll all be better off if you have some players who give you high entertainment value.

Finally, the glue. These players aren't always your most physically gifted, but they hold the team together. They have a good sense for the mental and emotional status of the team. They can cool tempers or motivate teammates, depending on what the team needs. They may also be your best ball-control players, offering steady play and rarely making errors. You need one or two of these players. You could have six studs, but they may not be able to play together and stay organized. They have the ability to drag others along to a win even when things aren't going well. They use their brains to find ways to beat drills and opponents. They give their teammates confidence and think for them at times. These players are often the unsung heroes because the box score contains no statistic for thinking. Let them know what a great job they're doing and tell them how important they are. Without these players you just have six people on the court. With these kids who are the glue, you have a team that can win championships.

Why Teams Fail

Successful coaches may have down years, but in the end their programs are always near the top of their divisions. They make some great decisions to help their teams win and constantly do things to avoid failing.

Some teams fail simply because the coaches aren't good at transferring what they know. Other coaches simply don't know much to start with. You can always learn more by reading books, going to clinics, and talking to colleagues. But some coaches who have been great players aren't very good at passing on what they know to players. The best advice I can give is to try a variety of methods. Players learn in a variety of ways. Some can listen to what you say and do it right away. Some need to see what you mean with a demonstration or on tape. I tend to teach the whole skill and tell them what the result needs to be. I'll help them tweak their techniques only to come close to the desired result. If they are getting good results, I generally won't change much. As a coach you should have a vision of the final goal, and then you should be creative in finding a variety of ways to lead your players to that goal.

Although we are busy teaching techniques, hitting balls, and taking stats, be sure to keep your eyes and ears open for the warning flags of danger. By this I mean the players or coaches who are undermining what you're trying to accomplish. They may be grumbling about something, putting down their teammates, or creating a divide between the players and the staff. The best thing for you to do is to hit the problem head on as soon as you know about it. If you think it will just go away, you're wrong. Day by day, the problem will fester and grow. Before you know it the problem will spread until it has more control over the team than you do. It's much easier to do damage control as problems develop than to try to save a team whose collective spirit is on life support.

An internal problem that is out of control or a lack of basic game skills can cause a team to implode. You've all seen it before. Sometimes the opponent causes the breakdown; sometimes your own team collapses. They are playing well for a while and then they crack, playing as if they've never seen a volleyball before. They shank balls. They don't flow to the ball. They hit every serve and shot out. Suddenly there is silence on the floor. It's not a pretty sight. The team is handing the game to the opponent. They've packed their bags and are heading home. If this is your team during a match, you might have to try something drastic to get them out of the funk. You need to take a serious look at what caused such a severe problem. You have a lot of work to do.

One simple answer to losing could be that the players aren't having much fun. Remember, volleyball is a game. Games are supposed to be fun, so find ways to make it enjoyable. Browbeating your players after every play is like hitting the puppy with a newspaper. Sure, they'll still do what you say—with their shoulders hunched and their tails between their legs. When players are afraid of making mistakes, they'll start doubting every move they make. You can identify teams that have coaches who make it enjoyable to play volleyball. The players have a spark in their eyes, and they're eager to jump on the court to play some ball.

Some coaches fail even though they may be doing many of the right things. What might be happening to them is that they're letting personal problems affect what the team accomplishes on the court. The team ends up dragging around a lot of extra baggage, which weighs heavier on them every day. Do what you can to limit how involved you are in their personal problems and limit how much you involve them in yours. They don't need to know your personal problems. You might think you're just getting to know them, but your job is to guide them to wins. Help them or get them help if the problem is severe. Becoming too involved will hold your team back.

Even winning teams can begin to fail if they are not able to redirect the negatives into positives. External forces can be the downfall of many teams as the staff puts more energy into putting out fires than coaching the team. Distractions from outside sources can divert teams from their goals. You and your team must be good at deflecting and protecting, at taking something that comes at you in a negative way and turning it into something positive. Here are four areas that can cause problems for your team if you don't handle them well.

1. Parents and friends often want what's best for the player, but you and the player know what's best for the team.
2. Media often search for the juice. They want to get the scoops and stir things up. Prepare your team with answers. Deflect the negative; direct to positive. Have your players hear and see your confident words.
3. Fans can be brutal on the road.
4. Officials try to be accurate, but you won't always agree with them.

To go deeply into these areas would take a whole chapter by itself. One area I do want to touch on is the media. Their job is to get readers, and readers like controversy. First, tell your players always to speak about opponents with respect. You don't want to supply a quote for their locker-room wall. Second, teach them how to answer questions in a way that puts a positive spin on things. An example from our 2001 season involved a player I had moved from right side to left side. She had been an all-American her junior year on the right, but we needed her kill production on the left. She is Jenny Maastricht, and she struggled early in the season. After a match we won, a reporter asked her if she was frustrated with her play. I was impressed that Jenny said, "No, I'm not frustrated. I think I'm getting a lot better, and the rest of the team is playing great." Jenny just deflected a negative question and turned the reporter to a positive direction. She also protected herself and the team by staying away from a negative topic. Here's another example. Before the Final Four, Meggan Kohnen sprained her ankle. She rehabbed for a week and still played in the semifinal match versus USC. Our sports information director, Diane Nordstrom, told reporters that one of our players was playing at 85 percent, and she meant Meggan. In the postgame interviews after beating Southern Cal, one of the reporters asked Sherisa, "So, Sherisa, you must be the player playing at 85 percent since you came out of the back row. Do you need the rest?". He clearly didn't know volleyball or the situation. Sherisa had just been named a first-team all-American. She could have been negative and created a bigger problem. Instead she said, "No, Jamie (Gardner) comes in to play for

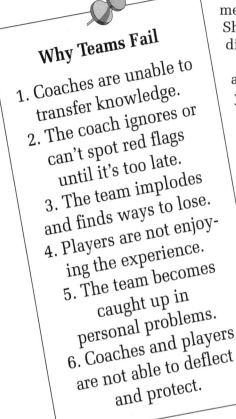

Why Teams Fail

1. Coaches are unable to transfer knowledge.
2. The coach ignores or can't spot red flags until it's too late.
3. The team implodes and finds ways to lose.
4. Players are not enjoying the experience.
5. The team becomes caught up in personal problems.
6. Coaches and players are not able to deflect and protect.

me because she's great in the back row." Sherisa turned that question in the right direction.

It's not just what your players say; it's also what you say. Most players read what you say to reporters in the local or school newspaper. Be positive, avoid singling out players, and don't put down the team's performance. Speak with confidence about your team and where they are headed. Plant in their minds the thoughts that will help the team move toward a championship.

The general concept is to avoid failure to give yourself a chance at success. Protect what you have. Put on the blinders, avoid the distractions, and stay on course. Don't waste energy on things that won't help you reach your goals. Use your energy to improve yourself, your team, and the situation they're in at the time.

Peak Performance

Everyone wants to know how to get his or her players to play at the highest possible level. You certainly can't do this all the time, but you want to avoid the big swings from great play to awful play. If you can keep them playing in the range from good to great, you're doing pretty well. The first challenge is to help them find their individual zones. Then you have to get them to peak at the right time as a team.

Individual players vary in how well they practice compared with how well they play in a match. Some always focus and hustle, whether they are practicing or competing in a game. They seem to find their ultimate playing level easily because they're internally motivated. Other players seem to coast in practice but then turn it on when it's game time. Externally motivated players seem to have a bigger variation in quality of play between practices and games. Your job as a coach is to get your players to play at a consistently high level in practice. Some days they'll be tired from school, travel, friends, or some other distraction. Those practices can be a waste of time. Get their attention early with drills that demand concentration. Some days, no matter what you try to do, players just can't put it together. Explain to your team that they may simply have to work harder to find the zone where they feel they are playing well. Just hustling more can increase the energy level. I think there is truth to the adage "Fake it til you make it." No one can always play at his or her best, but the good players learn how to get themselves up into the zone of strong performance.

The second part of peak performance is getting your team to win when it really matters. Conference tournaments or season-ending tournaments (high school state, NCAA, club nationals) are the times when your team must be playing its best. Make sure that the players are well prepared (playing with confidence), healthy (rested), and eager to play. Shorten (or eliminate) practices and back off the weights and conditioning. Help them to have their bodies feeling good and their minds fresh. The toughest decision you may have as a coach is knowing when to give them a day off. Look at their travel schedule and watch for signs of their wearing down. Be aware of when midterms occur and when major projects are due. You may think that they need more reps in the gym when what they really need is a day off. A fresh body and mind can come back strong the next day.

When tournament time rolls around near the end of the season, be sure that your team has fresh arms and legs. Going lighter on the weights and conditioning will get them moving better. Shortening practices a little will put everyone in a better mood, and they'll want to keep coming to the gym. Just when it begins to seem as if the season will never end, you need to make them feel that it's just beginning. And really, it is. Tournament time is what you've worked so hard for, what separates the good teams from the great teams. If you prepare your players correctly and take care of them, you may see your team do things at tournament time that you only dreamed about. When they find their zone and work together in a great rhythm, it can be magical. Reaching this paradise is why we all coach. Suddenly, you've won the championship, and all you did was make about a thousand critical decisions along the way!

The Winning Formula

Coaches ask themselves the same question in every sport: How can I get my team to win? Everyone is searching for the formula that gives his or her team a chance to win every time they compete. Without talking about strategy or physical techniques, I've put together a list of a few things that have worked for me over the years.

I grew up in Wisconsin during the first glory days of the Green Bay Packers and Vince Lombardi. I followed them every weekend and can still remember the announcer's call. "Dale to the left, Dollar to the right, Star drops back to pass . . ." I recently had a chance to read a book on Lombardi. What I learned from it was that he kept things simple. He made sure his teams did the simple things to perfection. I think that's the first part of the winning formula. Keep things simple and do the simple things well. Some coaches ask their players to do so many complicated things that they outsmart themselves. The team makes so many errors that the game becomes easy for the opponent to win.

Good coaches can identify the weak areas of their teams, and they have a vision of how they will eliminate them. If you can make each of your players stronger and more well rounded, your team will be more difficult to defeat. Watch every part of what they do and find creative ways to eliminate your weak areas. Give them the mental and physical skills to find ways to beat every drill and every opponent.

Sometimes coaches do too much as they lead their teams. Keep your players healthy and happy by avoiding overtraining, overmeeting, overcoaching, and overthinking. It's easy to think that we should do more of everything. That approach doesn't work, and the good coaches know when to back off. An example of the result of overcoaching happened to me outside the gym. I've been playing golf since high school and although I wasn't great, I did pretty well. I never really had a lesson until two years ago, and I thought it was finally time. It was beneficial to see what I should be doing. The instructor went down the list of things I should correct. Now when I play all I have to do is keep my knees from shifting, keep my left arm straight, cock my wrist at the top of my swing, swivel my hips around my pivot leg, turn my wrist over as I contact the ball, and follow through so that my hips face forward and my hands finish high. That's all. See my point? Sometimes it's better to teach the whole move and just change a little at a time. Did the lesson help? My golf game has never been worse! Understand that too much information may hurt more than it helps.

Winning teams are rarely outstanding in only one area. They tend to excel because of their balance, which can come in different forms. One way to look at it is by the number of veterans in the lineup. You need to look at your team, see what they need, and find a way to balance it out. If the team is young, give them plenty of playing experiences to help them mature quicker. If you have a veteran team, give them new challenges and variety to keep them eager. If the group doesn't know how to be serious, give them drills that create an intense atmosphere so that they focus on the task. If they're too serious, give them ways to relax in stressful situations. Your team may start out under one of these descriptions and over the season take on a different personality. You will need to make adjustments to continue heading in the right direction.

Above all, I think that the best coaches know when to push their teams and when to back off and be patient. You and your staff constantly critique your team and push them to improve. Sometimes the best thing to do is to be quiet and let the drill take its course. The team may need a while to figure out a drill and accomplish the goals. It's tempting to stop the drill and talk. More instruction, more attitude, better results, right? Sometimes, yes. But know when to step back and let the players learn on their own. Let them be creative and find ways to win. If we as coaches always give them the energy and help them out of jams, they'll never learn to do it themselves.

One thing that I started doing as a club coach still works for me today in practices or matches. Although I don't do it often, this approach makes a point. If my team is not playing together, or if nothing I say seems to be getting through to them, I pull them together and tell them they need to figure it out. Then I step aside, at least 10 feet away. They are stunned for a second, but then something takes place. Someone, a leader, starts things off with an opinion. Then the others pitch in with some thoughts. Suddenly, they start playing harder because they often listen to each other more than they do to the coach. Whatever they said in the huddle, they'll put a better effort into it because it came from them. They don't want to look bad when they're in charge. They'll show you just to prove that they can do it on their own.

The Winning Formula

1. Keep things simple and do the simple things well.
2. Eliminate your weaknesses.
3. Eliminate overtraining, overmeeting, overcoaching, and overthinking.
4. Find a balance. Know your team's needs.
5. Be patient. Allow your players to make mistakes and give them time to grow.

Make Steps up the Ladder

Every season is made up of a multitude of decisions and results. The best coaches find ways to help their teams make the journey to the top of the ladder, to guide them closer to their goals. A player or the team occasionally stagnates. Forward movement stops. Coaches have the job of finding out why progress has slowed and making the necessary changes to get back on track. In every season, setbacks occur. These events can crush weak teams or give mentally tough teams the incentive to surge forward. I believe that everything happens for a reason—to get us closer to perfection. No one can achieve perfection, but if you strive for it in the right way, you'll be amazed at how close you can get. Train the physical side of your team but be sure to spend as much or more time with the mental and emotional aspects. Once you learn how to do that, you'll see that the championships are great, but the satisfaction of getting the team there can be just as gratifying.

If you want to learn an approach to sport that encompasses more than just the physical technique, read *Thinking Body, Dancing Mind* by Huang Chunliang and Jerry Lynch (Contributor) I read it about three years into my first Division I head coaching job, and I felt that it related to my style of coaching. The best coaches are teachers, and we are teaching our players much more than how to spike, dig, or block a ball. Teach them to be in control of their minds and their emotions. Unlock the full potential of each of your players. Best of luck to each of you, and remember, it's still a game.

CHAPTER TWENTY–THREE

Scouting Opponents and Evaluating Team Performance

Jim Coleman

Volleyball statistics are boring and misleading. They are worshiped and misunderstood. They are difficult to record and more difficult to interpret correctly. Like a glass of fine wine, statistics are best appreciated in small quantities.

As a player, I too often remembered all the good plays I made but only the bad plays my teammates made, and I justified my importance to the team by this faulty statistical system. To be meaningful, a statistic needs to be comprehensive, accurate, and valid. Often we take only a brief look at the game.

One need not be a mathematical genius to understand volleyball statistics. Remember that the most important statistic is the final score! All others are relatively unimportant.

Reason for Statistics

There are many reasons for taking statistics. We must recognize which statistics are being taken and for what purpose they are being used. For instance, coaches often use media statistics to make team decisions, a purpose for which they are unsuited.

Types of Statistics

1. Media statistics. Recognize that the media are interested in simple numbers that they can rapidly accumulate and that the public can easily understand. For that reason, media statistics are generally simple totals and positive. Jennifer killed 12 spikes, blocked 6 balls, and served 3 aces. Seldom are the "stupid errors" reported.

Media statistics are rarely true indicators of the causes of wins or losses, nor do they measure the true value of a player to a team. Media statistics seldom offer a complete picture of the game.

The only semicomplicated statistic with which the public becomes familiar is spiking efficiency. We will discuss efficiency later in the chapter. The AVCA-NCAA statistics sheet (published by the American Volleyball Coaches Association) is a good summary for media statistics.

If you report team results to the same printed media for a prolonged period, such as a competitive season, you should develop a box score similar to that used by the media in basketball and baseball (table 23.1).

2. Team recognition. Teams often receive recognition by an extension of media statistics. Teams are recognized by wins and losses. Individuals are recognized by statistical totals such as "Mary had a match kill record of 57 kills in the five-game match against the Nawakwa Tigers on January 25" or "Coach Al Scates recorded his 1,000th collegiate win against Pepperdine University on February 3, 2001."

3. Match management. Most coaches are interested in performance during a match. They would like to make match decisions based on hard numbers accumulated during the match. For instance, when a player rotates to the net, should the coach leave the player in at the net or use a different front-row player? A coach needs to know things such as the player's current hitting percentage, what the player has done on the last five swings, and how the team has scored while the player is at the net.

Clearly, the type of statistics required to answer these questions are different from the statistics the media needs.

4. Match evaluation. The coach should analyze the results of each match to determine reasons for the win or loss. Each team should have statistical standards that, if reached, indicate success in that phase of the game. These standards are not easily determined, but they are critical for an accurate evaluation of team performance.

TABLE 23.1

Box Score

SCORES (USA VS. RUSSIA) 3-1: 25-19, 23-25, 25-23, 25-21

USA*	BLK	ACE	KILL	ERR	ATKS	EFF	POINTS	DIGS
Jones	1	0	17	3	33	0.424	18	1
Coleman	4	0	5	1	10	0.400	9	2
Greeno	5	1	9	4	16	0.313	15	4
Beal	0	3	12	1	24	0.458	15	7
Dunphy	2	0	5	3	10	0.200	7	3
Sato	0	0	1	0	2	0.500	1	6
Buck	2	0	10	2	25	0.320	12	2
Sambo	0	0	4	3	9	0.111	4	2
Dusty	0	0	1	0	1	1.000	1	1
Sye	0	0	0	0	0		0	10L
Opp err							16	
Total	14	4	64	17	130	0.362	98	38

(continued)

TABLE 23.1 CONTINUED

Russia	BLK	ACE	KILL	ERR	ATKS	EFF	POINTS	DIGS
Shukin	3	0	7	3	24	0.167	10	2
Fomin	0	0	14	1	18	0.722	14	7
Czrnklov	0	1	3	3	10	0.000	4	0
Modlevski	0	1	10	1	23	0.391	11	9
Andronovic	0	0	1	3	6	-0.333	1	10
Pojerek	0	0	1	0	1	1.000	1	1
Lapinski	2	0	11	3	27	0.296	13	3
Marvolski	0	0	0	0	3	0.000	0	0
Somolov	0	0	14	2	21	0.571	7	2
Modov	1	2	0	0	0		0	0
Lasko	0	0	0	0	0		0	14L
Opp err							17	
Total	6	4	61	16	132	0.341	88	48

Assists: USA Sato 52, Sambo 9
Russia: Pojerek 60
Attendance World League Record 16,591
Site: San Diego Sports Arena

Statistics Code for Box Score
*Team: Competing team; Blk: Number of stuff blocks by the player or the team; Ace: Number of service aces (there can be no second play of the ball); Kill: Number of attack kills; Err: Sum of attack errors and stuff blocks against the player; Atks: Total number of attacks; Eff: Spiking efficiency in decimal form; Points: Number of points scored by a player or team (sum of blocks, aces, and attack kills)

5. Practice goals and drills. Statistics ought to be a primary determinant of the nature of drills in practice. For instance, if in the weekend competition a team had an acceptable spiking performance from the left side of the court but not on the right, practice should emphasize hitting from right. If a team was able to side out effectively in rotations 2, 3, 4, and 5, but not in 1 and 6, practice should emphasize the weak rotations.

Statistics in Practice Drills

The design of drills in practice also has a statistical basis. For instance, if a team expects to side out two of every three times in competition, the following practice drill could be useful. The first team will only receive service. The second team will be on the court in specialized positions, with the net specialists at the net and the serving and defensive specialists in the back row. The serving specialist will serve 10 balls to the first rotation. If the receivers side out seven times, the first team wins. If the first team wins six or less, the second team wins. The team should perform this drill through all six rotations, repeating those that the second team wins.

I personally prefers drills in which we expect the team to win consecutive rallies. If in the previous scenario we expected the team to win consecutive rallies, we could make the following calculations.

The probability of the second team winning two consecutive rallies is

$$(1/3)(1/3) = 1/9 = 0.11$$

The probability of the first team winning two consecutive rallies is

$$(2/3)(2/3) = 4/9 = 0.44$$

Thus, the first team is four times more likely to win the competition. To make this competition more even, require the first team to win three consecutive rallies versus two for the second team:

$$(2/3)(2/3)(2/3) = 8/27 = 0.30$$

Still, the first team is three times more likely to win the competition. To almost equalize the teams' probabilities for winning, the first team must side out five consecutive times.

$$(2/3)(2/3)(2/3)(2/3)(23) = 32/243 = 0.13$$

The probabilities are about equal, and the competition is truly competitive.

The numbers quoted are good percentages for national teams, but not for most of us. The normal team should expect two versus three or maybe two versus four to be competitive probabilities.

The probabilities for siding out are easily determined. Considering only the score sheets from last year's important matches, calculate the side-out percentages for the winning team. This figure should give a good indication of what side-out and point-scoring goals a team needs to achieve to win.

It should noted that the USA Olympic men's team in 1988 would win with five side outs plus a free ball. They were, in fact, winning six rallies in a row. Their side-out percentage was expected to be around 70 percent. It is little wonder that they were Olympic gold medalists!

Statistical Validity

The concept of statistical validity is often difficult for coaches to incorporate into their statistical programs. Validity is equally difficult to explain, yet we accept statistical validity in everyday life quite easily.

For a statistic to be valid, the value given to the performance must be proportional to the probability that the performance will lead to winning a rally.

Take, for instance, the purchase of a $1 bottle of soda, ignoring taxes. It takes 100 of the coins we know as pennies to reach the goal of $1, to buy the bottle of soda. It also takes 20 nickels or 4 quarters.

Now let's suppose that a youngster shows up at the store with a new kind of coin. The kid tells the clerk that two of these coins are worth one soda. The clerk says that it will take five of the coins to buy the soda. Who is correct?

The clerk is correct. Why? Because, at the clerk's store, the kid needs five of these new coins to achieve the goal, to win the soda. The value of one of these coins is one-fifth of a soda. The same thing happens in volleyball.

No matter what the coach thinks, if the performance of a specific serve produces a point only once in five times, the value of each serve is one-fifth of a point. Too often coaches will give the serve some other value because it looked good, was served on target, was a jump serve, gave the other team only one option, and so on. Too often, the assigned value does not correspond to the probability of scoring a point.

The value that we should assign to any performance is the probability that the performance will lead to the winning of a rally. Numbers assigned to performance must have a probability basis to be valid! If performances are not based on probabilities, their values cannot be added, subtracted, multiplied, or divided. Performances not based on probabilities should be given values such as x, y, and z. Mathematical functions cannot combine these categories.

Statistical validity might be best explained by studying the most common system for the evaluation of serving and serve receiving.

In 1968 the U.S. Army loaned me Coach Bill Neville to become the statistician for the USA men's Olympic volleyball team in the Mexico City Olympic Games. Of course, Neville later became an Olympic gold-medal-winning volleyball coach working alongside Doug Beal with the 1984 men's Olympic team.

One of our goals was to create a system to evaluate serving and receiving. The first step in creating the system was to understand the concept that each serve was a competition in which the total value of the performance was always the same, like the value of the bottle of soda. For a service ace, the serving team received all the credit, won the entire soda. For a service error, the receiving team won the entire soda. If the served ball remained in play, the two teams shared the soda, with the amount of soda received by each team proportional to that team's probability of winning the rally.

As we developed the statistical system, we marked off the court to determine what the nature of serve reception really was. Figure 23.1 shows the court definitions we used for serve reception.

Because both Bill and I had spent most of our lives in school, it was reasonable to think of performances as grades in school. Thus, we developed a chart (table 23.2) that allowed us to calculate serving and passing grades in a manner similar to how a teacher would calculate grades in school.

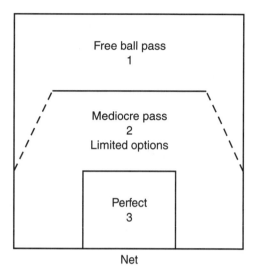

Figure 23.1   Serve-reception zones.

Then we reasoned that we could calculate a serving average from the evaluations. Thus, if a player served one A, no Bs, four Cs, three Ds, and one F, we could perform the following calculation to produce a serving average:

$$\frac{(1 \times 4) + (0 \times 3) + (4 \times 2) + (3 \times 1) + (1 \times 0)}{9 \text{ serves}} = 15/9 = 1.67$$

Similarly, the receiving team would have a passing average:

$$\frac{(1 \times 0) + (0 \times 1) + (4 \times 2) + (3 \times 3)}{8 \text{ passes (plus one error serve)}} = 17/8 = 2.13$$

TABLE 23.2

Evaluation of Serving and Receiving in Volleyball

Category of serve	Evalutaion of serve	Score of serve	Score of opponent's pass
Ace	A	4	0
Free ball to serving team	B	3	1
Mediocre serve or pass	C	2	2
Perfect pass	D	1	3
Service error	F	0	No pass

Thus, by the scoring system suggested, the serving player had a serving score of 1.67, and the opponent's passing score was 2.13.

This system has worked quite well for most teams since we introduced it many years ago. The system has two problems:

1. There was no proof of validity of the system.
2. Many coaches have changed the definitions of the passing zones.

Coaches used the system blindly, and successfully, for years before anyone challenged its validity. We had been instinctively lucky when we created the system. A series of studies in later years evaluated the validity of the system. The probability of scoring a point was calculated after each type of serve. The data are shown in table 23.3.

TABLE 23.3

Probability of Scoring Based on Serve Type

Category of serve	Grade evaluation of serve	Score of serve	Theoretical probability of scoring	Actual probability of scoring
Ace	A	4	100%	100%
Free ball to serving team	B	3	75%	71%
Mediocre serve or pass	C	2	50%	52%
Perfect pass	D	1	25%	30%
Service error	F	0	0%	0%

Because the theoretical and actual probabilities are so similar, the system has validity and is acceptable for use. If these numbers are not similar for a given team, the coach should reconsider the values used in the statistical system.

The second problem is much larger. Coaches have redefined the serve-reception categories. Most often, because coaches want to have more attacking options, the nonperfect categories have been redefined.

Often, the C class of serves has been subdivided into the categories given in table 23.4.

TABLE 23.4

Definition of service reception	Grade of serve	Score of serve	Score of pass
Receiving team has two offensive options	C	2	2
Receiving team has only one offensive option	B	3	1

As it turns out, these definitions are not valid. For most teams, the probability of winning a rally when the setter has one option is the same as when the setter has two options. Both are around 50 percent. Thus, we are giving a paper dollar and a silver dollar different values even though either one will buy the same soda. We are giving a basketball layup and a 15-foot jump shot a different number of points when they are each worth two points. Such definitions are not valid, and coaches should avoid using them. If statistical values are to contribute to winning, the statistical system needs to be valid.

An added benefit has been determined for the passing scores of a team. It has been generally shown that the passing scores determine the level at which a team can compete. Within the various levels, passing does not determine the winner, but it does establish the level at which a team can compete, as shown in table 23.5.

TABLE 23.5

Serve Reception Levels	
Level of play	Passing range
International teams	2.50 and over
FAA (low-level international)	2.30-2.50
AA (top-level clubs)	2.20-2.30
A (average clubs)	2.00-2.20
B and C levels	Below 2.00

What Statistics Should a Coach Take During a Match?

There is no general answer to the question, "What statistics should be gathered?" Candid answers include take what can be controlled, take what will help, take what can be understood, and count what counts!

What does the coach want to know? What can help him or her make decisions during the match? Do the statistics also have to serve as media statistics? Are statistics being summarized for season totals? How quickly can the statistician get meaningful statistics to the head coach?

Although one coach may choose to keep spiking as the first statistic, another coach may prefer points won and lost in each rotation. The answer is as individual as the personalities of the coaches.

The advent of the computer has changed the nature of recording and calculating statistics. In the beginning, statistics were kept by pencil on a clipboard, eyeballed during the match, and calculated with a quick mind and a slide rule after the match. Coaches were able to record and calculate only a few statistics.

The data-acquisition process improved as the data were eyeballed during the match and then summarized by computer after each match. Today, statistics are taken live during the match directly on the computer on the bench, and coaches are able to study them during interruptions of the match. In today's most sophisticated systems, a statistician away from the court can take statistics by computer during the match. As the statistics are being recorded, they are transmitted electronically to another computer on the bench for immediate study by the coaches.

Most computer programs are mouse driven and easily learned. The problem with mouse-driven programs is that the mouse is difficult to operate on the bench and so slow that operators can accumulate data on only one team at a time. With a faster touch-type program, however, a skilled typist can record every ball touch by both teams.

Voice-recognition statistical programs appear to be the next step. Current technology, however, does not allow the computer to filter out crowd noise, and data produced by such programs are inaccurate.

Spiking Efficiency

The results from many studies prove that what happens at the net determines who wins matches. Differences between the spiking and blocking of the teams determine which team wins a match. Historically, most coaches began by taking spiking statistics. In 1955 the term *spiking efficiency* was introduced, and the statistic has been used successfully ever since. Generally, spiking efficiency determines the winner of a match, a tournament, and a season. No easily understood blocking statistic was kept until approximately 1992, when the national teams introduced the statistic called *spiking efficiency against the block,* or *blocking efficiency.* Both spiking efficiency and blocking efficiency are valid statistics, and they are the most important statistics to keep.

Most coaches begin by recording spiking. Three important spiking statistics are kill percentage, error percentage, and spiking efficiency.

$$\text{Kill percentage} = \frac{\text{Kills} \times 100}{\text{Spiking attempts}}$$

Kill percentage is a good statistic, reasonably valid, but it does not take into account the number of errors that the attacker makes. A spiking attempt is any ball that an attacker hits or should hit. If an attacker believes that the ball is set too poorly to attempt an attack, the attacker should not swing. Once the attacker swings at the ball, the attacker is taking responsibility for what happens to the ball. If the attacker does not swing as often as the coach thinks that he or she should, the coach must judge the performance of the player and provide counsel. To the statistician, the recognition of a spiking attempt is clear.

$$\text{Error percentage} = \frac{\text{Errors} \times 100}{\text{Spiking attempts}}$$

A spiking error is an attack hit into the net or out of bounds, or an attack that an opponent stuff blocks.

Spiking efficiency is defined as kill percentage minus error percentage:

$$\text{Spiking efficiency} = \frac{(\text{Kills} - \text{errors}) \times 100}{\text{Spiking attempts}}$$

Many prefer to use the decimal equivalent and not multiply these terms by 100.

Spiking efficiency is a valid statistic and is normally the number-one determinant of winning in volleyball. A guide to the evaluation of spiking efficiency is given in table 23.6. Although the chart may not be accurate for a specific team, it is a good general guideline.

Initially, spiking efficiencies were kept as a general statistic to summarize all spiking for a player or a team. As the statistics became more sophisticated, the efficiencies were tabulated from various positions on the floor such as right, left, and middle. In the early 1980s a back-row position was added. Today we use two more sophistications. Often the statistics are kept by type of set, such as high ball, shoot, or quick. Significant differences in spiking efficiency have been found relative to the play situation. Generally, attacks are classified by

a. the first attack from service reception,

b. transition attack after service reception, and

c. transition attack after serving.

TABLE 23.6

Suggested Evaluation of Spiking Efficiencies

Spiking evaluation	Spiking efficiency
Superb (world-class)	50% and above
Outstanding	40-50%
Great goals—above expectations	30-40%
Normal goals	20-30%
Needs help	15-20%
Definitely hurting the team	10-15%
Better off bumping ball over net	0-10%
Should not be on the court	Below 0%

Spiking efficiencies on serve reception are nearly always higher than transition efficiencies. Figures 23.2 and 23.3 are sample hand-statistics data sheets used by national teams at one time or another. Coded ticks were used to indicate the following:

Attack from left: /

Attack from center: |

Attack from right: \

IP means attacked ball in play.

B means attack was stuff blocked.

E means attacking error.

Err means nonattacking error.

First Ball SO Pt Attacking is the first attack from service reception.

Transition SO Pt Attacking is transition attack after service reception.

Transition Sr Pt Attacking is transition attack after serving.

Note that with the recent change to rally point scoring (RPS) from traditional service point scoring (SPS), the names of the kinds of attacks will change (table 23.7).

— TABLE 23.7 —

Traditional name	New slang term	New technical name
Points	Real points	Service points
Side outs	Side-out points	Reception points

Notice that the RPS game is not significantly different from the SPS game. In RPS the number of reception points will be the same for each team, plus or minus one point. The "real points" scored by each team still determine which team wins. The game is different in that the team receiving the first serve of the game may win the game with an advantage of only one real point. The major difference between RPS and SPS is that the typical RPS game is shorter and has fewer rallies than the traditional SPS game. Probability theory tells us that the shorter the game, the more likely it is that upsets will occur. Thus, rally scoring is often blamed for more upsets, although this reasoning may be incorrect. The upset may be due to the shortened game.

In this game (figure 23.2), Sally Smythe did the following:

1. She attacked seven balls from the left, one from the middle, and two from the right.
2. She killed four, including the only set from the middle.
3. Her only two sets on the right were blocked against her.

#	Name	Attacking				Passing				Serving					Blks		Oth
		Kill	IP	B	E	3	2	1	0	1	2	3	4	0	+	–	errors
2	Franklin																
4	Smythe	/I//	///	\\	/												
5	Reynolds																
14	Barnes																
	Team total																

Figure 23.2   Sample statistics data sheet.

4. Her only hitting error was from the left.

5. Her overall spiking efficiency is $(4 - 3) \div 10 + 100 = 10\%$

6. Her efficiency from the left is $(3 - 1) \div 7 + 100 = 29\%$.

7. Her efficiency from the middle is $(1 - 0) \div 1 + 100 = 100\%$.

8. Her efficiency from the right is $(0 - 2) \div 2 + 100 = -100\%$.

9. Evaluations are that Sally needs work on right-side hitting. Her hitting from the left and middle is satisfactory, with a 37.5% efficiency.

Figure 23.3 shows a similar statistic sheet but divides the terminal attacks into three point-earning categories:

1. First-ball attacks from service reception (SR)

2. Transition from service reception (TS)

3. Transition for real points (TP)

#	Name	First Ball SO Pt Attacking				Transition SO Pt Attacking				Transition Sr Pt Attacking			
		Kill	IP	B	E	K	IP	B	E	K	IP	B	E
2	Franklin												
4	Smythe												
5	Reynolds												
14	Barnes												
	Team totals												

Figure 23.3 Sample statistics data sheet.

Blocking Efficiency

The most common blocking statistic is the number of stuff blocks. Blocking error is an extremely difficult term to define. To most statistical systems, blocking error means that the blocker hit the net or stepped beyond the centerline. To the coach, a blocking error may have an entirely different definition. Stuff blocks and blocking errors have little relationship to winning.

Although there are more sophisticated blocking systems, the most meaningful term seems to be blocking efficiency. At least, the numbers are expressed in terms with which most coaches are familiar. The system needs much research and refinement.

The general concept is that the spiking efficiency of the attacker is determined for every time that the blocker jumps. Each time the blocker jumps, the attacker is given a value of +, 0, or –, and the number of blockers is recorded. From these data, the blocking efficiency of each blocker is calculated.

Although the concept is simple, the accumulation of data and the calculations involved are complex. It is best to have a computer program perform the calculations.

The fundamental question in the calculation of blocking efficiency is how to compare a single blocker with a double or triple blocker. If Sam Blocker has the given blocking statistics, how do we calculate efficiency?

Sam Blocker: three single blocks—two attacker kills and one in play; and seven double blocks—three attacker kills, one stuff, two in play, one attacker error.

Spiking efficiency against the single blocks is

$$\frac{(2 - 0) \times 100}{3} = 67\%$$

Spiking efficiency against the double blocks is

$$\frac{(3 - 2) \times 100}{7} = 14\%$$

The question now is how to combine these efficiencies. Some statisticians prefer to combine all numbers:

Total spiking efficiency against Sam Blocker is

$$\frac{(5 - 2) \times 100}{10} = 30\%$$

On the other hand, research indicates that the preferred technique for combining the single and multiple blocks is to divide the credit for blocking to all the blockers participating. Thus, Sam Blocker gets full credit for the single blocks, but only receives half values for the double blocks. The calculation would then be:

Total spiking efficiency against Sam Blocker is

$$\frac{(3.5 - 1) \times 100}{6.5} = 38.5\%$$

Of course, the better the blocker, the lower the spiking efficiency—that is, spiking efficiency against the blocker. One of the early studies using this blocking statistical system took data for the USA men's and women's national teams (table 23.8).

The results for the men were as expected. The greater the number of blockers, the better the defense (blocking) became. On the other hand, the results for the women were surprising. The greater the number of blockers, the poorer the blocking became.

The results showed men's and women's volleyball to be quite different games. It is likely that the women were not as skillful at blocking as were the men relative to their competition. In addition, the women were probably employing a blocking system that did not fit their specific skills. They probably should not have used a three-person block. A competition some years earlier had produced similar results.

TABLE 23.8

Blocking Efficiency 1991 Study

Number of blockers	1	2	3
USA Men	45%	30%	15%
USA Women	15%	30%	45%

Positional Prejudice

Positional prejudice is one of the most serious limitations of any volleyball statistical system. This means that the performance expectation for a given technique varies from position to position. For instance, in the highest level of men's volleyball, the middle hitters are expected to have spiking efficiencies about 10 percent higher than the outside hitters.

There can be many reasons for positional prejudice. In the case of the middle hitters, the middles tend to hit mostly quick sets that pass the blockers before they have a chance to react. The outside sets tend to be slower, and the extra time allows one or more blockers to attempt to stop the attack and one or more diggers to attempt to dig the attack.

In the back row on defense, the libero is often middle back and designated to handle any free ball. Thus the libero makes a number of extremely easy plays. On the other hand, the wing diggers are often hit by attacks from the quick hitters and have no time to react. For these and other reasons, defensive statistics are often less than meaningful to the coach than offensive statistics.

Setting Statistics

A statistical system for setting is probably the most difficult system to create. The most common media statistic is the assist. When an attacker kills a ball from a set, the setter receives a statistical assist. Numerous problems reduce the value of this statistic:

1. Setters in long games tend to get more assists.
2. Setters whose teams play long matches tend to get more assists.
3. Setters playing on teams that use only one setter have an advantage over setters who play on teams that use more than one setter.
4. Setters who have good hitters are more likely to get more assists than those who have weak hitters.

Attempts have been made to classify setting into categories similar to those used for service reception (table 23.9).

— TABLE 23.9 —

Classification of Setting

Category of set	Evaluation of set
Perfect set	3
Mediocre set	2
Set leading to free ball to opponent	1
Set giving opponent a direct point or rally	0

These evaluations are reasonably valid. A perfect set leads to about three times the number of rally wins as does a free ball to the opponents. Three main problems affect the value of this system:

1. The definition of a perfect set varies. A perfect set in one offensive system may not be perfect in another. The perfect set to one spiker is not perfect for another spiker.
2. The statistician is often influenced by whether the attacker kills the ball rather than the absolute quality of the set.
3. When defined in this manner, setting is not a major determinant of winning. The coefficient of correlation between setting scores and winning is often in the range of -0.10 to $+0.10$.

The only setting statistic that seems to relate to winning is the ability of a setter to convert a mediocre pass into a perfect set. Setters on winning teams seem to be able to do this better than setters on poorer teams.

The evaluation of setting seems to be more of an art than a science. There is much more to setting than can easily be tabulated. Elements such as deception, game plans, and psychological factors make evaluation of setting extremely difficult.

Evaluation of Digging

The evaluation of digging is similar to the evaluation of setting. No adequate system seems to have been devised for this phase of team defense. The most common statistic taken is the total number of digs. This system contains many flaws. Long games and long matches produce more digs. Good blockers produce more digs. Positional prejudice affects digging totals. The degree of difficulty of the attack being dug varies considerably.

A system of evaluating digging similar to the system for reception of service is logical (table 23.10). When these definitions are used, the coefficient of correlation between digging and winning often falls in the range of 0.30 to 0.60. This means that digging can explain about 10 to 40 percent of a team's winning. These numbers are seldom consistent.

---TABLE 23.10---

Evaluation of Digging

Category of dig	Evaluation of dig
Perfect pass to setter	3
Mediocre pass to setter	2
Free ball to attacking team	1
Digging error	0

Analysis of Point Scoring

A team can earn points in three ways—attacking, blocking, and serving. A team may also gain points on the opponent's errors. Normally these errors are subdivided into opponent's attack errors and other errors.

The more sophisticated computer programs are able to produce a chart of point scoring by rotation. Such charts as that shown in table 23.11 can reveal much about the strengths and weaknesses of each rotation. Creating this kind of chart by hand is difficult and time consuming.

┌─ TABLE 23.11 ─────────────────────────────────

Point* Scoring by Rotation**

USA MEN'S VOLLEYBALL TEAM

Skill	Rot 1 + −	Rot 2 + −	Rot 3 + −	Rot 4 + −	Rot 5 + −	Rot 6 + −
Serve	18 11	19 12	7 13	8 12	10 5	6 7
Attack	44 36	44 38	31 40	37 21	53 33	33 31
Block	18 25	15 30	11 20	16 16	16 23	19 23
Opp attack errors	18 21	15 18	22 18	12 12	15 21	22 21
Opp other errors	9 4	10 4	9 8	10 3	11 3	8 2
Totals	107 97	103 102	80 99	83 64	105 85	88 84
Differentials	10	1	-19	19	20	4
Number of USA rotations	208	202	195	193	184	196
PPR*** USA	0.52	0.51	0.41	0.43	0.57	0.45
PPR opp	0.47	0.51	0.51	0.33	0.46	0.43

*Please note that these are service points, real points. An analysis using rally points would be equally valuable but would yield different numbers from which the same conclusions could be reached.
**Rotation 1 is the position in which the setter is in the right back of the court. In rotation 2, the setter is center back, etc.
***PPR is points per rotation.

Points Per Rotation

One rotation is a term of service for a player. Points per rotation is the average number of real points scored per each player's term of service. If a server serves three balls and scores two points, the PPR is 2 ÷ 1 = 2.00. In the world championships, Lloy Ball, the USA setter, served 315 times and scored 107 points, including 18 aces. There were 208 side outs. His PPR was 107 ÷ 208 = 0.51. The average opponent had a PPR of 0.47 when Ball was in position 1, right back, on the court. This position was a positive one for the USA.

One of the great benefits of the use of PPR is that it can be calculated directly from the score sheet. Each coach is entitled to a copy of the score sheet after a match. The statistic is free!

An analysis of tables 23.11 and 23.12 can yield a number of observations that should challenge the team in competition and practice.

The first question is whether the team measured up to its expectations of points per rotation. The goal of the USA team is to have a PPR of 0.50. With a PPR of 0.48, as shown in table 23.11, the USA almost met its goal as a team, but only three rotations met that goal. Therefore, the team should practice its point scoring in rotations 3, 4, and 6.

The USA goal is to hold its opponents to a PPR of 0.40. The team met its goal only in rotation 4. Clearly, the USA needed side-out practice.

Because the USA had a greater number of rotations in rotations 1 and 2, it is clear that the USA probably started often in rotation 1. If this is true, the USA presented three below-average rotations to its opponents before rotating to rotations 4 and 5, which were the rotations in which they scored the greatest positive point differentials or PPR differentials.

Note that the study of PPR is not a precise science because opponents often rotate the dial to create particular matchups against a team. On the other hand, it is common for a team to start in the same rotation every time, although the rotation may not be high scoring. The data indicate that it would have been unwise for the USA to start a game in rotations 6, 1, 2, or 3.

TABLE 23.12

Point-Scoring Summary by Skill

USA Men's Volleyball Team				World Championships 1998	
Skill	**+**	**%** *		**−**	**%**
Serve	69	12		60	11
Attack	242	43		199	37
Block	95	17		137	26
Opponent attack error	104	18		111	21
Opponent other error	57	10		24	5
Total points	566			531	
Point differential	35				
Total number of rotations			1,178		
Points per rotation	0.48			0.45	

*The percentage of the team's points scored in this manner.

It also appears, from table 23.12, that the USA performed better than its opponents in attacking but gave the advantage right back in blocking. The USA gained by not giving away so many other errors.

Statistics do not tell the entire story of a team's winning and losing. To gain more information, coaches have devised many scouting charts, tables, and reports to supplement information not learned from statistical data. The following are suggestions used by many coaches.

Points Won Chart

Points won charts are easy to keep and give an indication of how points are won or lost during a match. They are simple enough to be kept by virtually any player or spectator. They are also good to create news stories for the media. Table 23.13 is the simplest of points won charts.

—TABLE 23.13—

Points Won Chart

Place			Date	
Team USA	**Score**	**Point**	**Team Russia**	**Score**
SR kill by #3	1-0	1	SR kill by #14	1-1
SR kill by #3	2-1	2	SR error by opp #7	4-2
Block by #3	3-1	3	SR back-row kill by #1	6-3
Ace by #7	4-1	4		
Sr error by opp #14	5-2	5		
Trans kill by #4	6-2	6		
		7		

Scouting Reports

The coach without a scouting report will soon be looking for another job. Whether or not that statement is true, the well-prepared coach will either have a scouting report before a match or prepare a shot chart during the match, or both. Shot charts along with statistical reports can give a team an advantage over an unprepared opponent.

Descriptive commentary of each player normally accompanies shot charts. Such commentary might be similar to this:

"Number 7, Juri Lapinski, is a right-handed jump-float server. Serves effectively down the left sideline then plays defense in position 5. He moves slowly in the back row but digs well when he can touch the ball. Does not hit back row. Dink in the middle on him.

"At the net he blocks well on the left. In all positions he hits junk shots off the block. He does not hit very hard. He gets only about 20 percent of sets while at the net. Do not block him too high; turn him in toward the center of the court."

Shot charts have many forms. For instance, figure 23.4 shows the Russian service receivers and their passing averages.

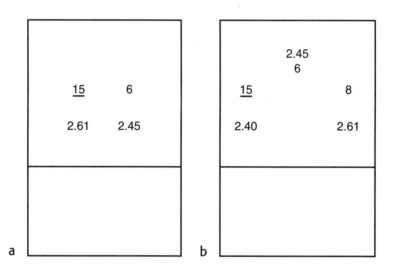

Figure 23.4 Russian passing averages in rotation II (underlined players are front row): **(a)** pattern versus float serve; **(b)** pattern versus jump serve.

Often a coach will have on the bench a notebook with one or two pages about each rotation. This notebook may take several forms. Among these will be a page with the diagram on the left having shot charts from previous matches and the diagram on the right showing what is happening in the current match. This setup will help a coach know whether the opponent is following a normal game plan or has made changes.

Accompanying the chart for the match being played will be a table that includes the following information:

a. Rotation number

b. A set of +s at the top of the chart to indicate which players are in which position in this rotation

c. Opponent's play information including the following:

    1. Reception number

    2. Number of passer

    3. Value of the pass. If there is no number, a default is assumed. At the national team level, the default is expected to be a perfect pass, a 3.

    4. A name or a description for the play being run. For instance, in figure 23.5, if the common play is an X/4/D, this means that player 7 goes for a quick (71) set, 15 for an X (62), 10 for a 14, and 8 for a back row D.

    5. Which player actually attacks the ball.

    6. The result of the play:

      + A kill by the attacker

      − A hitting error or stuff blocked (indicate which player stuffed the ball).

      o, + The ball stayed in play, and the attacker eventually won the rally.

      o, − The ball stayed in play, and the defender eventually won the rally.

A play on this chart may be coded in this manner (figure 23.5):

15, 3, X/31/A, 8, o,+

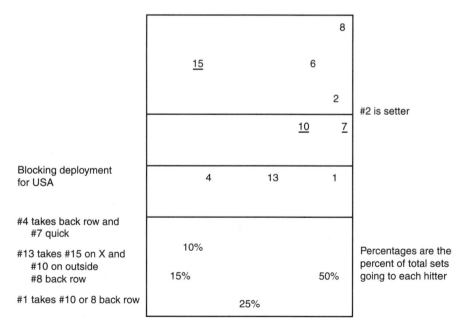

Figure 23.5   Primary offensive in Russian rotation II.

The preceding describes the following play. Serve reception number 6. Player 15 passed a 3 pass. The play was an X with player 7 hitting quick, 15 on the X, 10 hitting a 31, and player 8 hitting an A. The ball stayed in play, and the serving team eventually won the rally.

With experience, a coach will develop various shortcuts and codes. A team may often use more than one serve reception pattern in the same rotation. In this case, two or more shot charts must be available for the offense (figure 23.6).

The coach may attempt to keep all shot data on one six-court chart (figure 23.7).

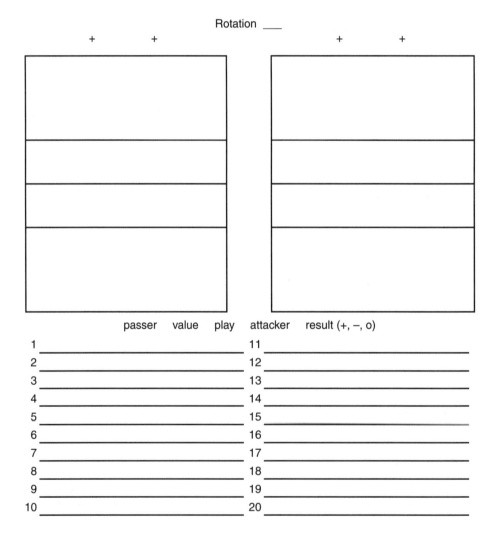

Figure 23.6 Multiple shot charts.

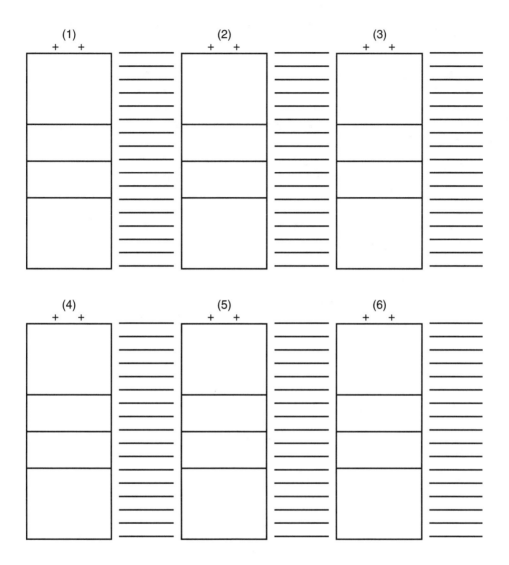

Figure 23.7   Six-court chart.

Summary

There are several reasons for taking statistics:

1. Providing information to the media
2. Individual recognition for execution of specific skills
3. Match management (assisting the coach in making game decisions)

4. Match evaluation (at the match's conclusion)

5. To use in practice to measure the efficiency of practice goals and drills.

It is important to remember that for a statistic to be valid, it must be proportional to the probability that the performance will lead to the winning of a rally.

The complexity of the statistical system being used should be based on what the coach wants to know. At the beginning level of play, the most critical skills are serving and passing (successes or failures). These are simple to chart by relatively untrained statisticians because the result is very objective and simple to measure.

Advanced level statistics, whether being kept on your own team or on your opponents, require trained statisticians because this level of charting requires valid subjective judgment.

In conclusion, it must be remembered that the validity of a statistic is dependent on the recording proficiency of the person recording the data. Those recording at the advanced level need to be trained carefully if the collected data is to be valid and useful in making proper coaching decisions.

CHAPTER TWENTY–FOUR

Handling Game Situations

Al Scates

Less than two weeks before the playoffs began, we lost at Long Beach State in five games before 1,935 partisan Long Beach fans. Although Long Beach was the number-one team in the country, our team and staff were disappointed with our performance in this important match.

After the loss, I quickly got the players into the team room and had them stretch out on the floor. The reporters had to wait until I talked to the team. I did not go over the match or blame a player for the loss. Instead, I assured the team that I knew what the problems were and that together we would fix them on the practice floor the next day. I made sure that the players calmed down before I released them. A worked-up and angry player can embarrass the team and the institution.

After releasing the players, I gathered the statistics, which my statistician was printing out in the arena, and reviewed them before going to bed. After I had answered all questions about the coaching and playing, I could sleep peacefully. For 35 years, I taught full-time in the Beverly Hills School District while I coached at UCLA. I always had a first period class at 8:00 A.M. Early on, I found that it was better to stay up after a match and decide what I was going to do the next day before retiring. It is better to sleep with a peaceful mind for four hours than it is to toss and turn with unresolved problems on your mind. The lucky collegiate coaches who have no morning classes may not feel the same urgency to solve all the problems before going to bed. Although I retired from teaching, I still need to have the answers before going to bed.

Reviewing the Last Match

Win or lose, a coach must review the last match to prepare for the next one. If a practice day is available, the coach can correct problems and work on a new strategy. I particularly like to review our first spike after our pass, our transition and our hits after we serve by rotation, game, and match. I look at our front row, back row, and total attack. I review each player's attack according to the type of set he received. I look at our float and jump-serve reception and at our side-out percentages by player and rotation. I look at our serving average, team attack, pass, block, dig, and point information by rotation and by game. I want to know our point scoring by each player's serve and points scored by jump serves and float serves. Next I look at the videotape and I may break it down by our serving rotation and our side out rotation.

Preparing for the Next Match

My assistants look at videotape of our next opponent, if one is available, and provide me with a preliminary game plan, which I usually embellish. Once we finalize a game plan, I develop a practice schedule to implement that plan. The team also sees the videotape of the opponent (when we have it) and receives a full explanation of the game plan on the practice floor and during our pregame meeting.

Being Healthy for the Playoffs

Throughout the regular season, a coach must teach techniques and tactics while continuing to condition the team, but the most important thing a coach can do for his or her team at the end of the season is to try to make sure that the team is healthy and rested. Let me tell you about a choice I had to make during the 2000 season.

UCLA's key player for the 2000 NCAA playoffs was our all-American setter, Brandon Taliaferro. Brandon was experiencing back pain during practice, so I referred him to our team doctor, who ordered an MRI. The MRI showed that Brandon had a degenerative disk problem in lumbar disks two through five. His pain was aggravated when he had a heavy workload in training or competition.

When we learned the diagnosis, we were in the middle of our regular league competition. To earn home-court advantage in our first league playoff match, we had to be seeded in the top four, and if we did not win three league playoff matches, we would not get an automatic bid to the NCAA playoffs. Without an automatic bid, we probably would not get in at all.

After consulting with the doctor, I had two options. First, I could give Brandon a reduced training load and continue to play him. This plan meant that he would go into the playoffs at less than 100 percent. Second, I could rest him until his symptoms disappeared and he became healthy. This option could potentially cost us the home-court advantage in the playoffs. I decided to rest him and use our true freshman setter, Richard Nelson. We did not allow Brandon to practice, lift weights, or suit up for matches. Making this decision was easy for me because our goal was to win the NCAA championship, and I did not believe that we could accomplish that goal unless Brandon could play to his full potential. I picked a weak part of our schedule, and while Brandon was out we won two and then lost to Cal State Northridge at home, a team we were 40-2 against until that point. I took a risk and continued to rest Brandon despite the bleak situation as we slid toward the fifth seed and a playoff opener on the road. Our rookie setter improved, however, and we defeated UC Irvine 3-1 on the road to hold onto the fourth seed and first-round home-court advantage. Brandon rested for five matches and finished the regular season in good health with the help of a greatly reduced training regimen.

Resting Brandon was risky because in the previous season we played our first-round match against Hawaii on their home court, in front of 10,250 enthusiastic fans. Our postseason tournament ended right there. In 2000, we played our first-round match against defending conference and NCAA champion, BYU, in UCLA's Pauley Pavilion and swept them. If we had lost one more match during the regular season, we would have played BYU in Provo, where five of our starters would find their jump serves traveling about four feet farther because of the altitude. We would have had to serve more floaters to cut down on errors. BYU would have been favored to win with their small gym jammed over capacity with 5,000 fans. At sea level in Pauley Pavilion, our jump servers served 67 balls and we scored 42 percent of the time. Our float servers served 60 balls and we scored 28 percent of the time. That performance was enough to win.

Reviewing Your Passing and Your Next Opponent's Serving Tendencies

We had three days to prepare for the second round of playoffs against Loyola, who was having the best season in their long history. They had beaten us 3-1 two weeks earlier, their first win ever against UCLA in 60 tries! Now they believed in themselves and were a real threat. As my assistants prepared the preliminary Loyola game plan, I reviewed our passing throughout the last six matches, which had occurred over a three-week span. I found out that outside hitter Mark Williams had passed 248 serves and we had sided out 65 percent of the time, whereas libero Matt Davis had passed 358 balls and we had sided out only 61 percent of the time. After reviewing the video, I saw that Matt had taken more court than usual. Of the 3,900 balls we passed during the 2000 season, Mark and Matt passed 3,535 serves, or 91 percent of the total. These figures included a few games in which Matt did not play. At this point, I instructed Mark to pass more of the seam because Matt was becoming too aggressive. I also reviewed our recent loss to Loyola and found out that of the 84 float serves we passed, we sided out only 54 percent of the time. We had an average side out of 68 percent on balls served in during the last six matches, so 54 percent was well below the average. Previously, Loyola served only 39 jump serves in against us, and we sided out at a 69 percent rate. We emphasized float-serve reception in our three days of practice by having the second team simulate Loyola's float-serve tendencies, using the same side of the court and the same depth behind the service line that their servers used.

Next, I looked at our spikes in scoring situations during the last six matches and found that pipes or balls set to our backcourt hitter in area 6 were our best high-ball options with a 42 percent efficiency and 50 percent kill average. In the frontcourt, fast sets to every hitter were working well. I shared this information with our setters.

During the Loyola playoff match, our outside hitter, Mark Williams, passed 69 serves, and we sided out 64 percent of the time. Our libero, Matt Davis, passed 69 balls, and we sided out 74 percent of the time. Obviously, Matt's percentage went up when he let Mark take more of the difficult serves. This was not much of a risk as Mark later played libero for the Australian Olympic team. The float-serve reception practice paid off as we passed 107 floaters and sided out 73 percent of the time. However, our jump-serve reception suffered, showing 38 serves in for a 55 percent side-out average. If you neglect part of the game in practice, it usually shows up during the next match. We eliminated Loyola 3-1, and shortly thereafter Loyola eliminated their men's volleyball program. They had been in our conference since I started it in 1964, and they had the best team in their history. Unfortunately for Loyola volleyball, their baseball program lost an estimated $600,000 and their basketball team won only two games and lost a bundle as well. They cut men's volleyball to reduce the projected deficit of the baseball and basketball programs in the succeeding year by about $200,000.

Do Not Change a Good Game Plan

In the third round, we faced Pepperdine at their place in the league finals. Pepperdine had beaten us in five games on their court, and we had beaten them in four games at home during regular league play. For the 2000 league finals, a capacity crowd of 3,000 fans packed the arena close to the court. After they beat us 15-6 in the first game, I explained to the team that Pepperdine had just played the best game they were capable of playing and that we were going to stick to the game plan and win the match. I pointed out that Andre Breur, their key player and a member of the German national team, had been jump serving and hitting a lot of balls and would lose effectiveness as the match progressed. I reminded them of Pepperdine's individual jump-serving tendencies and told the players that we should keep shifting our passers into their tendencies. Finally, I reminded our blockers to stop Pepperdine's middle attack by bunching into the center of the court and said that we would stop their outside hitters with one blocker if necessary. Before this match, our staff compiled Pepperdine's side-out offense during their matches against USC and us. We knew their routes and tendencies and placed our blockers at their points of attack. Eric Daly, our statistician, compiled their statistics, which suggested which Pepperdine blockers to avoid, who to serve to, and what to expect from their offense. We accumulated the same statistics for our players and knew how each player's style stacked up against Pepperdine. We had a great game plan, and I was not about to change it because we got beat up in the first game.

I knew that our best rotations against Pepperdine were 2 through 5, with which we had scored 28 more points than we gave up in our two previous matches. We started in rotation 2 because we were negative 6 points in rotations 6 and 1. After all the preparation for this match, it came down to our four-time all-American setter, Brandon Taliaferro, setting a great match and having 10 kills in 16 attempts. Brandon led our team with 11 digs and had a few blocks as well. It was also helpful that our second-team opposite, Ed Ratledge, came off the bench in game one and had 27 kills in 50 swings.

Conditioning Is Key in Traditional Scoring

It is important to train for a long match by making practices more intense than matches and then practicing with medium to light intensity for the two days before the match. Because the NCAA men's teams were still using traditional scoring with six substitutes, teams won long matches on conditioning. When your hitting statistics go up in the latter part of a long match, it usually indicates that your team is rested and has good endurance. With the exception of the practice on the day before the match, our practices required more endurance from the players than the matches did. Note the game scores and hitting statistics in tables 24.1 and 24.2.

Now the men's teams and the rest of the world are using rally point scoring. Endurance will no longer be as important because five-game matches will usually be played in about two hours.

TABLE 24.1

Game Scores 4/29/2000

Game scores	1	2	3	4	Team records
UCLA	6	15	15	15	27-5
Pepperdine	15	11	4	9	22-5

TABLE 24.2

Team Attacks per Game

UCLA					Pepperdine				
Game	K	E	TA	Pct	Game	K	E	TA	Pct
1	17	7	44	.227	1	24	6	39	.462
2	20	12	45	.178	2	18	12	44	.136
3	19	4	41	.366	3	21	16	50	.100
4	31	5	53	.491	4	25	11	51	.275

Team blocks: 21   **Team blocks: 14**

Who Starts?

Ed Ratledge had a brilliant match against Pepperdine, and many coaches thought I was going to start him against Penn State. After playing him as both a starter and a substitute, I knew he performed better off the bench (table 24.3). I also believe in holding something in reserve. Therefore, I held our most explosive hitter in reserve and started Evan Thatcher, who was the better blocker and digger.

This situation was similar to the one we experienced in 1998, when junior middle blocker Danny Farmer came into the NCAA semifinals for our senior captain, Tom Stillwell. Danny had 16 straight kills to lead us to a come-from-behind victory over Lewis University. Many people thought we were going to start Danny in the finals, including his parents, who flew from Los Angeles to Hawaii to watch. I decided to start Stillwell because throughout his career he had an uncanny ability to dig the spikes of Pepperdine star George Roumain. Although Tom was usually a mediocre to average defensive player, he was exceptional against Roumain's thundering blasts. As a junior, Tom led the nation in blocking. He was strong at the net and deserved a chance to start in his last collegiate match. Tom played well in the frontcourt and converted many of Roumain's spikes into our points with great defense. We beat Pepperdine 3-0, but had we lost a game, Danny would have been ready to turn it around. Danny understood my logic and became a starting middle blocker his senior year. He is currently a wide receiver with the Cincinnati Bengals.

— TABLE 24.3 —

Ed Ratledge off the Bench

	GP	Kills	Times Attacked	Pct.	Opponent
01/28/00	5	43	65	.408	@ Hawaii
02/17/00	3	46	86	.384	Cal State Northridge
03/01/00	4	36	60	.467	BYU
03/08/00	3	10	20	.400	@ UC Santa Barbara
03/31/00	3	19	28	.607	@ Cal State Northridge
04/29/00	4	27	50	.380	@ Pepperdine

So Evan Thatcher started ahead of Ed Ratledge and in the next match had 16 kills in 28 attempts, 10 digs, and 4 blocks in a short three-game match. Even under the pressure, Evan had the most sets, best hitting percentage, and the most digs of any player on either team. Had he started weakly, he would have gotten the hook and become one of the pine brothers while Ed got the playing time. By comparing a player's statistics off the bench and as a starter, it will become clear what to do.

Preparing for the Semifinals

Next we had to prepare for the biggest match of the year thus far—the NCAA semifinals. At the start of the season, we played Penn State at the Outrigger Tournament in Hawaii and defeated them 15-4, 15-3, 11-15, and 15-2. Although we had not seen them for 14 weeks, we had monitored their scores and statistics.

After rewatching our Penn State match on video, I noticed their setter constantly misdirecting our middle blockers by running the quick hitter in one direction and then setting the other way. The setter did not set the second man through on the combination plays and set quick or high. On double quicks, he set the middle attacker. That was at the beginning of the season, so I just made a note of it on the first page of my game book and decided that we would not adjust our defense for this match. Instead, we would create a scoring plan during the contest, based on taking away whatever they wanted to do.

We had three practice days before the NCAA semifinals, so I reviewed our side outs by rotation from the last three playoff matches to find out who was hot and who was not. At this stage in the season, the head coach only needs to talk to the setter to change the side-out offense. I prepared a chart showing our six rotations for him, with everyone's hitting attempts and efficiencies on their various routes.

I decided that in rotation 1 (side out 70 percent) we would misdirect Penn State's middle blocker by running back ones and gaps and setting the left-side hitter over the gap and the long way. Because our quick hitter's best route was a front one, we would feed him on that route. In rotation 2 we were siding out at 77 percent and everything was working, so we did not change anything. If it is not broken, do not fix it. In rotation 3 (side out 65 percent), our outside hitters were hot, so we planned to set the outside whenever the end blockers were helping on our quick hitter. This included a go over the gap to our left-side attacker and a red, or fast, set to the right-side attacker. When the area-4 blocker was bunching, we would watch this from the bench and let our setter know what the block was doing. We left rotation 4 alone because we were siding out at 75 percent. In rotation 5 (side out 66 percent) I encouraged our setter to keep jamming the pass, and he agreed to do so (much to his delight). In rotation 6 (side out 63 percent) we planned to set the middle on a good pass with a backcourt set to our opposite as the first option.

I thought Penn State was a year away from being an outstanding team, so I was just looking for us to have a focused match. I tell my players the truth about our opponents. I told them, "If we play well, we will not need any special strategies." We defeated Penn State 15-11, 15-8, and 15-10 (the third game took 42 minutes). Penn State was a much better team in 2001, with five returning starters. I did not try to get the team up for the semifinals because they were already extremely focused for the match.

Analysis of the Semifinals

While reviewing the statistics after the semifinal match, I found that we sided out at 73 percent (65 percent on serves that landed in) and scored at a 37 percent rate. We usually win when our side-out and scoring percentages total 100 or above, and we had scored 110 percent. We sided out better as the match progressed, but I was alarmed that we gave up four of Penn State's six aces in rotation 1. They were serving tough jump serves, but we passed 73 of the 79 in jumpers for a side-out percentage of 63 percent. They served only 11 float serves, and we sided out at 82 percent. Their game plan was to take risks and serve tough, and they had 6 aces and 22 errors. Our goal was to serve normally (tough) and to keep our aces-to-errors ratio at 1 to 3. We had 8 aces and 18 errors, so I was satisfied. Setter Brandon Taliaferro had 4 aces and 6 errors. He served 17 balls for a 42 percent scoring average. Outside hitter Mark Williams had 3 aces, 6 errors, and 19 serves for a 37 percent scoring average. With these serving statistics in mind, I decided to match them up against Ohio State in good situations for their particular jump-serving preferences and try to prevent one of Ohio State's good jump servers from matching up against us in our rotation 1. I noted that after I benched outside hitter Matt Komer in the second game, Cameron Mount came in and lit it up with 9 kills in 14 attempts and was ready to contribute again.

Preparing for the Finals

Our next match was the NCAA finals against Ohio State. Our staff and players had 48 hours to prepare. I reviewed our side-out percentages by opponents in serves for the last five matches and found that rotations 1 and 6 were our weakest, so I decided not to start there, even though our setter, Brandon Taliaferro, was a big-time server in rotation 1.

We had scouted Ohio State at USC and Pepperdine six weeks before the finals. We charted their serves, passes, plays, and spikes. We knew where

TABLE 24.4

Points by Rotation in the Last Five Matches

Rotation	Average side-out % by in serves	All in serves by extreme matches		Points
		Low side-out %	High side-out %	
1	59%	53%	83%	+2
2	65%	69%	90%	+22
3	68%	60%	100%	+22
4	65%	50%	80%	+18
5	62%	56%	80%	+11
6	58%	54%	67%	+3

they started and what their strong and weak rotations were. We knew when the setter went the long way, who he set to in the clutch, and who got set to in transition in each of their rotations. We watched them defeat Pepperdine in three straight games, and then my two assistants received the ESPN videotape of the match and started to develop a game plan for my review. That night, I reviewed our scoring tape against Penn State because I still had a practice day to correct any technical problems. We had won almost all of our 18 NCAA championships by dominating the net, so as usual I focused on our blocking.

I shared the following information with the players as we reviewed the tape together the next morning. I told them what to look for before I rolled the tape:

Middle blocker number one

Good job!

Middle blocker number two:

1. Lose the four slide steps to the left. Keep your body a foot away from the net and use a crossover step. Close the seam on the left by getting shoulder to shoulder with the end blocker.

2. When moving right, make the left hand cross-court move as you are running by the cross-court spikes.

3. Do not drop your hands or squat as the setter releases the ball, or you will never block a quick set.

4. Close the seam moving left and do not overrun the cross-court shot moving right.

Outside hitter number one:

1. When moving from the bunch to the spread, you must get to the pin and *still* take the seam with your right hand. Take big steps. When you get to the pin, your arms are too close together; keep your seam hand in the seam.

2. Squat before the setter releases the ball; you are late versus the quick sets.

Outside hitter number two:

Work on bunch to spread steps; keep your spine straight when jumping (weight on trailing foot).

Opposite:

Keep seam hand in the seam and penetrate.

Setter:

Watch the hitter sooner when blocking.

The secret of handling big-game situations is to prepare your team thoroughly before the game begins. When the team is technically sound, the coach merely has to remind the team to focus on what they already know about themselves and their opponent.

Getting the Information to the Players

Our specific player preparation for the finals began the Friday morning before our Saturday afternoon match. That old cliche that players should focus on one match at a time is definitely true. We did not mention Ohio State until we defeated Penn State, and our players were eager for the new information. As the staff and team reviewed the videotape of the Ohio State victory over Pepperdine, we had our libero, Matt Davis, and our primary passer, Mark Williams, memorize the serving tendencies of every Ohio State starter. With this information, we shifted our receiving formation slightly for each server to decrease the chance that Ohio State would serve to our weaker third passer, who was only allowed to pass balls directed to his navel and was always standing on one of the sidelines. I would occasionally tell my two primary passers to shift a step to the left, right, forward, or back during the match.

Ohio State entered the Final Four hitting an awesome .402 as a team. As usual, we reviewed the tendencies of the hitters who received the most sets on the videotape. Sometimes you can win the game by shutting down just one hitter. The Ohio State opposite received an average of 10 sets, made 5.31 kills, and hit .359 per game. Their main outside hitter received 9 sets, made 4.8 kills, and hit .324 per game. Both middle blockers hit over .500 but had only 3.7 and 3.6 kills per game. I told our three big jump servers to serve tough. I would be happy with our usual goal of one ace for every three service errors. During the finals, in their three rotations, we had 7 aces and 18 errors, so we exceeded our goal. When we jump served, we almost always got two or three blockers on their outside hitters. Our game plan was to read block the entire game. I felt that as long as the Ohio State middle attackers received about one-third of the sets, we could control their outside hitters with two blockers and win the match.

During the game, I often gave blocking instructions to our players when we served. These directions usually pertained to their starting positions. I gave occasional reminders regarding the opponent's hitting tendencies. Blocking instructions can be given orally when it is quiet or with signals in loud venues.

We kept statistics on Ohio State's serve reception in the semifinal match against Pepperdine and found that they passed 71 jump serves for a 2.23 reception average (on a three-point scale). During the season, UCLA passed jump serves at 2.45, so we knew we would get them in passing trouble with our jump serves. In their previous match, Ohio State's Pieter Olree passed 51 of 100 total serves, and they sided out 67 percent of the time when he passed. This was slightly better than the team's 66 percent side-out average versus Pepperdine. Their libero did not pass many float serves, and Eric Daly, our statistician, graded his 17 jump-serve receptions at 1.94 with a 62 percent side-out average. Our plan was to jump serve at their libero and float serve Pieter Olree in the seams of responsibility and make his attack routes difficult. The players knew this before the game began, but if the server needed help, he would look to the bench and I would signal a serving area for him. Olree was hitting .324 for the season, but we held him to .162 in 37 attempts in the finals by serving him out of his attack routes and making sure that we had two blockers on him. We went one-on-one with their middle blockers and did not commit on them. We conceded big hitting percentages to their middle attackers because in the semifinals they only set them 42 of 143 total sets and had 23 of 77 kills. If Ohio State's middle blockers had neared 50 percent of their team's kills, I would have changed our blocking strategy. I monitored the official volleyball box score that the match statistician distributed after every time out, and I did not change our blocking tactics. Had we lost a game or had the middles received more sets, we would have committed occasionally and gone one on one on a perfect pass.

Summary

After a loss, the coach should hold a brief meeting to make sure the players cool down and do not embarrass the program or the institution. During this meeting, the coach should not place blame on individual student-athletes. The meeting should end on a positive note. To ensure a good night's rest, the coach should review the match and make decisions about the next practice before retiring. After the match, one of the assistant coaches should provide the head coach with a game plan for the next opponent so that the head coach has the option of incorporating it into the next practice session.

The head coach should insist on a written injury report from the trainer about the treatment and status of each player at least twice a week during the season. Having healthy players for the playoffs is crucial to having a championship season.

When finalizing your game plan, be sure to match up your best passing rotations against your opponent's best servers. Your statistician should keep track of each rotation's side-out percentage versus float and jump serves to facilitate this matchup. If you are confident that you have a good game plan, stay with it even if you lose the first game. The better conditioned teams usually win long matches. Therefore, make your practices more intense than the matches.

Determine who comes off the bench well and who does not. To learn this, you will have to use many combinations early in the season. You want to have confidence in your substitutes before you reach the playoffs. Try to schedule the best teams early in your season so you will know what you have to do to beat them during the single-elimination phase. Go with the players who are hot at the end of the season, regardless of their season averages. Finally, keep coaching hard until the final whistle, because in the immortal words of Yogi Berra, "It ain't over til it's over."

ABOUT THE EDITORS

Donald S. Shondell is a legend in USA volleyball. As coach at Ball State University for 34 years, he won an impressive 769 games, the second highest all-time victory total by a men's team coach. Shondell was selected as an All-Time Great Volleyball Coach by the United States Volleyball Association and was the American Volleyball Coaches Association's Coach of the Year in 1995. He has coached many of the nation's top coaches, including former USA women's national team coach and current USC coach, Mick Haley. He served as president of the USVA in 1978 and is the former president and co-founder of the Midwestern Intercollegiate Volleyball Association. Shondell was a 1996 inductee into the Volleyball Hall of Fame. He retired from coaching in 1998. Shondell lives in Muncie, Indiana.

With 630 wins and 26 years of collegiate coaching experience, **Cecile Reynaud** ranked among the top nine in career victories among active Division I coaches when she retired from Florida State University after the 2001 season. In May of 1996, Reynaud received the George J. Fischer Leader in Volleyball Award presented at the USA Volleyball National Meetings. This award recognizes long-time, significant contributions to volleyball programs and activities in the United States. She is a member of the Volleyball Hall of Fame selection committee and served 12 years on the USA Volleyball board of directors and three years on the executive committee. Reynaud was also a former president of the American Volleyball Coaches Association. She is an assistant professor in the sport management program at FSU. She lives in Tallahassee, Florida.

ABOUT THE CONTRIBUTORS

Doug Beal is the head coach for the U.S. Men's National Volleyball Team. His team won the gold medal at the 1984 Olympics in his first tour with the team (1977-85). He returned to coach the men's national team in 1997 and will remain with the program through the 2004 Olympics in Athens, Greece. Beal was a national team player for seven years after graduating from the Ohio State University in 1970. He was a five-time United States Volleyball Association All-American selection and the MVP of the 1975 USVBA National Championships. Before joining the nationa team program as a coach, Beal served as head coach at Bowling Green University and The Ohio State University.

Jona Braden is the women's volleyball head coach for the University of Kentucky. She entered Kentucky with eight years' experience as the head coach for Butler University. Under Braden's direction, Butler won two Midwestern Collegiate Conference volleyball championships and finished as conference runner-up four times. Braden earned the MCC Coach of the Year honors in 1986 and 1987 and the Coach of the Year in the North Star Conference in 1985. Before coaching, Braden played volleyball for Ball State and compiled a remarkable record of 115-43 over three years.

Teri Clemens was the women's volleyball head coach at Washington University in Missouri from 1984-1996. In addition to compiling a 457-67 record, Clemens led the Bears to win 28 consecutive postseason matches, setting an NCAA record with a tournament record of 37-3. Clemens led her team to eight University Athletic Conference titles and seven Division III national championship titles during her 12 years as head coach. She has claimed the Tachikara/American Volleyball Coaches Association Division III coach of the year award three times, in 1991, 1994, and 1996.

Jim Coleman founded the field of volleyball statistics and has authored many books and articles on it. Coleman had four decades of experience with national volleyball before retiring in 1998. He served as head coach of the men's team from 1965-1970, 1978-1980, and 1990 as well as the general manager for the USA National Volleyball teams. Coleman also served as head coach for Washington State University women's volleyball from 1982-1986. Jim Coleman passed away in August of 2001.

John Cook entered his first season as head coach of the University of Nebraska women's volleyball team with a perfect season and the national title. Before Nebraska, Cook was the head coach at the University of Wisconsin. During his seven-year stint with the Badgers, he amassed a 161-73 record, shared a Big Ten title in 1997, and took his team to six postseason tournaments. Cook has been awarded with the Big Ten Co-Coach of the Year and the American Volleyball Coaches Association District 2 Coach of the Year. Cook also served as first assistant for the U.S. Men's National Volleyball team and won a bronze medal in the 1992 Olympic Games.

John Dunning joined Stanford University's women's volleyball program after spending 16 seasons with the University of Pacific. Dunning was very successful at Pacific, posting a 437-102 record. He led the Tigers to capture two NCAA titles, five Big West Conference championships, and 16 consecutive NCAA postseason tournament appearances. Dunning has been honored as the Big West Coach of the Year two times and as the Volleyball Monthly Coach of the Year after his first season at University of Pacific. His 2001 Stanford team won the program's 5th national championship and Dunning was selected the 2001 Division I National Coach of the Year.

Peter Hanson is the men's volleyball coach at The Ohio State University. Since taking the reins in 1985 he has captured eight Midwestern Intercollegiate Volleyball Association (MIVA) championships and has appeared in the NCAA tournament five times. In 1998 he was named Volleyball Magazine Coach of the Year and in 2000 he was named the American Volleyball Coaches Association Coach of the Year. Prior to Ohio State, Hanson enjoyed a coaching stint at the University of Wyoming (1982-1984). He began his coaching career at Ball State University in 1980 after playing there for two years.

Mike Hebert, women's volleyball head coach at the University of Minnesota, has coached for 26 years and has joined the very few who have won more than 700 games. Entering the 2001 season, Hebert was 121-48, participated in four NCAA tournaments, and came within one point of winning the Big Ten Conference title. Hebert came to Minnesota after 13 years with the University of Illinois. He led the Fighting Illini to four Big Ten titles and 11 consecutive NCAA tournament appearances. Hebert was honored as National Coach of the Year in 1985 and Big Ten Coach of the Year in 1985, 1986, 1988, and 1999. He also served as president of the American Volleyball Coaches Association from 1985 to 1988.

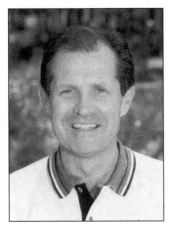

Taras Liskevych coached three USA women's volleyball teams and captured a bronze medal in 1992. Liskevych holds the record among USA women's volleyball coaches for most wins, longest tenure, and most international matches as a coach. Before his head coaching job with the USA volleyball team, Liskevych headed the University of Pacific women's team and brought the program from the intramural level to a national contender. He led the team to six NorCal Conference titles and was awarded Conference Coach of the Year five different times. In 1983, Liskevych was named the 1983 Collegiate Volleyball Coaches Association National Division I Coach of the Year.

Bill Neville has coached volleyball for more than 30 years. In 2001 he retired from the University of Washington where he was the women's volleyball head coach. While coaching at the University of Washington, he led his team to back-to-back postseason tournament appearances and a second place finish in the Pacific 10 Conference, the toughest volleyball conference in the nation. In addition to his success at Washington, Neville led the 1984 U.S. men's volleyball team to an Olympic gold medal. Prior to Washington, Neville held the head coaching position at Montana State University where he brought a previously unknown volleyball program into the top 20 national rankings.

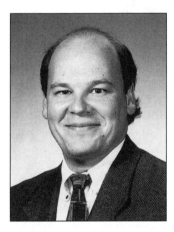

Mark Pavlik's involvement with Penn State University's men's volleyball began as a player. Before Pavlik's head coaching career began, he was Tom Peterson's assistant during a five-year span when the Nittany Lions were 111-39 and appeared in the NCAA tournament four times, winning the national title in 1994. In 1995, Pavlik was named head coach and, in the same year, was nominated for the American Volleyball Coaches Association Coach of the Year award.

Mary Jo Peppler is currently the director of coaching at Coast Junior Volleyball Club in San Diego. Peppler had head coaching jobs at Utah State University, University of Kentucky, and University of Florida as well as coaching the No.1 women's beach volleyball team in the world from 1991-1996. Her playing career included the Olympics, the Pan American Games, and professional beach volleyball. Peppler was inducted into the Hall of Fame for USA Volleyball, the Women's Sports Foundation, and California State University California Beach Volleyball Association. She was also awarded the Founders Award from the American Volleyball Coaches Association.

Terry Pettit was the women's volleyball head coach at Nebraska University for 23 years before retiring. He finished his career with over 700 overall wins of which more than 650 come from Nebraska. He was only the fifth coach to hit the 650-win mark at one school. Pettit was honored as National Coach of the Year by the American Volleyball Coaches Association in 1986 and 1994 and claimed the Big 12 Conference Coach of the Year title eight times. He led the Huskers to 16 consecutive NCAA tournaments and won the school's first national volleyball title in 1995.

Tom Pingel has been serving USA Volleyball's youth division since 1991. He has held many roles, including Youth and Junior Olympic Volleyball Division vice president, head of the delegation for the U.S. women's national team during the World Grand Prix, head of the girls' junior national team in 1994, and most currently the director of High Performance National Programs. Pingel has also directed the Circle City Volleyball Club in Indianapolis.

Russ Rose, the women's volleyball head coach at Penn State University, has a record of 795-140 and an 85 winning percentage. After 11 years in the conference, the Nittany Lions have captured six Big Ten titles under Rose and have made five Final Four appearances. Rose has been awarded the American Volleyball Coaches Association Coach of the Year twice and the Big Ten Coach of the Year four times.

Al Scates, five-time national coach of the year, has led the UCLA men's volleyball team to 18 national championships in 32 years. His overall coaching record is an unbelievable 1,109-167. He is the inaugural recipient of USA Volleyball's All-Time Great Volleyball Coaches Award. Scates was inducted into the California Beach Volleyball Hall of Fame and became the first active coach to be inducted into the Volleyball Hall of Fame. Al is a U.S. Olympic Committee Coach of the Year. He was an outstanding player for UCLA and the U.S. National team and played on six USA championship teams. He was named both a UCLA All-American and a nine-time volleyball U.S.A. All-American.

Dave Shondell has had great success coaching both girl's high school volleyball and girl's club volleyball. In his 11 years at Muncie Central High School, Shondell has brought three state championships and five top 10 national rankings to the school. He has coached club volleyball for 16 years, winning three National Club Championships. Shondell also coached the Indiana High School All-Star Team five times and the Mizuna All-American Team once.

Steve Shondell, head coach of girl's volleyball at Muncie Burris High School, has posted an outstanding 891-63 record in 26 years. Shondell's teams have claimed 25 conference championships and 13 state championships. He also brought three national championships to the school in 1990, 1992, and 1997. Shondell was inducted into the Indiana Volleyball Hall of Fame in 1996. Has coached club volleyball for 28 years and has won 15 national champaionships with the Munciana Volleyball Club.

Jim Stone started his career at The Ohio State in 1981 as the women's volleyball head coach. In 20 seasons, he has led the Buckeyes to three Big Ten Conference championships and 12 NCAA Tournaments, reaching the semifinals in 1991 and 1994. Stone was awarded Big Ten Coach of the Year in 1989, 1991, and 1994 as well as American Volleyball Coaches Association Coach Mideast Region Coach of the Year in 1989, 1991, and 1998.

Fred Sturm was the head coach for the U.S. men's volleyball team from 1991 to 1996, but his involvement with USA Volleyball started as a player in 1976 until 1977. Before coaching USA Volleyball, Sturm spent 12 years as the head coach at Stanford University, where he was voted the most successful coach in the school's history with over 300 victories as both the men's and women's head coach. Sturm was elected NCAA men's volleyball coach of the year in 1989. Sturm played for UCLA during his collegiate career and helped the Bruins win three NCAA championships, in 1972, 1975, and 1976.

Rudy Suwara began coaching volleyball in 1971, when he was named men's volleyball head coach at the University of California at Santa Barbara where he placed second in the National Tournament twice and placed fourth once. From 1976 to 1992, Suwara coached the women's volleyball team at San Diego State University and led his teams to the National Championship Tournament 13 times. Suwara also coached the men's team from 1977 to 1980 and again in 1988. In 1993 Suwara began his six-year stint as an assistant coach for the USA men's volleyball team and as a head coach for the team in 2000. His involvement with USA Volleyball originated as a player when he was a member of the U.S. gold-medal Pan Am and Olympic volleyball teams.

Pete Waite is head coach for the University of Wisconsin. After just three seasons at Wisconsin, Waite has become the winningest volleyball coach in UW history with an 84-16 record. The Badgers finished second in the 2000 NCAA Tournament and won the Big Ten in 2000 and 2001. Waite was named Big Ten and Mideast Region Coach of the Year in 2000 and 2001. Before heading up the Badgers, Waite spent 11 years at Northern Illinois University, where he was the all-time winningest volleyball coach in the school's history. He had a 266-102 record with the Huskies and made four NCAA tournaments.

Paula Weishoff is currently the top assistant at the University of Southern California, where she played and became an All-American. While playing at USC, Weishoff led the Women of Troy to a 46-4 record and the AIAW national championship. She was a member of the U.S. Olympic Volleyball Team, winning a silver medal in 1984 and a bronze in 1992. Weishoff was voted MVP of the Olympic Games in 1992. In 1998, she was inducted into the U.S. Volleyball Hall of Fame.

Mary Wise, head coach of the University of Florida women's volleyball team, has compiled an impressive 333-36 record at Florida in ten years, including eight undefeated regular seasons. Since Wise's arrival in 1991, the Gators have made the NCAA national semifinals five times in nine seasons. Wise was rewarded the Southeastern Conference Coach of the Year eight times and the American Volleyball Coaches Association Coach of the Year twice. Before arriving in Florida, Wise spent five years at the University of Kentucky as both the assistant coach and head coach. During that time, Kentucky won two SEC titles and advanced to the NCAA tournament three times. Wise was hired as the head coach at Iowa State after she graduated from Purdue University, where she played as a setter and aided Purdue to two Big Ten Championships.